PRINCELY TREASURES

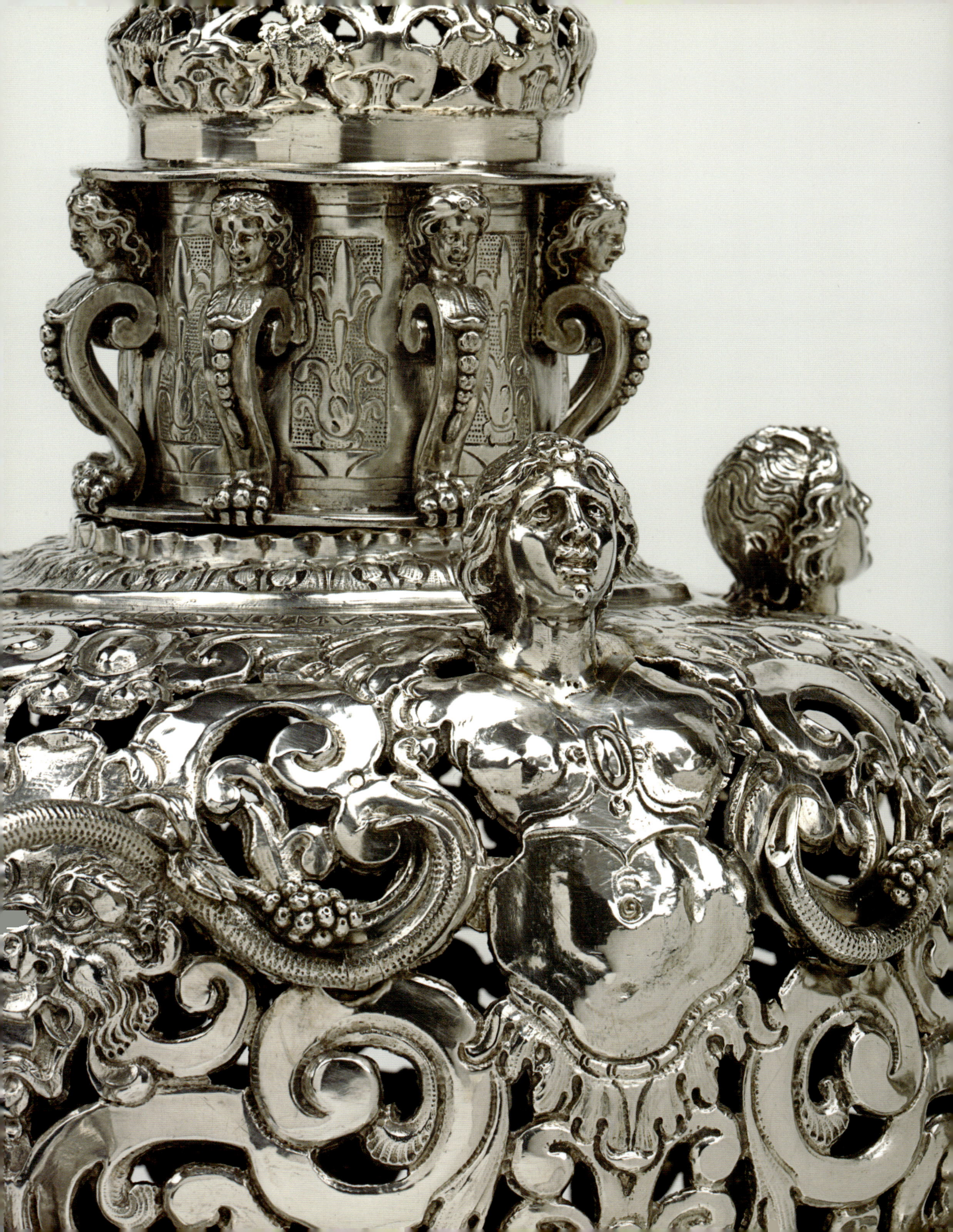

PRINCELY TREASURES

EUROPEAN MASTERPIECES
1600 — 1800

FROM THE VICTORIA AND ALBERT MUSEUM

Edited by Sarah Medlam and Lesley Ellis Miller

V&A Publishing

First published by V&A Publishing, 2011
Victoria and Albert Museum
South Kensington
London SW7 2RL
www.vandabooks.com

Distributed in North America by
Harry N. Abrams Inc., New York
© The Board of Trustees of the
Victoria and Albert Museum, 2011

The moral rights of the authors has been asserted.

ISBN: 978 1 85177 633 7

Library of Congress Catalog Control Number 2010937396

10 9 8 7 6 5 4 3 2
2014 2013 2012 2011

A catalogue record for this book is available from the British Library.

Printed in Hong Kong

Designed by Joe Ewart for Society
New V&A photography by Richard Davis, and the V&A Photographic Studio

FRONT JACKET Armchair (detail, see page 144)
BACK JACKET Chasuble (detail, see page 74)
PAGE 2 Perfume burner (detail, see page 136)
PAGE 6 The Ceramic Staircase, part of the nineteenth-century buildings of the V&A. Designed by F.W. Moody in 1871 and manufactured by Minton, Hollins & Co.
PAGES 14–5 *Design for a projected Church of the Ordre du Saint-Esprit, Paris* (detail, see page 68)

The objects in this book reflect the themes of the exhibition which it accompanies. For this reason, they are not organized chronologically or geographically but illustrate different aspects of European courtly life in the period 1600 to 1800.

CONTENTS

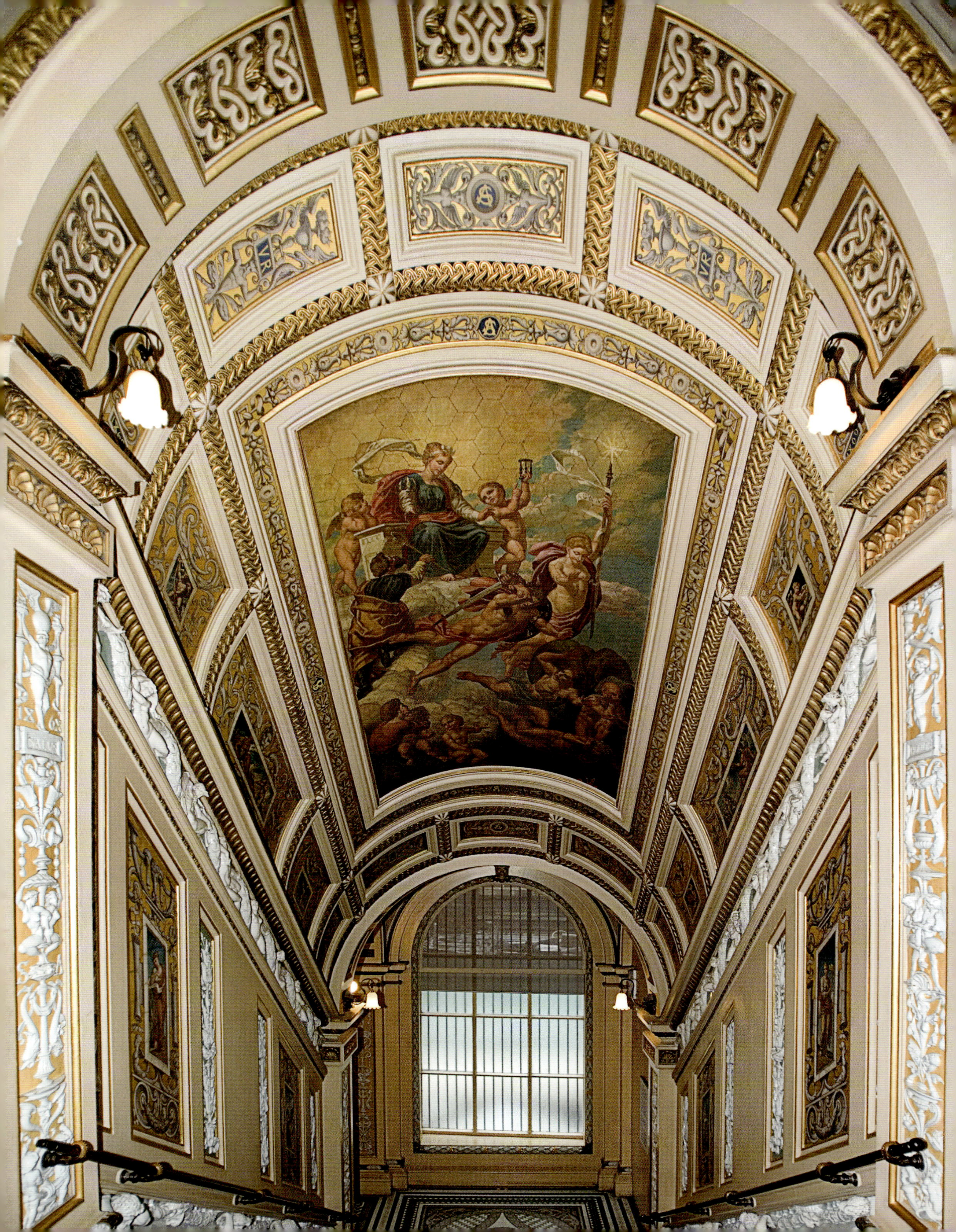

FOREWORD

The Victoria and Albert Museum has one of the greatest collections of European decorative art of the seventeenth and eighteenth centuries. From the miniature to the monumental, it encompasses many different materials and techniques, including painting and sculpture, ceramics and glass, metalwork and furniture, textiles and dress, prints and drawings. Eighty masterpieces have been selected for this touring exhibition. They were acquired and used by European men and women of power, wealth and taste. Many were made by Europe's finest artists and craftspeople, using precious materials from around the world. They come from all corners of the continent – from Sweden in the north to Spain in the south, from Portugal in the west to Russia in the east. A few, made in Asia specifically for the European market, demonstrate European states' great appetite for Asian art.

The richness of the V&A collections is due principally to the foresight of the founders of the Museum. As Sarah Medlam's essay in this volume reveals, these men looked beyond their own local British manufacturing context in their efforts to create a collection of works of art available to all, to educate working people and inspire British designers and manufacturers. The V&A was established in 1837 as the teaching collection of the School of Design and became a public museum after the enormous success of the Great Exhibition in 1851. Following the Museum's move to its present site in 1857, its collections expanded rapidly as it set out to acquire the best examples of decorative art from all periods. It also acquired fine art – paintings, drawings, prints and sculpture – in order to tell a more complete history of art and design. In 1899 Queen Victoria laid the foundation stone of a new building designed to complete the Museum and endow it with a grand entrance façade. To mark the occasion the Museum was renamed the Victoria and Albert Museum, in memory of the enthusiastic support that Victoria's husband Prince Albert had given to its foundation.

The V&A collections span 2,000 years of art in virtually every medium, from many parts of the world, and continue to grow today.

After exploring the topic of *Princely Patronage in Europe, 1600–1800*, and introducing some of the key patrons and taste-makers who commissioned luxury objects or were immortalized through them, who gave and received lavish gifts and acted as the conduit through which design ideas circulated, four thematic sections follow, each of which focuses on a different aspect of courtly life. After considering the fate of the arts during war, *Power and Glory* explores how representations of war were used to decorate objects commissioned for courtly use, from armour and weapons to tapestries and painting. *Religious Splendour* reveals the nature of objects made for worship, commissioned by secular and ecclesiastical patrons for public or private devotional use, while *Display in the Interior* presents furniture, textiles and ceramics made for use in the home, either for decorative or social purposes, for display or personal indulgence. Finally, *Fashion and Personal Adornment* reveals the care and attention that aristocratic men and women devoted to their dress and to the accessories with which they surrounded themselves.

The refurbishment of the 'Europe 1600–1800' galleries at the V&A is currently under way. In the spirit of all V&A projects, this reinterpretation aims to reveal and celebrate the beauty of these and many other works of art, while making them accessible to as wide an audience as possible. This redisplay also offers the opportunity to tour these key pieces, in the hope that they will inspire a passion for *objets d'art* and a desire to see more of such treasures in the V&A in London during the next decade.

Sir Mark Jones
Director, Victoria and Albert Museum

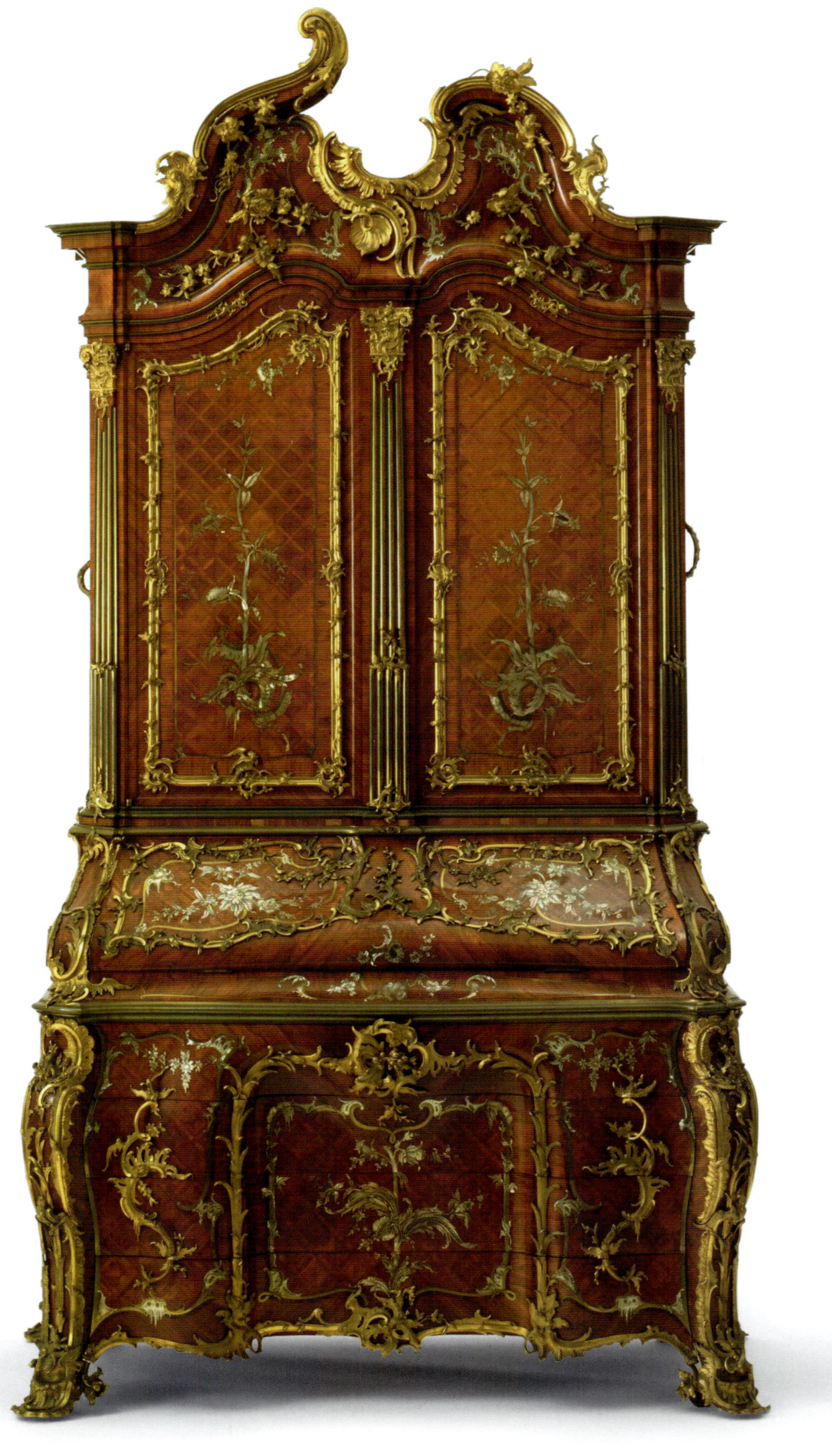

A PRINCELY COLLECTION FOR THE NATION: EUROPEAN DECORATIVE ARTS IN THE V&A

SARAH MEDLAM

THE V&A IS NOW CELEBRATED AS a treasure house of princely magnificence. Its origins, however, were not dynastic. Elsewhere in Europe, many national museums developed from royal or ducal collections that were made available to the people either by revolution or by strategic generosity, in an age of developing democracy in the mid-nineteenth century. The origins of the V&A were very different, and its unrivalled holdings of international art and design are the result of more than 150 years of collecting by a public institution for public benefit.

The V&A had its roots in government initiatives on education in the 1830s, the decade that saw the first successes of electoral reform in Britain. Manufacturers and government alike were concerned that the failure to develop adequate education for designers and artisans in the many manufacturing industries on which Britain's growing wealth depended, represented a threat to Britain's pre-eminence as a manufacturing nation. Whereas, in several European states, a tradition of design academies had been well established in the eighteenth century, in Britain art education was still dominated by the Royal Academy, offering only a traditional training in the fine arts of painting and sculpture. There was also a lamentable lack of opportunity for those working in design and manufacture to see the best examples of decorative art. The architect C.R. Cockerell (1788–1863) enthused about the opportunities available to such people in continental Europe:

… the leisure of the artizans [sic] *in most of the cities, of France especially, is passed in the palaces and gardens of the king, where they have beautiful works of art before their eyes, in architecture, sculpture and painting.*

The aspirations of the founders of the Museum thus challenged the first Director to create, in the shortest possible time, collections to rival the princely riches of Paris, Munich or St Petersburg. The design of the first Museum buildings at South Kensington reflected their ambitions. The galleries were decorated with mosaic and tiling (page 6) to create a palace for the masses. The South Kensington Museum, as it was called until 1899, was at once a place of training, with students from the School of Design moving freely between the galleries and the adjacent studios and lecture rooms, and a place where the public came to enjoy the new collections, with refreshment rooms (the first in any museum) to add to the social pleasure of a visit.

From the beginning, the Museum set out to show the art and design of Europe, North America and Asia. The international range of the collections has remained its greatest strength. In Europe, most national museums concentrated largely on the products of their own state. The V&A's collections started from quite a different point, with early acquisitions coming largely from continental Europe, in particular from Italy. Individual items were purchased on the London art market, such as the bust of Pope Innocent X, after a model by Alessandro Algardi (page 22), or the silver binding for a prayer book made in Germany in 1731 (page 96). As the collections grew and became better known, donations began to augment the Museum's holdings. It was, however, a major undertaking to create a museum from scratch, to match princely

1 Writing cabinet made for Augustus III, King of Poland. Dresden, *c.*1750–55 (V&A: W.63–1977)

collections in Europe that had been amassed during centuries of commission, purchase and gift.[1]

The early curators were active travellers in pursuit of material. Henry Cole (1808–82), the first Director of the Museum, made a journey to Italy in 1858–9, and the following year his colleagues Richard Redgrave (1804–88) and John Charles Robinson (1824–1913) were also there, actively buying for the Museum. In 1864, and again in 1865, Robinson travelled extensively in Spain, sending back purchases including sculpture, jewellery and metalwork, ceramics, fans and ivories. In so doing, these men emulated many private collectors in an era when antique-collecting had become not just the preserve of kings and princes, but also the hobby of many who had made their money through successful commercial activities.

One technique that Cole used very astutely in the development of the new Museum was the acquisition of complete collections. As early as 1853 the Museum purchased the Bandinel collection of ceramics, which included everything from ancient Greek pottery to eighteenth-century porcelain from Vienna, or Doccia in Italy. This collection had been created by James Bandinel (1783–1849), a friend and supporter of the engineer Sir Isambard Kingdom Brunel and a civil servant who had served as superintendent of the Slave Trade Department at the Foreign Office. A few years later the Museum went in pursuit of the collection (chiefly of Renaissance objects) formed by the French lawyer Jules Soulages (d. 1857) in Toulouse. It finally came to the Museum on loan in 1856, but difficulties over funding the purchase meant that the acquisition of all the objects was not completed until 1865.

The Museum also bought large numbers of objects from collections that came to public auction. In 1854 Parliament made a special vote of funds to purchase items from the collection of British Liberal politician Ralph Bernal (1808–82). More than £8,000 was used to acquire 730 items, ranging from the pair of pistols made for Louis XV of France in 1750–60 by Jean-Baptiste La Roche (page 62) to Meissen porcelain, Venetian glass and German leatherwork, and including Chinese ceramics.[2]

Although work on the formation of the collections was energetic, it was hardly systematic, and acquisitions undoubtedly reveal the personal preferences of the curators and their advisors and current fashions in collecting, as well as the Museum's stated aims of displaying excellence in design and technique. The first 20 years at South Kensington saw, for instance, the creation of a fine collection of lace (page 74), reflecting not only the historical importance of such textiles from the seventeenth to the nineteenth centuries throughout Europe, but also the astonishing popularity of historical lace with collectors in the mid-nineteenth century. Porcelain was acquired in great quantity, not only because the ceramics industries were a powerful element in the national economy, requiring investment in the training of designers and craftsmen, but also because the collecting market was lively. The number of fine examples on the market encouraged the acquisitive instincts of curators, as much as those of private collectors such as Lady Charlotte Schreiber (1812–95), whose magnificent collection of ceramics (largely British) was donated to the Museum in 1884.

By the 1870s, in one popular, yet expensive, area of collecting, the Museum felt that it was falling behind. The taste for French decorative arts from the late seventeenth and eighteenth centuries had been dominant among fashionable British collectors since the 1820s, following the lead of George IV (1762–1830) and members of his court. The Museum's curators were only too well aware of the importance of this taste in creating 'French Style' as the dominant contemporary commercial style in everything from ceramics to furniture and textiles. Individual pieces of French porcelain and furniture did come to the

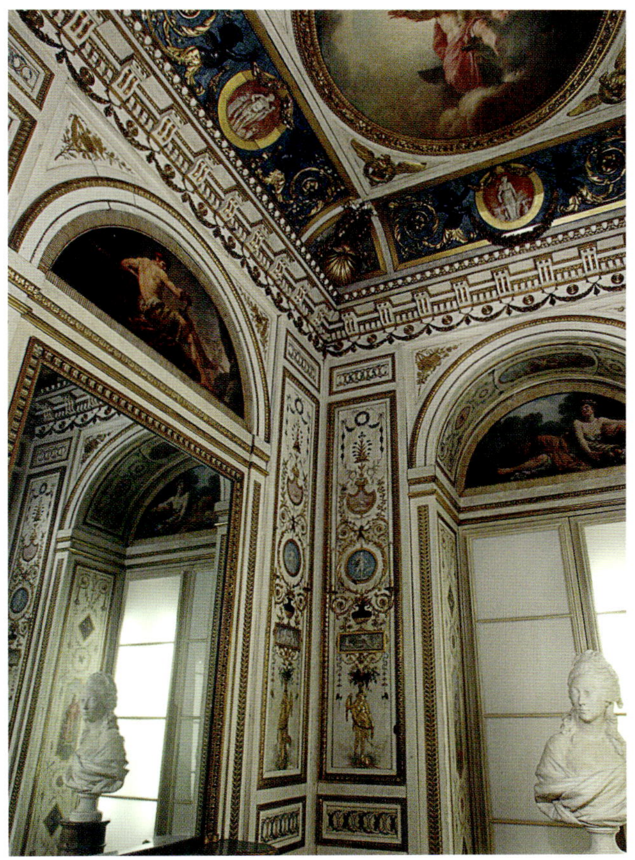

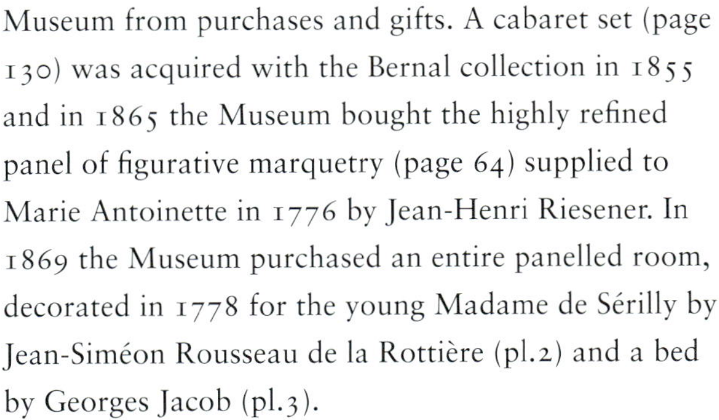

2 The boudoir or cabinet designed by Jean-Siméon Rousseau de la Rottière (1747–1820) for Madame de Sérilly. Paris, 1778 (V&A: 1736–1869)

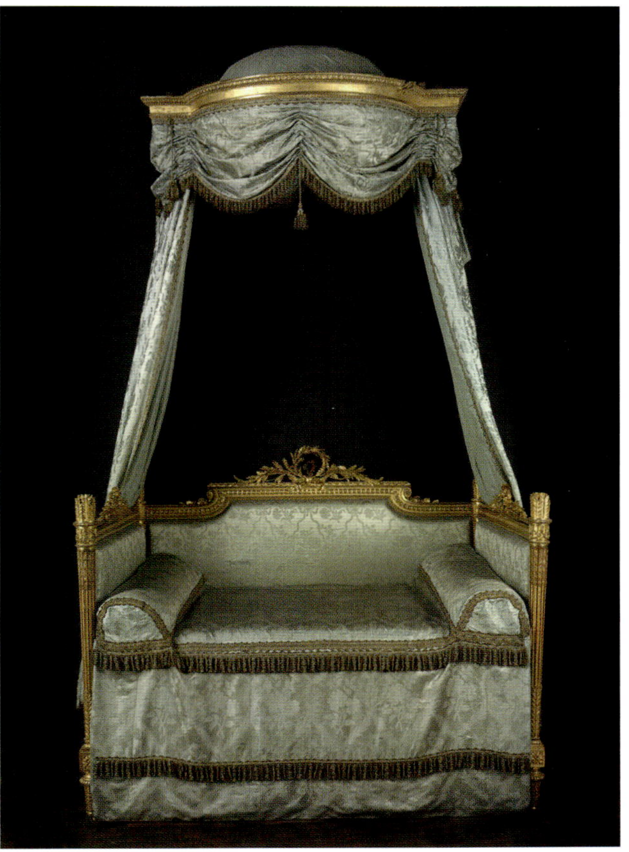

3 Giltwood bed by Georges Jacob. Paris, c.1780 (V&A: 8459–1863)

Museum from purchases and gifts. A cabaret set (page 130) was acquired with the Bernal collection in 1855 and in 1865 the Museum bought the highly refined panel of figurative marquetry (page 64) supplied to Marie Antoinette in 1776 by Jean-Henri Riesener. In 1869 the Museum purchased an entire panelled room, decorated in 1778 for the young Madame de Sérilly by Jean-Siméon Rousseau de la Rottière (pl.2) and a bed by Georges Jacob (pl.3).

It was clear that the Museum could not hope to compete with the major private collections in the area of French decorative arts. Apart from the royal collection and a number of ducal collections, outstanding collections had been formed by the Marquess of Hertford and his son Sir Richard Wallace (the origin of the Wallace Collection, London), by John Bowes and his wife (the origin of the Bowes Museum,

County Durham) and by several members of the Rothschild family (the collections now in the care of the National Trust at Waddesdon Manor, Buckinghamshire being the best surviving example). Museum staff began actively to court the somewhat reclusive London collector Mr John Jones (1799–1882), the proprietor of a military tailoring business who had quietly devoted himself for some years to the collecting of French decorative arts, English and French portraits, and miniatures (pl.4). The range of his collecting is evident here in the miniature of Peter the Great with a Black Page (page 38), the miniature of Hortense Mancini (page 32), the portrait of Madame de Pompadour (page 34), the snuffbox now thought to have been made in Germany (page 58), the marquetry commode attributed to Charles Cressent (page 116), the porcelain-mounted reading stand (page 140) and

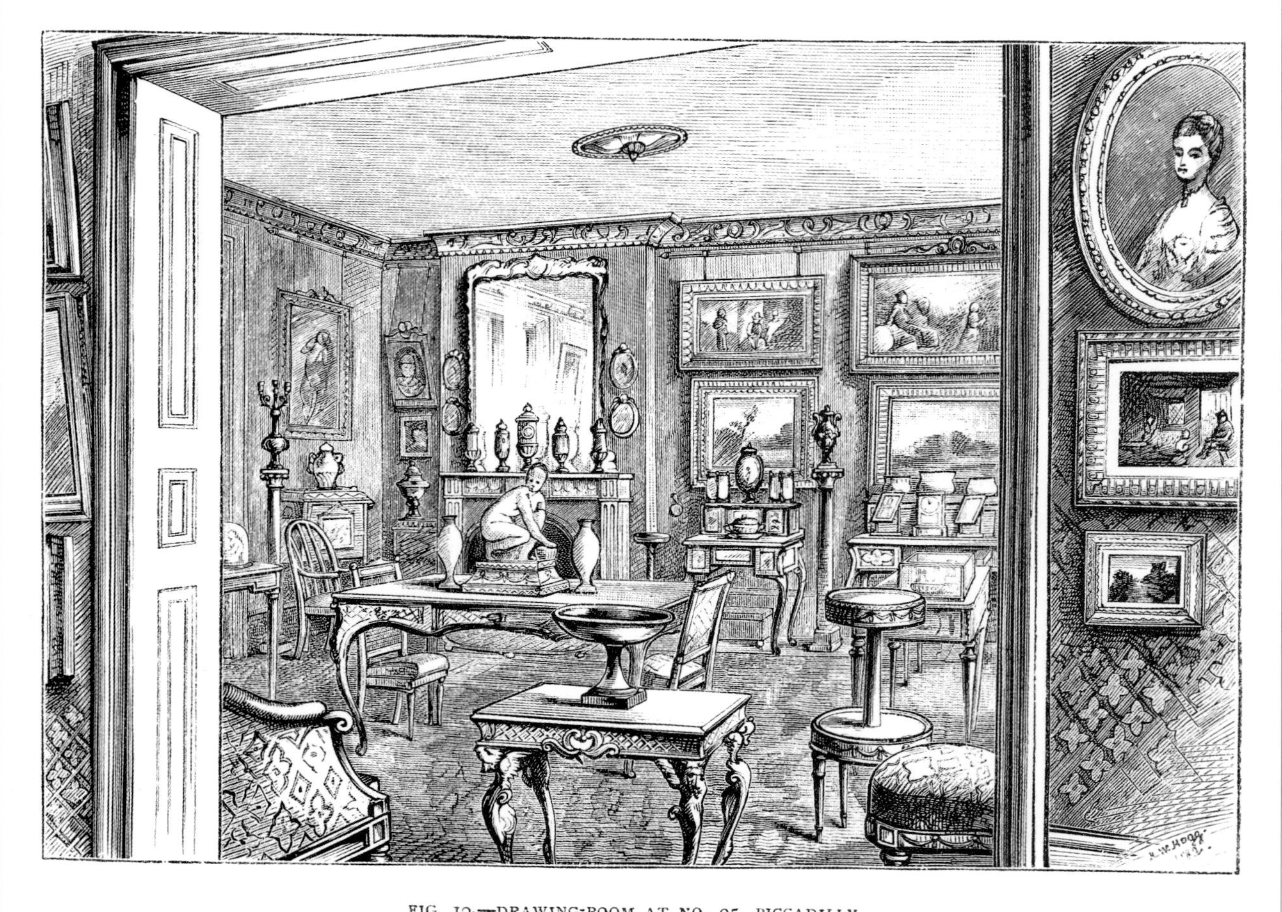

4 Illustration of the drawing room of John Jones at 95 Piccadilly,
*c.*1882, from the first guidebook to the Jones Collection

the painting by Nicolas Lancret of *The Swing* (page
120). In 1882 Jones's entire collection came to the
Museum as a bequest and, at a stroke, brought it one
of the most important collections of French furniture
and porcelain in any museum in the world.[3]

After this major addition, the pace of acquisition
slowed. The Museum also began to change the direction
of its collecting, concentrating between about 1885
and the beginning of the First World War in 1914
to a large extent on building up the holdings of
British decorative arts and developing its interest in
fashionable dress as well as textiles (pages 176, 178).
Even in this period, however, there were acquisitions
of exceptional pieces, such as the covered cup made
to commemorate Gustavus Adolphus of Sweden

(1594–1632) (page 24) and the design for a church
by Juste-Aurèle Meissonnier (page 68).

During the twentieth century the Museum
continued to enrich its international collections,
although purchasing was necessarily restricted at times
by the financial constraints of two world wars and the
intervening years of depression. The global conflicts
also undoubtedly discouraged curators from acquiring
pieces from the German states, their actions reflecting
popular prejudice. It was not really until the 1960s
that government funding once again reached levels
that enabled the Museum to collect more freely, with
the additional support of The Art Fund and many
individual supporters. By the early 1970s plans were
in hand to redisplay the galleries for European Art

1600–1800. In this new arrangement the richness of Jones's collection of French decorative arts inevitably dominated the galleries, and stimulated an interest in developing the collections with acquisitions from other centres of European production in the luxury trades. Several new acquisitions, such as the tapestry from *The Art of War* series (page 54), the tile panels from the Quinta Formosa, Portugal (page 112) and the ewer and basin with the arms of the Lomellini family (page 134), enriched the galleries in the 1970s. In 1977 the celebrated sale of Mentmore Towers, Buckinghamshire, brought new pieces into the collections, including a writing cabinet made for Augustus III, King of Poland (pl.1).

At the beginning of the twenty-first century the collections continue to grow. As in a princely collection, each generation brings new purchases, and new gifts to enrich the whole. The V&A continues to be very fortunate in the support of so many benefactors in enlivening its displays with new pieces to inspire and please its visitors. In 2003 the Museum acquired a King Vulture in Meissen porcelain, from the collection originally made for the 'Japanese Palace' in Dresden for Augustus the Strong (pl.5), with the help of the Heritage Lottery Fund, The Art Fund and the Friends of the V&A. More recently, the outstanding loans from the collection formed by Sir Arthur Gilbert (1913–2001) and his wife Rosalinde (1913–95) (pages 26, 28, 60, 70, 80, 98, 100) have created a whole new gallery in the Museum. And in 2009 the Museum was additionally given the fine pair of *rimmonim*, or decorative bells from a Torah, made in the Netherlands in about 1780 (page 104) by Lady Marjorie Gilbert through the American Friends of The Art Fund. In 2010 we started work on the planning of new galleries that will give these, and other riches of the collection, the setting they deserve, for a new generation to enjoy.

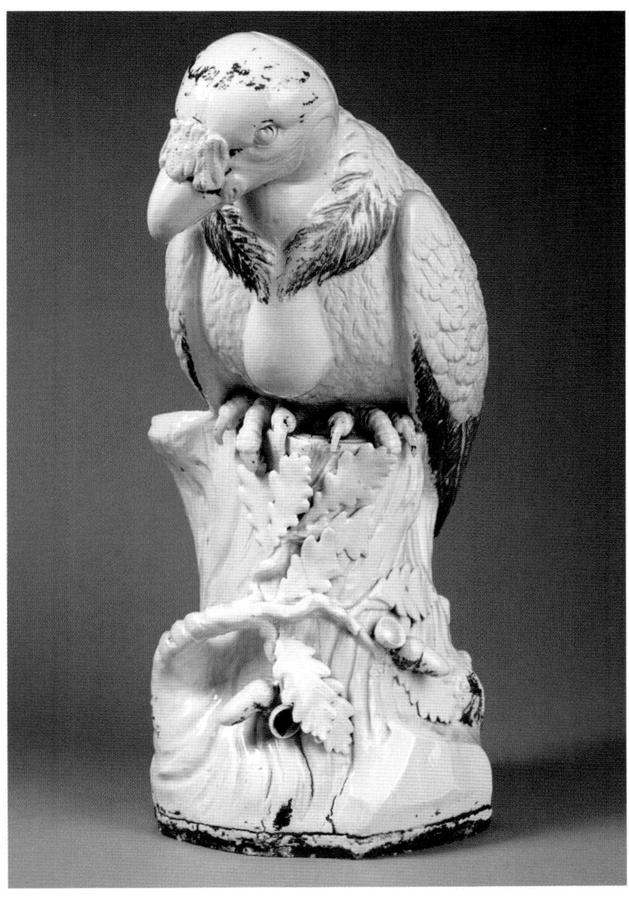

5 Figure of a King Vulture or Condor, modelled by Johann Joachim Kändler and made at the Meissen porcelain factory, *c*.1731, for Augustus the Strong, Elector of Saxony, for the Japanese Palace in Dresden (V&A: c.11–2003)

1 Anna Somers Cocks, *The Victoria and Albert Museum: The Making of the Collection*, London, 1980

2 'A Brief Account of the Formation of the Art Collections', in *Inventory of the Objects in the Art Division of the Museum at South Kensington ... For the Years 1852 to the end of 1867*, London, 1868, pp.v–vi

3 See Carolyn Sargentson, *French Furniture: 1640–1800. A Catalogue of the Victoria and Albert Museum Collection*, London, 2011, introductory essay

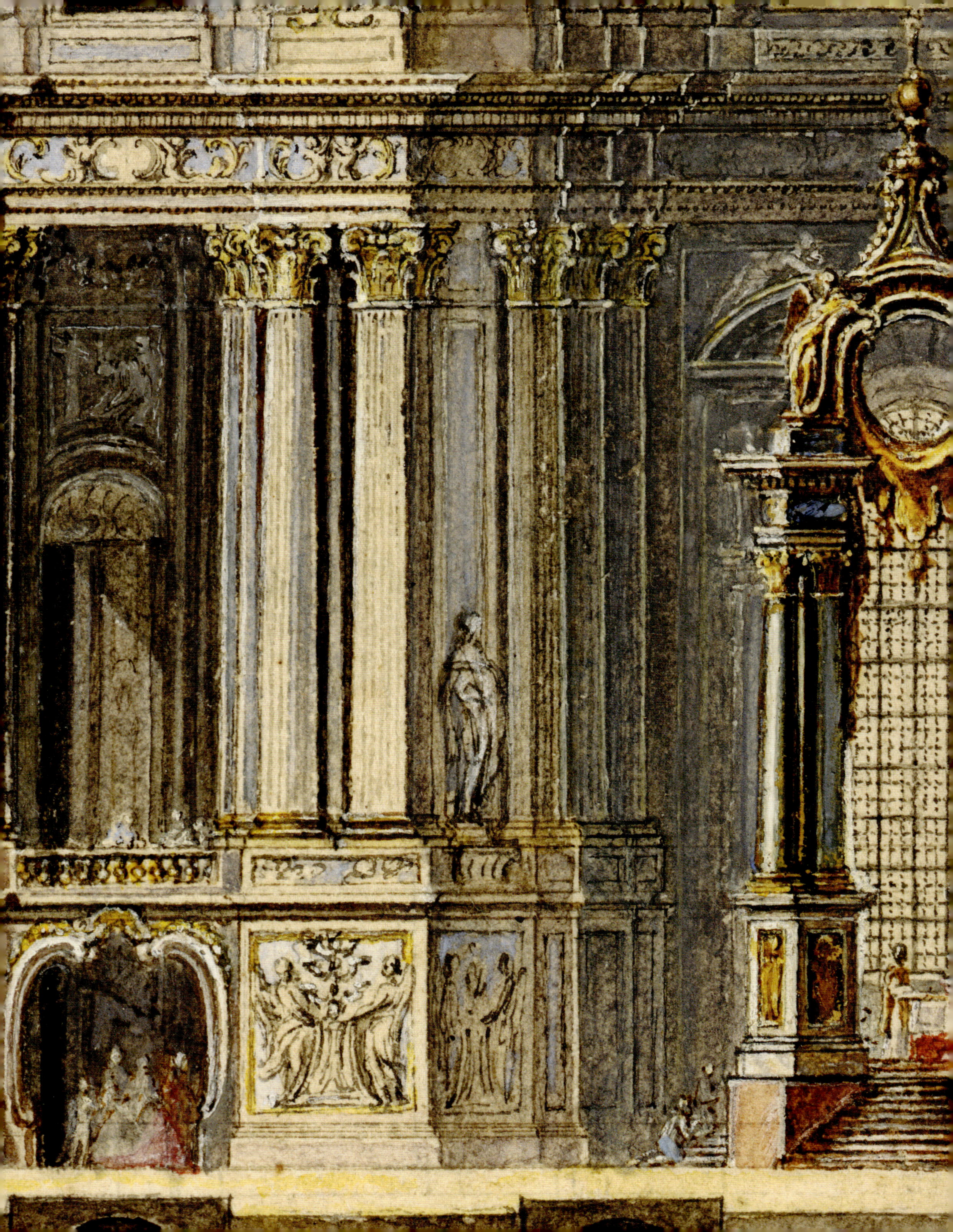

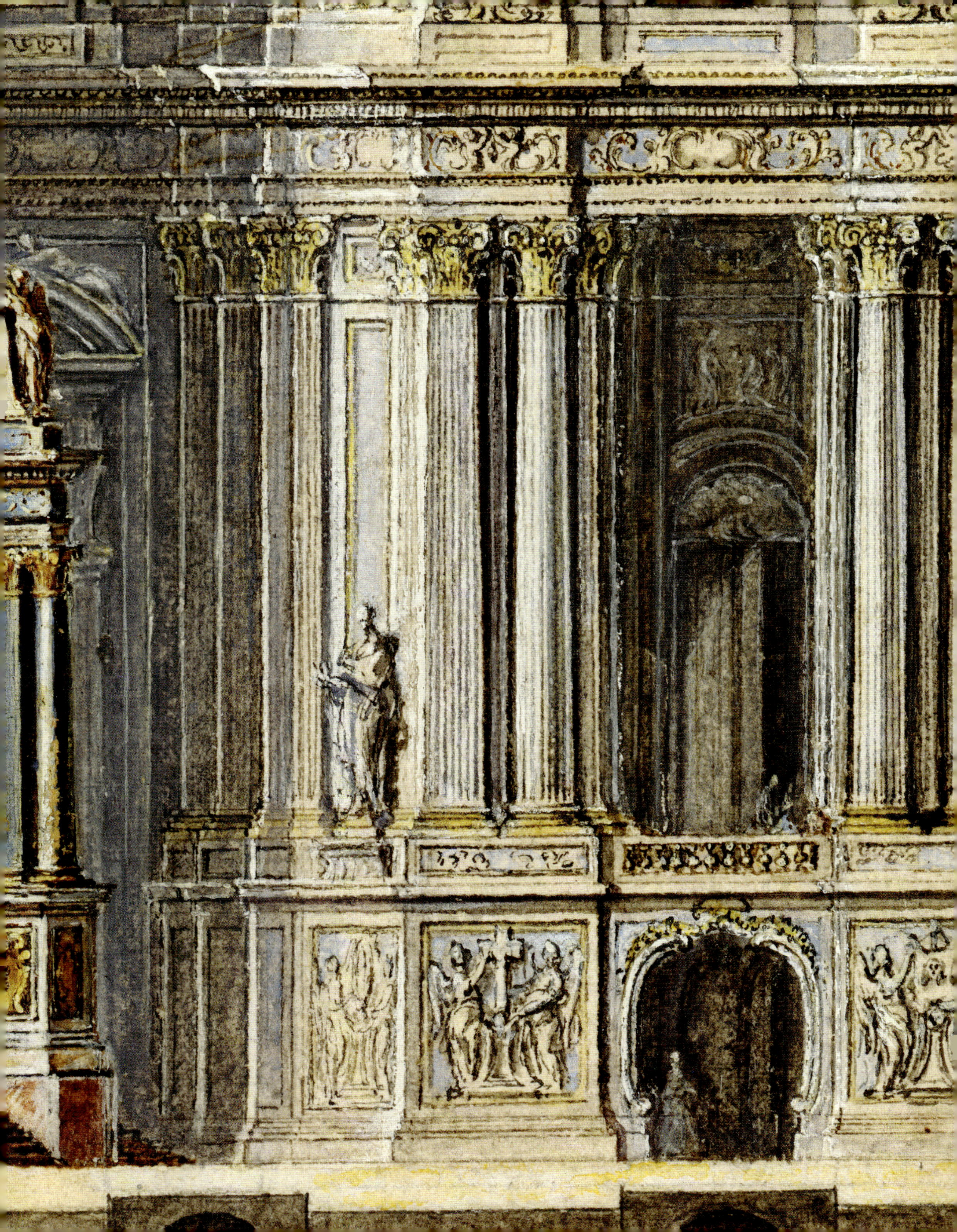

PRINCELY PATRONAGE IN EUROPE, 1600–1800

ANGELA McSHANE

IN 1767 CATHERINE THE GREAT (1729–96), Empress of Russia (a state that covered one-sixth of the world's land mass), opened her address to the Russian Legislative Commission with a stark but highly significant statement: 'Russia is in Europe.'[1] This statement was no mere lesson in geography. Rather, it indicated that Catherine (following in the footsteps of her illustrious predecessor, Peter the Great, 1672–1725) (page 38) saw being European as the epitome of being 'modern'. It was also a declaration that Russia intended to take its rightful place at the table and on the battlefield with European and world powers and would play a full role in the theatre of power by embracing the noble virtues, manners and education that European states so valued. Just as all her fellow monarchs and princes worldwide did, Catherine was to demonstrate fully her ambitions for her state through magnificent ceremony, artistic patronage, exchanges of gifts and lavish self-adornment and portrayal.

Before 1600 the whole continent of Europe could be represented in the shape of a single ruler (pl.6) – that of the Habsburg Holy Roman Emperor, Charles V (1500–58). In 1516 he claimed dynastic authority over most of the European continent, as well as 'lordship' over Africa, Asia and the new lands of America. By the turn of the century, however, this image belonged to the past. The Habsburg Empire was riven and bankrupted by religious and dynastic warfare and Europe had been divided into numerous, ambitious sovereign states. During the century that followed – despite worldwide troubles that ranged from prolonged international warfare, civil and religious strife and persecution, to a mini ice-age and near-universal outbreaks of plague and other infectious diseases – many European states benefited from developments in trade, technology, agriculture and governmental institutions that served to improve the prosperity and life expectations of large numbers of its relatively stable populations.

This prosperity led to a rise in the 'conspicuous consumption' of wealthy and powerful elites across Europe. Spain, the Low Countries and the Italian states were leaders of fashion and taste in the early 1600s, but by 1700 France reigned supreme in political and cultural spheres, with the figure of Louis XIV (1638–1715) looming large over European affairs. Yet even Louis could not have everything his own way. Former backwaters, such as Britain and the Netherlands, had benefited from large immigrant populations forced to flee persecution elsewhere. They brought with them vital new skills and capital. Entrepreneurs in these states set up rival 'East India' Companies to exploit the wealth of Asia. Their naval and military might created new global empires that revolutionized European trade and tastes. Equally dynamic new ruling dynasties in Sweden, Prussia and Russia sought to augment the prosperity and assert the political significance of their own states. In part they did this by attracting European artists, artisans and scholars with offers of patronage, pensions and tolerance. There was no 'national' craft aesthetic as such. European artisans had always been peripatetic, many being driven from their native countries by religious persecution. Great artists and thinkers, from René Descartes (1596–1650) to Voltaire (1694–1778), were wooed and won over by Queen Christina of Sweden (1626–89) and Catherine the Great.

Despite the incessant conflicts that ravaged and remodelled Europe from 1600 to 1800 – a period that ended with the great French Revolution of 1789 and the Jacobin massacres of the 1790s – this was also an age of growing social civilization and taste, of

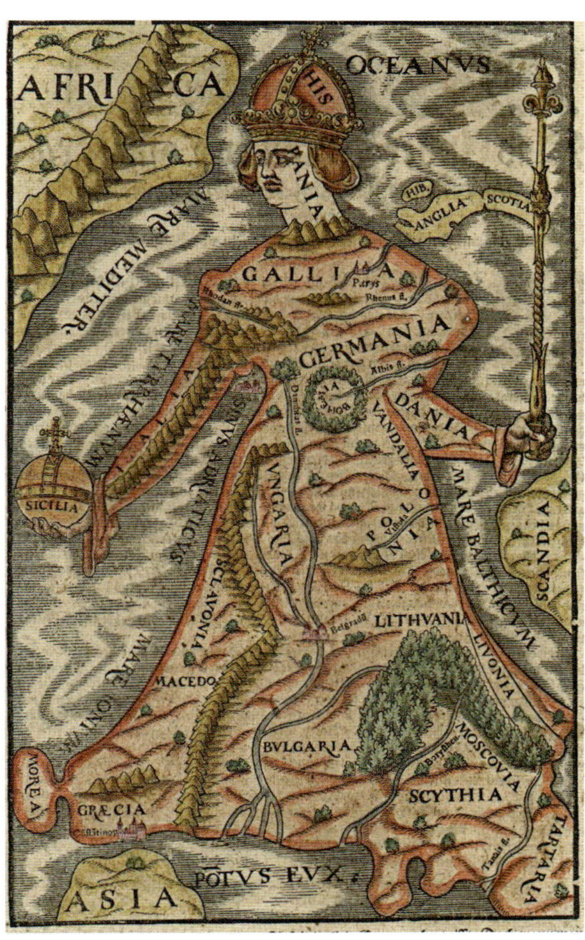

6 'Europa Regina' map, published in *Cosmographiae universalis* by Sebastian Münster. Coloured woodcut. Published Basel (first edition 1544)

intellectual 'Enlightenment', of increasing global connections, trade, travel and discovery. Cultural developments and the ever-present experience of warfare were not unconnected. The strategic demands of warfare were often a driving factor behind the cultural, scientific, industrial, technological and medical developments of the period. The movements of armies, the forcible clashes of cultures and the experiences of ordinary people forced tens of thousands to see and experience 'difference' and 'change'. Indeed, warfare created opportunities for innovation. Even the parallel development of 'politeness' or 'civilization' of manners might be seen as a necessary foil to the brutality engendered by conflicts over politics, trade and religion.

The needs of war also played a part in the development of the princely capitals of Europe. Success in military logistics required a stable centre for control, command and supply, which it was impossible to achieve with the peripatetic model of the medieval court, where courtiers followed the Prince, and government could not operate without him. By 1700 most major European states had established a fixed place for the court in existing urban centres, such as Madrid, Paris, Stockholm, London, Prague and Vienna. Not all took this approach, however. Dissatisfied with the entrenched cultures of Moscow and Kiev, Peter the Great – at huge cost in money and lives – chose to build the epitome of a modern European capital city from scratch. St Petersburg, captured from Sweden and giving sea access to western Europe, was created out of a swamp in fewer than 10 years (1703–13) (pl.7).

By the eighteenth century the typical capital city consisted of a vast monarchical residence that housed, or was surrounded by, new institutions of state, such as ministries of justice, war and finance, as well as

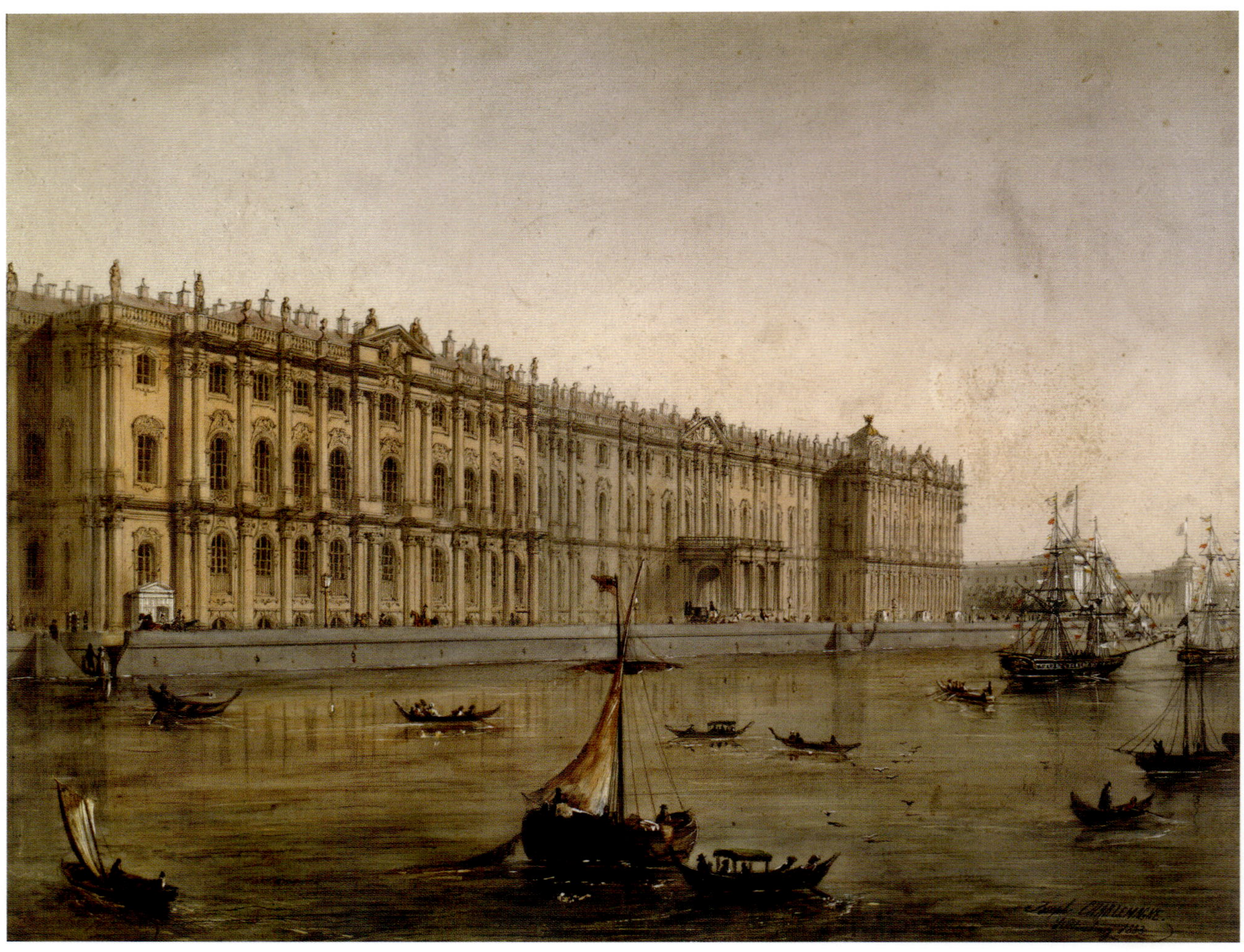

7 *View of the Winter Palace in St Petersburg, from the Neva,* by
Joseph (Jossif) Ivanovich Charlemagne. Watercolour. Russia,
1853 (State Hermitage Museum, St Petersburg)

hundreds of elegant residences. All these buildings
needed good-quality interior furnishing and decoration,
while their inhabitants required rich clothes, jewels and
objects of every kind. Thousands of ancillary services,
such as workshops and fashionable retail areas, as well
as assembly rooms, concert halls and even galleries
and the first museums, surrounded the courtly buildings.
The wise prince still travelled to see and be seen by the
people, but the court and the institutions of government
could function on their own, regardless of the ruler's
whereabouts. Louis XIV's great palace of Versailles
(pl.8) offered a different model of kingship. This
astounding royal residence, which was set apart from

the city, influenced some rulers, such as Frederick
the Great of Prussia (1712–86), but the majority
of European courts still remained closely in contact
with their capital cities and their social and cultural
institutions.

Some courts were led by kings, others by minor
princes and princesses, by nobles and statesmen, even
by businessmen or bankers. Courts were also led by
prince bishops, who combined a temporal and religious
function – and none was more powerful than the Pope.
His religious position was as spiritual head of the
Catholic Church, but he was also the secular ruler of
the Vatican States in Italy. The rise of Protestantism in

northern Europe meant that his position was much reduced, but it was still thought vital for all states, of whatever religious persuasion, to have representation at his court. The courts of Ottoman sultans, of Indian maharajas and of Chinese and Japanese nobles, warlords and rulers all took part in the same process of cultural posturing and competition between states. On the one hand, this could mean the mutual exchange of great treasures; on the other, it could lead to attempts to replicate, or 'steal', styles, techniques and recipes – as in the case of porcelain.

Women, too, created courts that dictated fashions and taste. In England, James I's Danish Queen Anne (1574–1619) welcomed many European painters and artists to her court. Charles I's French queen, Henrietta Maria (1609–69), brought with her the tastes and fashions of France. In France itself, not just queens but also royal mistresses had a key role to play in offering patronage to new artists and commissioning new works. Perhaps the most influential was Madame de Pompadour (1721–64) (page 34), who commissioned

8 *View of the Palace of Versailles, from the Place d'Armes*, by Pierre-Denis Martin. Oil on canvas. Paris, 1722 (Musée national des châteaux de Versailles et de Trianon)

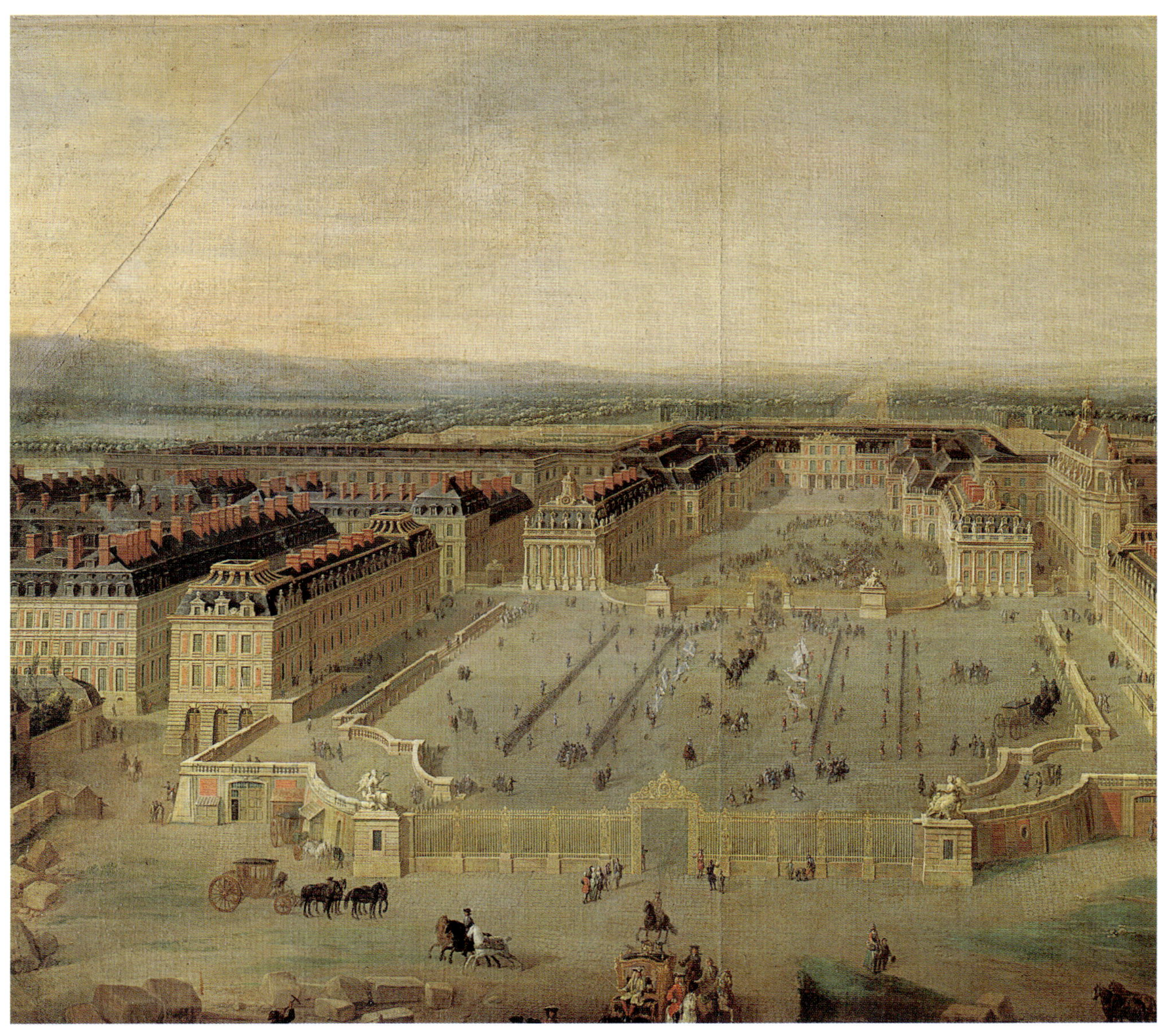

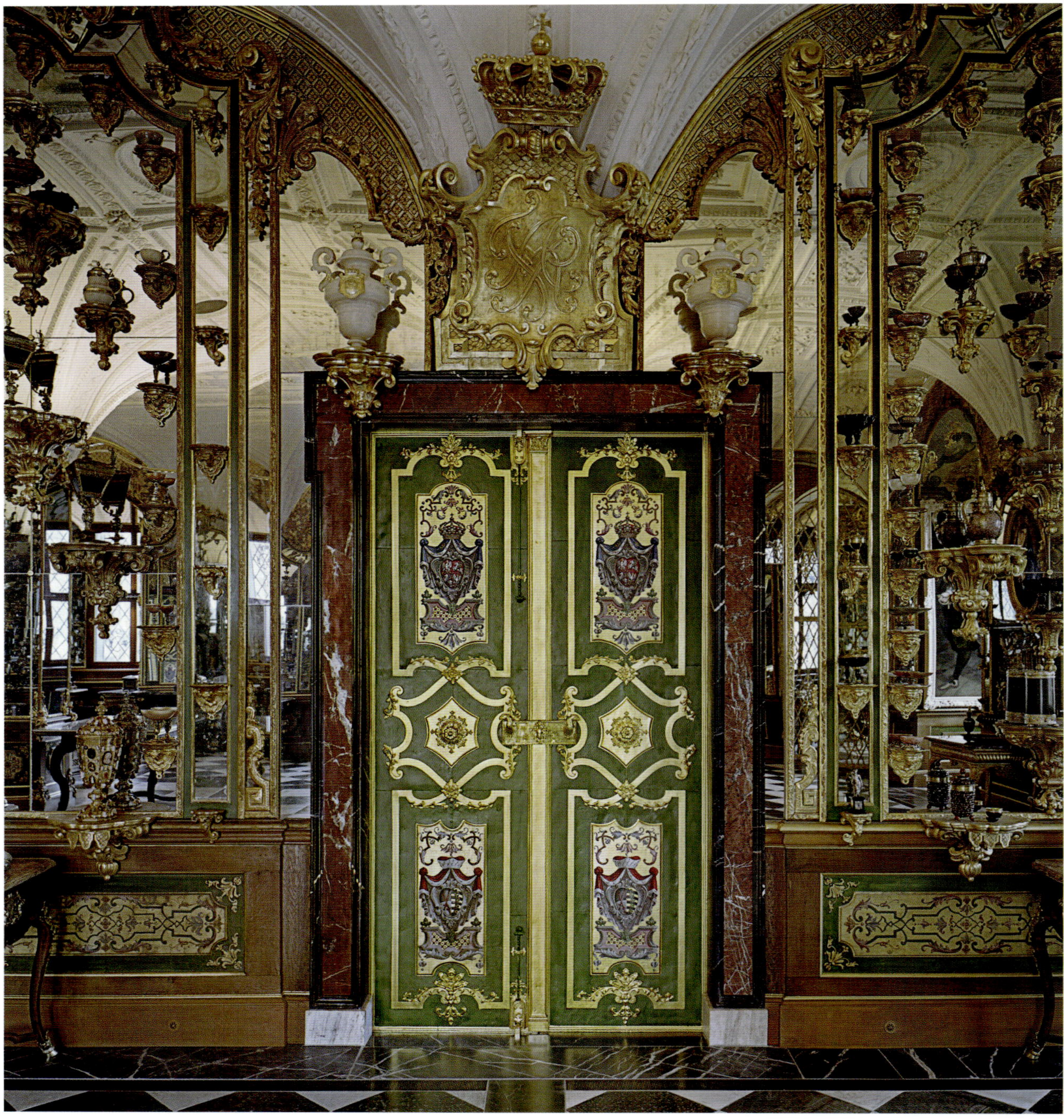

9 The Hall of Precious Objects, Historic Green Vaults, Dresden, before 1729 (Staatliche Kunstsammlungen Dresden)

hundreds of paintings and beautiful objects, staged theatrical events and supported writers and philosophers. Of her early death Voltaire wrote: 'I was indebted to her and I mourn her out of gratitude. It seems absurd that while an ancient pen-pusher, hardly able to work, should still be alive, a beautiful woman, in the midst of a splendid career, should die.'[2] Less-exalted women held salons at which some of the great minds and talents of Europe would meet. Others, such as the 'blue-stockings' of England, preferred to patronize the work of women.

Even the most ordinary person might have dealings with the court in some way. It offered an immense pool of patronage and opportunity, not only for soldiers or statesman and for the most brilliant of artists or scholars, but also for the most humble of tradesmen. Courts needed coalmen as much as goldsmiths, maids as well as merchants, but most of all 'this increasingly sophisticated elite created unparalleled opportunities for artists and craftsmen of every variety: hydraulic engineers who created fountains, painters, architects, goldsmiths, musicians, jewellers, furniture- and tapestry-makers'.[3] In some cases, as with the successful Gobelins workshops in Paris, the state attempted to take control over methods of production and taste. In other areas, such as the Netherlands and England, it was left to the market to hone and develop new skills and techniques.

Treasures had multiple roles to play at princely courts. They served to beautify the working and living interiors of buildings and the personal appearance of courtiers. They also acted as a means of unlocking patronage, of establishing links and networks and of displaying appropriate levels of luxury and taste to impress superiors, equals and social inferiors alike. This performance was finely tuned – too much opulence could inspire suspicion or opprobrium, while too little could be socially and politically disastrous. A gift to a superior needed to be finely judged, to act as a compliment to the taste, interests or beliefs of the patron rather than as too aggressive a display of the giver's own knowledge and wealth.

For princes themselves, the desire to awe their immensely rich subjects at home and key foreign visitors from abroad led to the most astonishing examples of 'art' shopping (and looting) in bulk and to the development of a European art market, staffed by courtly but ruthless agents. In 1627 the financially hard-pressed Charles I (1600–49) bought a large number of pieces from Duke Vincenzo II of Mantua (1594–1627) for £30,000 (more than his annual revenue from landed income), diverting funds away from the relief of the French Protestants (Huguenots) in La Rochelle. Ironically, this same collection was later to be sold in turn, after Charles's execution in 1649, with Philip IV of Spain (1605–65) selecting with alacrity key pieces for the Spanish royal

collection. In the late eighteenth century Catherine the Great was renowned for her expansive purchasing policy. Vast numbers of crates arriving at the Hermitage contained thousands of pieces of Chinese porcelain or Wedgwood (page 128). Catherine was magnanimous in her collecting, however, famously buying up the library of the great Enlightenment scholar Denis Diderot (1713–84) and then leaving it with him to enjoy for the rest of his life.

The desire of European monarchs to amass huge collections of art, including paintings, statues, medals, engravings, books, manuscripts, decorative furnishings and objects (pl.9), pushed to new limits the idea of the Renaissance 'cabinet of curiosities' – a path that led in the eighteenth and nineteenth centuries to the development of public museums, such as the V&A. Where monarchs went, courtiers had to follow, and soon nobles and gentry were developing the necessary knowledge (or at least the social connections) to ensure that they could make a fine show of artistic taste and discrimination. Treasured objects of every kind acted as a language of loyalty and allegiance – between monarch and subject, noble and client, husband and wife, parent and child – and so were retained and passed down by families. In fact, given the lamentably poor survival rate of documentary evidence from noble families across Europe, it is frequently the case that only surviving objects reveal something of these varied human relationships.

1 See *Catherine the Great's Instruction (Nakaz) to the Legislative Commission, 1767*, trans. and ed. Paul Dukes, Oriental Research Partners, Newtonville, MA, 1977; see also Isabel de Madariaga, *Catherine the Great*, New Haven and London, 1990; Simon Dixon, *Catherine the Great*, Harlow, London and New York, 2001

2 Christine Pevitt Algrant, *Madame de Pompadour: Mistress of France*, New York, 2003, p.291

3 John Adamson, 'The Making of the Ancien Regime Court 1500–1700', in John Adamson (ed.), *Princely Courts of Europe 1500–1750*, London, 1999, p.8

BUST OF POPE INNOCENT X (1574–1655)

Domenico Guidi (1625–1701) after a model
by Alessandro Algardi (1598–1654)
Rome; about 1690 (model about 1654–66)
Cast bronze
V&A: 1088–1853; h. 97.5 cm, w. 87 cm

PAPAL POWER WAS BOTH SPIRITUAL AND temporal, as was papal patronage of the arts. Princes of the Catholic Church commissioned major works in a variety of media for religious purposes, and they also built their own reputations through commissioning likenesses of themselves. This bust of Pope Innocent X, born Giovanni Battista Pamphilj, celebrates a prince who ruled the papal states from his election in 1644 until his death in 1655. Born in Rome, Innocent trained there as a lawyer, graduated from the Pontifical Gregorian University and then followed a conventional ecclesiastical pattern of service, before becoming Cardinal in 1629 and then Pope. He is considered one of the most politically astute pontiffs of the era, who much increased the temporal power of the Vatican. Initially he clamped down on papal expenditure and on art patronage in order to improve his court's financial situation. In the longer term he embellished Rome through a variety of commissions. His preferred sculptor was Alessandro Algardi.

This portrait bust refers directly both to Pope Innocent's family background and to his papal position. He wears papal robes, a *berrettino* on his head, a *mozetta* (or *capuccio*) around his shoulders and a stole around his neck. The embroidery on his stole derives from his family's crest, the fleur-de-lis and doves enclosed in scrolls of olive branches. Doves and olive branches are also Christian symbols of peace. The bust is one of a pair commissioned by Pietro Vito Ottoboni (1610–91), whom Pope Innocent elevated to the position of Cardinal in 1652, and who subsequently became Pope Alexander VIII in 1689. It was a companion to Alexander VIII's own bust by Domenico Guidi. This bronze of Innocent X is therefore posthumous, and was probably based on a terracotta model (now in the Palazzo Odescalchi in Rome) by Innocent's favoured sculptor Algardi, who was Guidi's late master. Guidi modified the original model, particularly the folds of the drapery, so that it matched his own style in his bust of Alexander VIII.

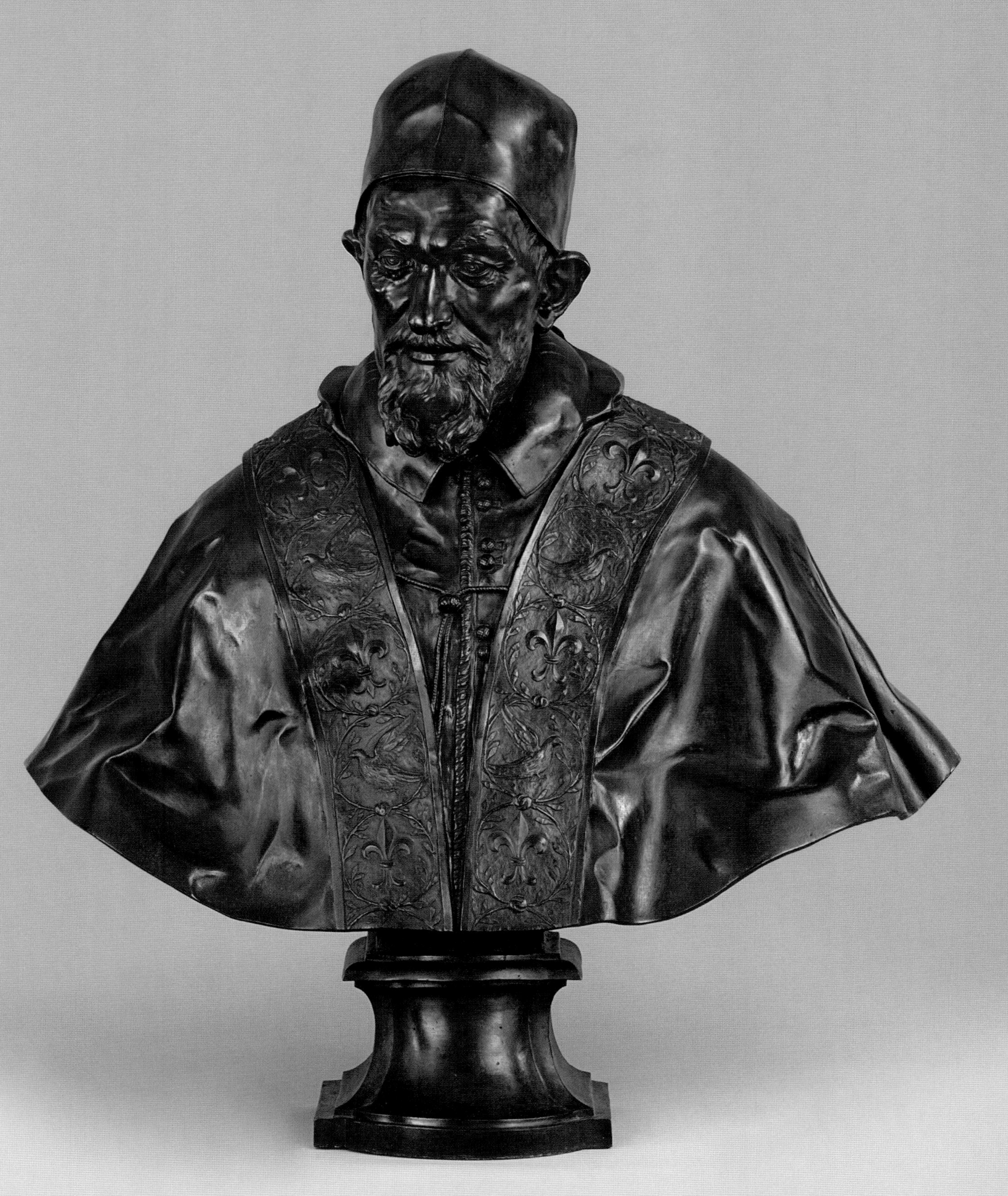

STANDING CUP AND COVER WITH A BUST OF GUSTAVUS ADOLPHUS OF SWEDEN (*1594–1632*)

Probably by Paul Birckenholtz (1561–1634)
Germany; after 1632
Silver, parcel-gilt, with applied figures cast in silver
V&A: 1885–1898; h. 34.9 cm, diam. 10.1 cm

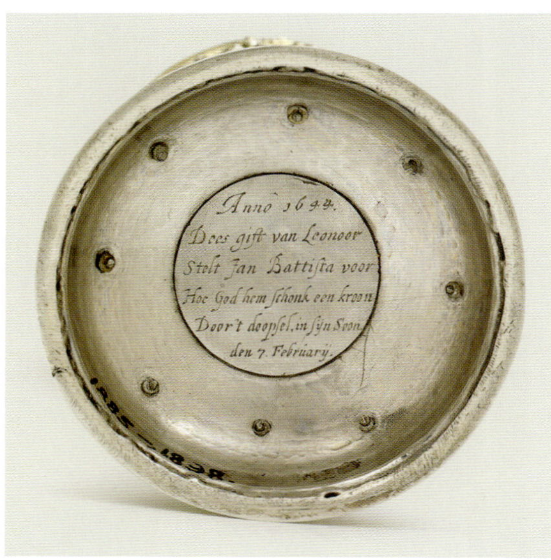

THIS CUP COMMEMORATES THE DEATH OF King Gustavus Adolphus of Sweden, founder of the Swedish Empire. A champion of the Protestant cause, he led his nation to military supremacy during the Thirty Years War (1618–48). He helped to determine the political as well as the religious balance of power in Europe at that time, and was poised to become a major European leader when he was killed at the Battle of Lützen, near Leipzig in Germany, in 1632. Despite his death, the battle was a decisive Protestant victory.

The cup bears a bust of the bearded king on its knop (ornamental knob), while the base is decorated with military trophies, and the stem of the cup is in the form of a lion rampant holding a shield and sword. Personifications of the Eight Virtues (Faith and Justice; Hope and Temperance; Prudence and Fortitude; Charity and Patience) are represented within oval frames of scrollwork and stems adorned with fruit. A plaque inside the lid contains a German inscription referring to the battle and to the:

> *almighty pious Lord ... most conquering of Heroes*
> *And the great Victor*
> *Who came from the Middle of the Night*
> *And fought for God's Honour*
> *Religion and Germany's freedom.*

A later inscription, engraved on a second plaque attached to the base of the cup, shows that by 1644 it had passed into Dutch ownership and appears to have been given as a christening present by 'Leonoor' to an unknown recipient.

Only five commemorative cups of this design are known to have been made, attributed to the Frankfurt goldsmith Paul Birckenholtz the Elder, based on stylistic similarities with another commemorative cup by him for the University of Marburg in 1629.

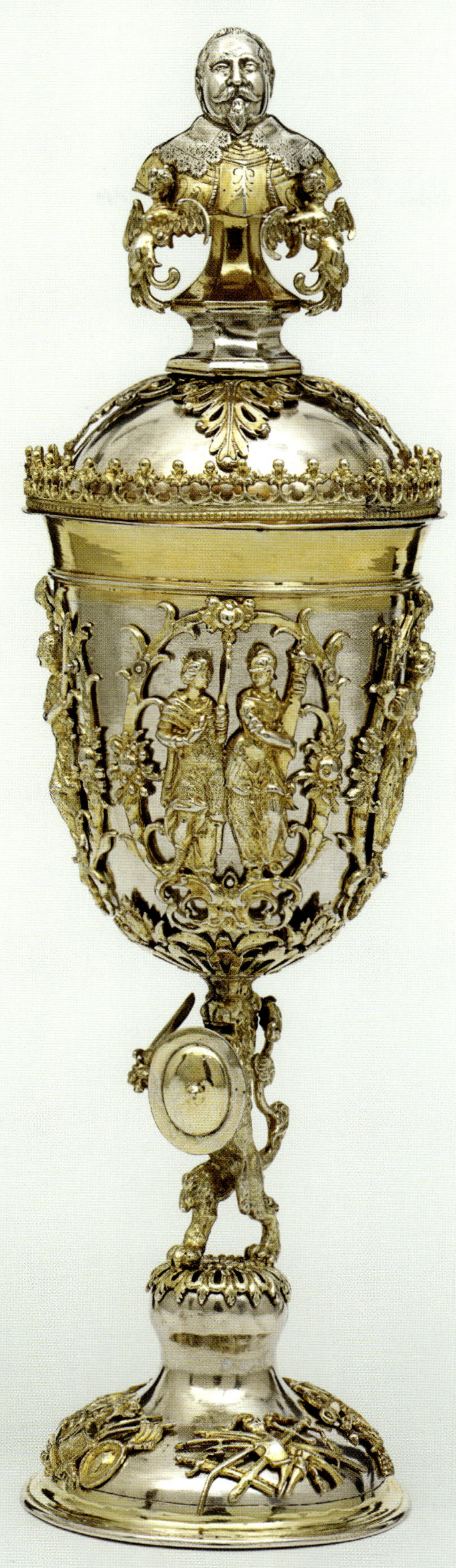

TOBACCO BOX WITH A PORTRAIT OF CHARLES I (*1600–49*)

London; 1670–85

Gold

V&A: LOAN:GILBERT.545–2008; The Rosalinde and Arthur Gilbert Collection on loan to the Victoria and Albert Museum, London; h. 1.6 cm, w. 6.4 cm, d. 7.9 cm

THE LID OF THIS GOLD BOX IS DECORATED with a profile bust of Charles I, King of England, Scotland and Wales, who was executed in 1649 during the Civil Wars (1642–51). Charles's understanding of kingship was based upon the concept of 'the divine right of kings'. This theory of royal absolutism held that the monarch's authority over his subjects could be tempered only by God. Charles's insistence on this right – complicated by religious differences within the three kingdoms – led him to fund his authoritarian policies with illegal taxation that ultimately provoked civil war. After his execution, republican rule continued until the restoration of the monarchy in 1660.

Charles I went to his execution proclaiming that it was the 'liberty of the people of England' for which he stood. A justification of his position, *Eikon Basilike* (Greek for 'Royal Portrait'), was both a publishing and propaganda triumph, selling more than 30 English editions by the end of 1649 alone. Charles was perceived by royalists as a martyr and in 1660, on the restoration of his son, was the only person to be made a saint by the Church of England.

This box is one of many objects in different materials, cheap as well as expensive, made for those of royalist sympathies to commemorate Charles's life and support his political agenda. Surrounding the image of the King is inscribed the motto: VIVAT REX, CURRAT LEX, FLORE[A]T GREX ('Long live the King, may the law run its course, may the flock flourish'). Around the border are symbols of the British monarchy: the lion and the unicorn from the royal coat of arms, and three plaques containing a rose (England) with a thistle (Scotland), a harp (Ireland) and fleurs-de-lis (France – a claim perpetuated on the royal arms until 1801). Above his head two putti (cherubs) support his crown, illuminated by a glorious sunburst engraved in Latin: *Video*, 'I see'. Charles is depicted directly beneath the all-seeing God by whose authority he believed that kings ruled.

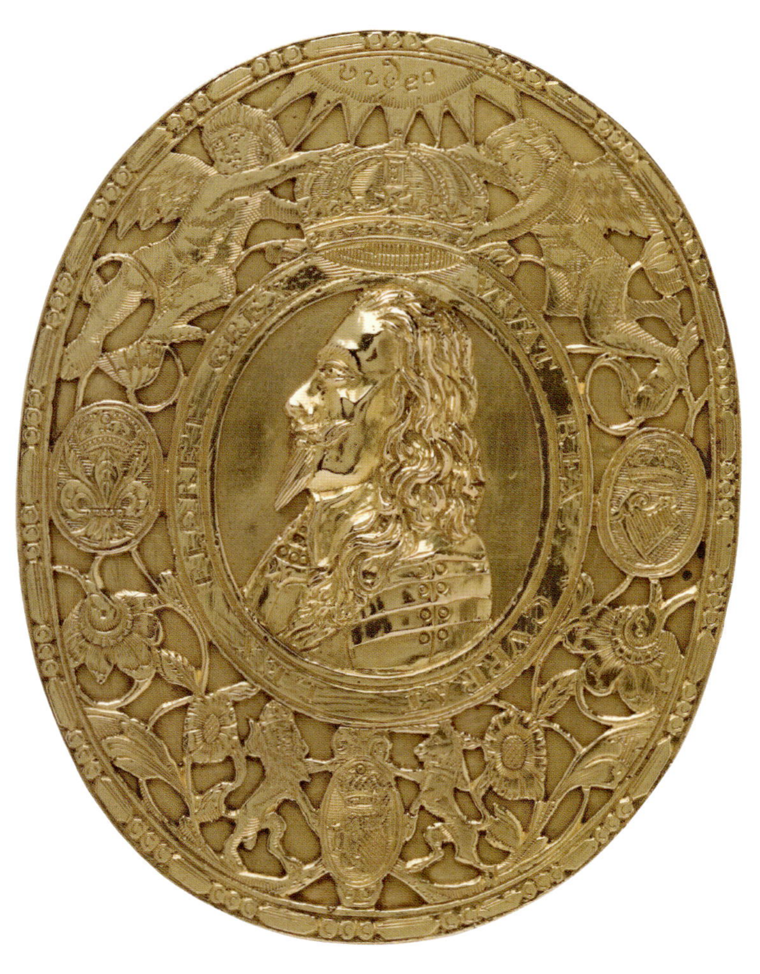

SNUFFBOX

Berlin; about 1765
Chrysoprase, gold, foiled carnelians and foiled
diamonds
V&A: LOAN:GILBERT.412–2008; The Rosalinde and
Arthur Gilbert Collection on loan to the Victoria
and Albert Museum, London; h. 5 cm, w. 7.8 cm,
l. 10 cm

THIS SNUFFBOX FROM THE PRUSSIAN ROYAL collections is typical of the great jewelled boxes commissioned by King Frederick II (the Great) of Prussia (1712–86). Frederick was a proponent of enlightened absolutism – absolute royal authority tempered by the principles of Enlightenment philosophy. These principles led him to modernize the Prussian bureaucracy, civil service and army, promote religious tolerance throughout Prussia, and patronize artists and philosophers. After many military campaigns, Prussia was by the end of his reign one of the most powerful states in the Holy Roman Empire, occupying double its original area, and was a major force in European politics, comparable to Austria.

Frederick, a passionate snuff-taker, is said to have had a collection of more than 300 boxes. On his accession he stopped the importation of French boxes and took a close interest in the design and manufacture of boxes in Berlin. Each year when he moved from Potsdam to Berlin for the carnival, he had a selection of his boxes transported carefully on a camel. He was particularly fond of the green gemstone chrysoprase, a form of quartz that was mined in Silesia, which he conquered in 1740. During his final illness he had laid out before him rough and polished chrysoprase, as well as boxes and jewels.

The body of the box is carved from a single piece of chrysoprase and set with a broad band of scrolls and flowers in diamonds, of which some are set over pale-pink, green and lemon-yellow foils. The base and lid are similarly encrusted with diamond-set flowers. The two red flowers on the lid are carved from carnelian.

The taking of snuff – a form of pure, powdered scented tobacco, which was inhaled through the nose – became increasingly fashionable during the seventeenth century. Frederick the Great's father, King Frederick William I (1688–1740), hosted a club at which snuff-taking followed strict rules of etiquette.

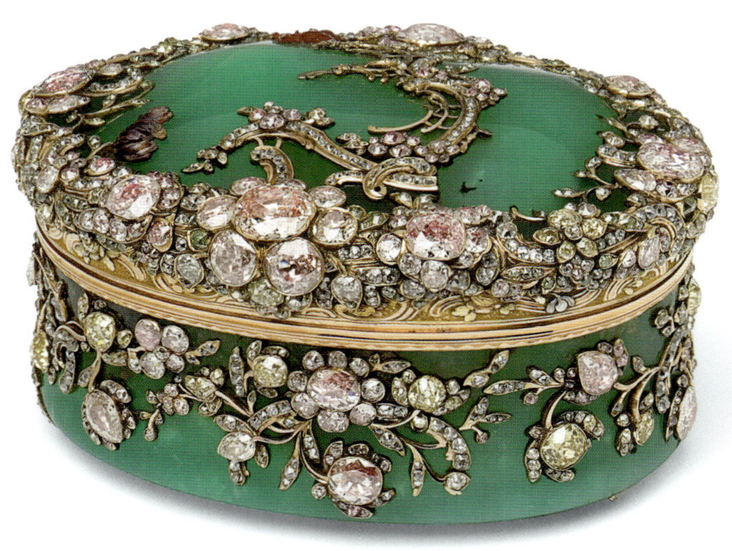

FAN LEAF (EXTENDED)

France; possibly about 1673–4
Gouache on two thicknesses of vellum, mounted
on a copper sheet, highlighted with gold and silver
V&A: P.39–1987; h. 27.5 cm, w. 47.5 cm

THE FIGURE IN THE CENTRE OF THIS IMAGE is almost certainly Françoise-Athénaïs de Rochechouart de Mortemart, Marquise de Montespan (1641–1707), *maîtresse en titre*, or official mistress to Louis XIV (1638–1715), from about 1670 until around 1680. She reclines amid the most luxurious furnishings available at court at that time, brought before her as if in tribute to a monarch. They probably adorn an apartment in the Trianon de Porcelaine, a single-storey brick pavilion that gained its name from the blue-and-white pottery tiles from France and Holland with which its walls were clad. Louis created this elegant entertaining complex in the gardens of Versailles for his mistress, and it became a favourite retreat away from the pomp and public ceremony of court life in Paris. This image is particularly precious because the Trianon was demolished in 1688.

Madame de Montespan was the most celebrated of Louis's mistresses. Born into a noble family, like most of her predecessors as royal mistress, she married the Marquis de Montespan in 1663, just four years before she caught the King's eye at a ball at court. She thus rose from her position as lady-in-waiting to the King's sister-in-law, the Duchesse d'Orléans, to hold considerable influence at court. Indeed, she was sometimes called 'the true queen of France'. This image was possibly painted as early as 1673–4 when the first three of Louis's children by Madame de Montespan were legitimized. It was possibly created as a love token to Louis to celebrate her ascension to the position as his undisputed chief mistress, since, rather provocatively, she is depicted bare-breasted. The child in the bath surrounded with doting putti is probably her son, the Duc de Maine, who would have been three years old in 1673.

Small gouache paintings such as this one are generally described as fan leaves, and were indeed painted on parchment or vellum prepared for fans, though this example was painted on the fan arc and surrounding areas at the same time, and may always have been intended as a decorative picture. In seventeenth-century France fans were a status symbol of the ruling and wealthy classes.

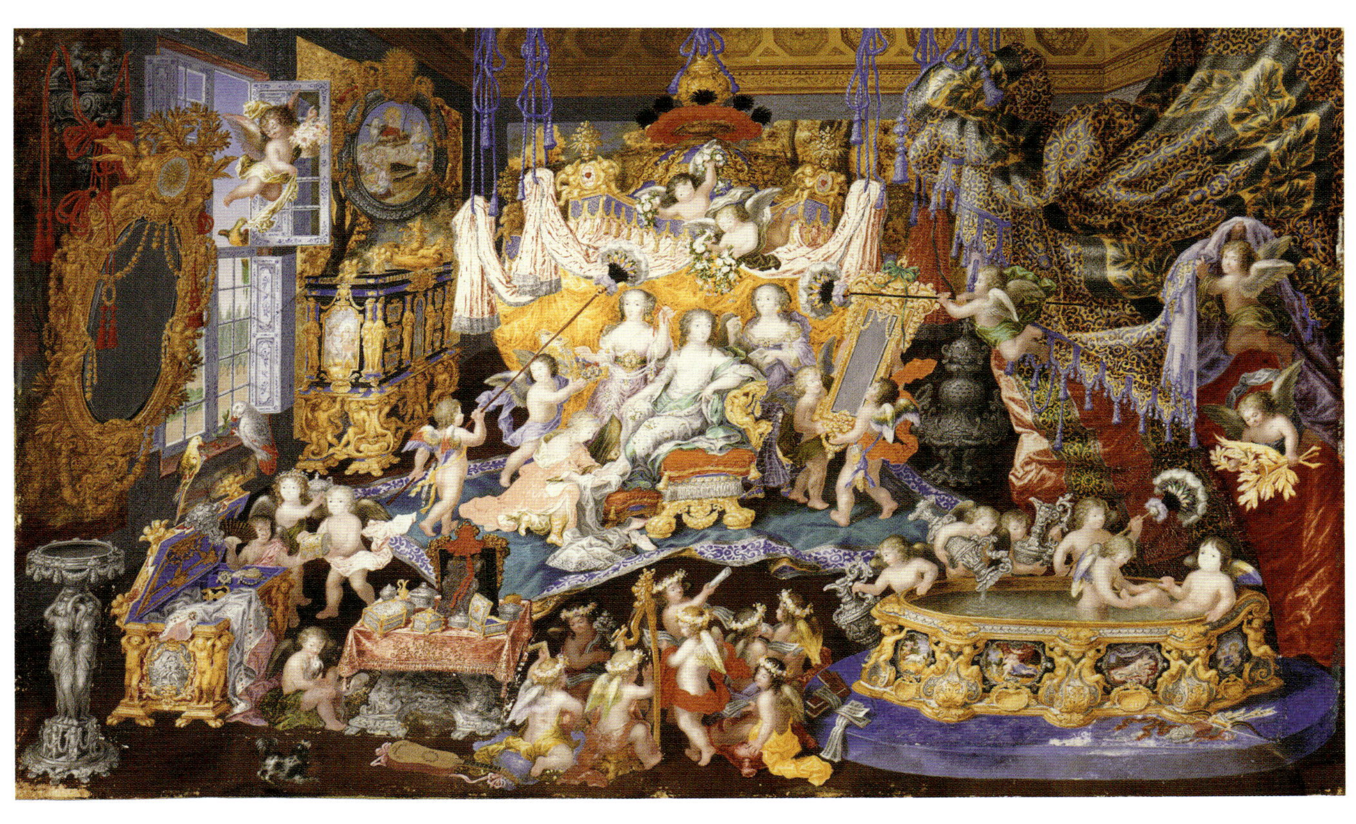

HORTENSE MANCINI, DUCHESSE DE MAZARIN (1646–99)

Jean Petitot (1607–91)
Paris; about 1675
Enamel on metal
V&A: 671–1882; bequeathed by John Jones;
h. 2.6 cm, w. 2.3 cm

THIS ENAMEL MINIATURE HAS LONG BEEN accepted as a portrait of Hortense Mancini, Duchesse de Mazarin, and as a particularly fine example of the work of the Swiss-born enameller Jean Petitot. Hortense Mancini, remembered as 'an extraordinary beauty and wit, but dissolute, and impatient of matrimonial restraint', led a colourful life, during which she travelled across Europe, gaining the protection of more than one influential prince. Her uncle Cardinal Jules Mazarin (1602–61), who effectively ruled France from 1651 until the King reached his majority in 1660, arranged an advantageous but ultimately unsuccessful marriage for her in Paris with one of the richest men in Europe, Armand-Charles de la Porte, Marquis de la Meilleraie. Louis XIV (1638–1715) made him Duc de Mazarin in 1662 in honour of the Cardinal. Between 1672 and 1675 Hortense lived under the protection of the Duke of Savoy (an independent state between southern France and northern Italy), and on his death she travelled to the court of Charles II (1630–85) in London, where her young cousin had just married the King's brother. Her affair with Charles secured her a place at the English court and a pension that continued until her death.

Hortense had many admirers, for whom such a small, intimate, yet durable portrait might have been a highly desirable memento. Jean Petitot, who created it, excelled in such portraits (see page 184 for the technique). His enamels are particularly notable for emulating the rich colour and gloss of oil. Unlike traditional miniatures, enamels do not fade, and this one retains all its original brilliance. The prototype for the enamel was probably painted before Hortense left for England in 1675, as her hairstyle was fashionable at that time. Like Hortense, Petitot had travelled in search of patronage, training initially as a goldsmith and enameller, working at the English court before the English Civil Wars (1642–51), subsequently as Court Painter in Enamel to Louis XIV of France, until the Revocation of the Edict of Nantes in 1685 banned the practice of the Protestant faith. He fled to his birthplace in Geneva, where he died in 1691.

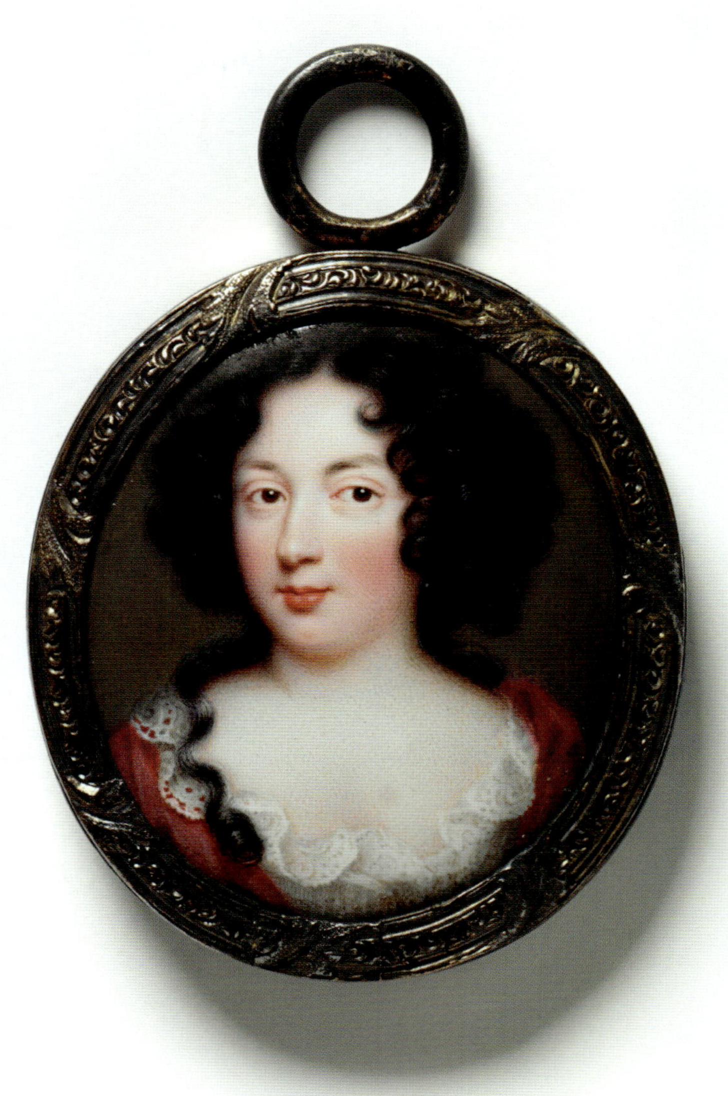

*JEANNE-ANTOINETTE POISSON, MARQUISE
DE POMPADOUR (1721–64)*

François Boucher (1703–70)
France; 1758
Oil on canvas
V&A: 487–1882; bequeathed by John Jones, 1882;
h. 52.4 cm, w. 57.8 cm

THIS PORTRAIT DEPICTS JEANNE-ANTOINETTE Poisson, Marquise de Pompadour, Louis XV's official mistress from 1745 until her death in 1764. Fashionably and expensively educated at the expense of Charles-François Lenormant de Tournehem (1684–1751), her mother's former lover, Pompadour moved in the most cultured Parisian circles. In 1741 she married into the ranks of the nobility and entered the royal court. She was the first royal mistress from a bourgeois background to retain such an elevated position over so many years. As Louis XV's mistress, she had a remarkable influence on all aspects of royal policy – court patronage, domestic and international affairs – which attracted a great deal of censure.

The Marquise's role as a patron of the arts and avid collector of luxury objects influenced taste throughout the French court. After her death, a team of evaluators took more than a year to list her possessions, which included fine paintings, sculpture, engravings, books (bound with her arms), furniture, metalwork, ceramics and porcelain, tapestries and carpets, and a substantial wardrobe of fashionable dress and accessories. These objects had come from the many mansions that she had remodelled or redecorated, and from the few that she had built for herself, notably the Château de Meudon at Bellevue (built 1748–50).

The Marquise skilfully used portraiture to establish her reputation for beauty, refinement and learning. Her patronage bolstered the careers of several leading artists. François Boucher, the King's artist, painted no fewer than seven portraits, each posed in different indoor and outdoor surroundings, and each displaying her taste, learning and skills. For all that this portrait appears simple and direct – a contrast with many society portraits of the Marquise – it is carefully staged. The natural setting evokes her love of gardens. The sumptuous plain satin dress is artfully informal in style and modestly covers her to the neck, yet is accessorized with bejewelled buckled shoes and pearl jewellery. The book in her lap, and the heavy volumes on which she rests her left elbow, suggest her cultural interests, even in this pastoral setting.

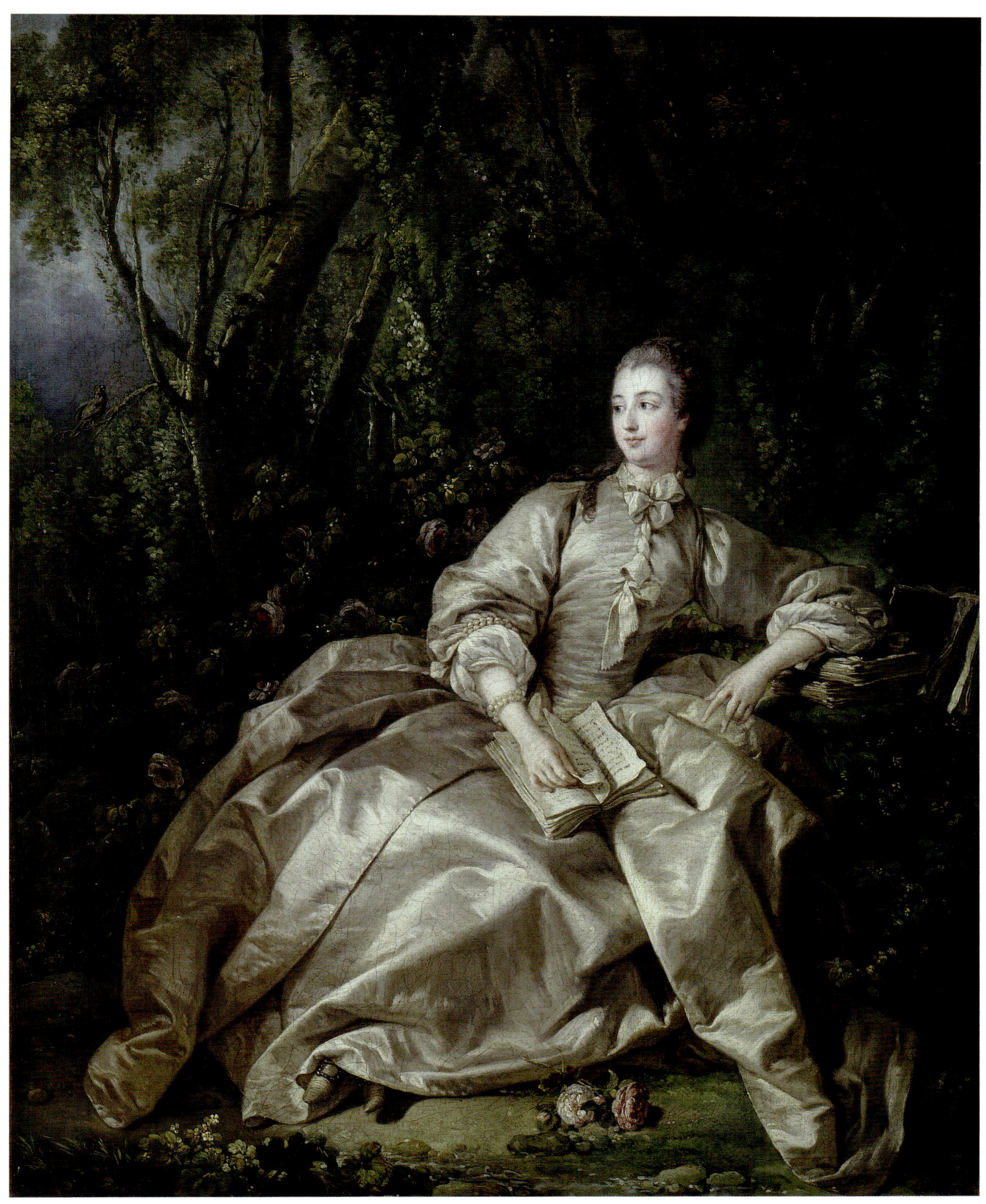

IVORY PORTRAIT OF LOUIS XIV OF FRANCE (*1638–1715*)

Michel Mollart (1641–1713)
Paris; before about 1683
Carved ivory
V&A: A.44–1935; h. 10.2 cm, w. 7 cm

THE SUBJECT OF THIS RELIEF PORTRAIT, Louis XIV (known as the Sun King), was one of the greatest patrons of the arts of the period. An absolute monarch, he believed in the 'divine right of kings' and deliberately promoted an image of himself, based on classical iconography and the visual language of the ancient Greek and Roman Empires, that would impress his power and legitimacy upon his often rebellious subjects and rivals.

Michael Mollart, from Dieppe, was lodged at the Louvre in Paris as an ivory-carver and medallist from 1684 to 1703. His small relief portrait combines contemporary French and ancient Roman symbols. Louis wears the helmet of a classical warrior, with a contemporary wig. His armour, too, is classically inspired, though decorated with the French royal fleurs-de-lis and cockerel, and edged with fine contemporary lace. He wears several medallions portraying members of his family, thus making clear his most significant dynastic connections. His wife Queen Marie-Thérèse (1638–83), daughter of the Habsburg emperor Philip IV of Spain (1605–65), lies prominently on his chest, while his mother Anne of Austria (1601–66), Philip IV's sister, hangs above his ear. His paternal grandfather Henry IV (1553–1610) (page 44), the first Bourbon King of France, and his father Louis XIII (1601–43) adorn his helmet. A figure of Fame surmounts the medallion of his mother, while personifications of Justice (holding scales) and Fortitude (with a pillar) appear on his shoulder. Two further cardinal virtues, Prudence and Temperance, may be the figures at his throat. The letters L and M appear along his chest, presumably standing for Louis and Marie-Thérèse. This iconography suggests that the ivory was probably made before the death of Marie-Thérèse in 1683. In addition, Apollo the sun god, with whom Louis identified himself, drives his chariot in victory across the helmet. Such ivory portraits were popular in the seventeenth and eighteenth centuries, prized for their virtuoso carving.

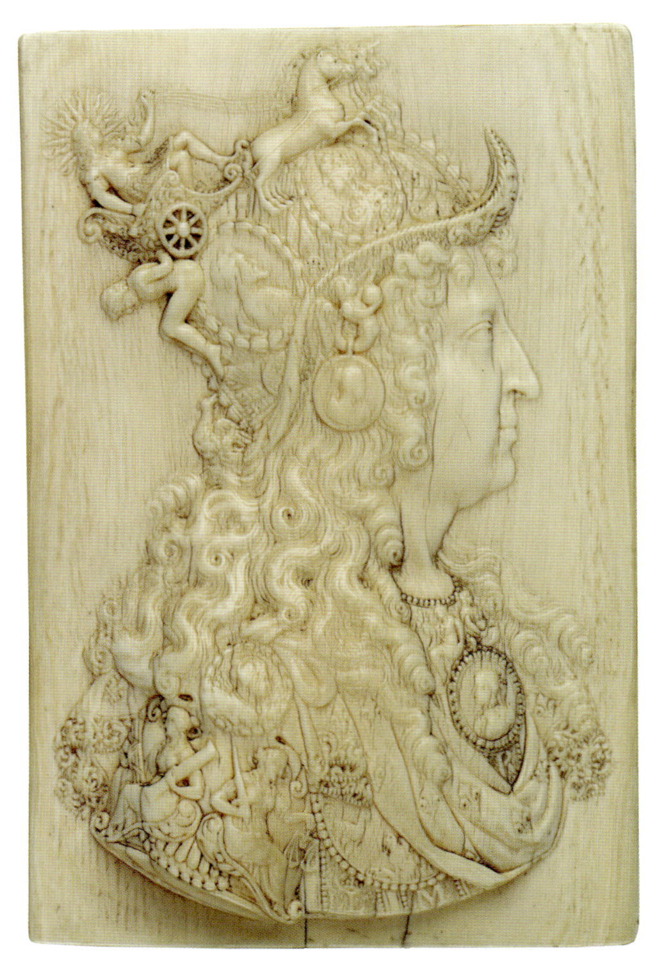

PETER THE GREAT OF RUSSIA (1672–1725)
WITH A BLACK PAGE

Baron Gustav von Mardefeld (about 1660–1729)
Probably Russia; about 1720
Watercolour on vellum
V&A: 605–1882; bequeathed by John Jones;
h. 21.6 cm, w. 16.5 cm

DURING HIS REIGN (1682–1725), PETER I of Russia embarked upon a programme of military, religious and administrative reforms that began the modernization of Russia, and its development as a great European state. In 1721, he was accorded the title of Emperor of All Russia, Great Father of the Fatherland and 'the Great', the title by which he is best known in western Europe. Peter's reforms were partly inspired by the many ideas he had gleaned during his remarkable travels in Europe, in 1697–8, some of which are incorporated into the iconography of this miniature.

The painting probably dates to around 1720 when the artist, Prussian diplomat and soldier, Baron Gustav von Mardefeld, was sent to Russia as his state's ambassador. A diplomatic gift, it cleverly combines a Western classical inheritance with references to Russia's indigenous cultural traditions. War is the dominant theme and battle rages in the background. While some of the warriors are clad as traditional Russians in Cossack hats, others wear fashionable Western three-cornered hats. All are clean-shaven, in reference to one of Peter's many cultural reforms that attacked the traditional Russian orthodoxy of wearing long beards by enforcing shaving on all polite society. Another 'Westernizing' touch is the depiction of Peter alongside his well-dressed black slave, denoted by the silver collar that he wears around his neck and by his sword. But here too a Russian touch is found – the frog-fastening on his coat is typical of traditional Eastern attire.

Depicted as a secular figure and bare-headed, Peter's political and military standing is made evident in his attire: a baton of office in his right hand, and over his fashionable western European coat he wears the ribbon of the Russian Order of St Andrew (which he had founded), a tricolour military sash and a breastplate carrying the Russian insignia of the double-headed eagle. The decorative helmet is classical in inspiration, a Western artistic convention indicating ancient lineage and tradition.

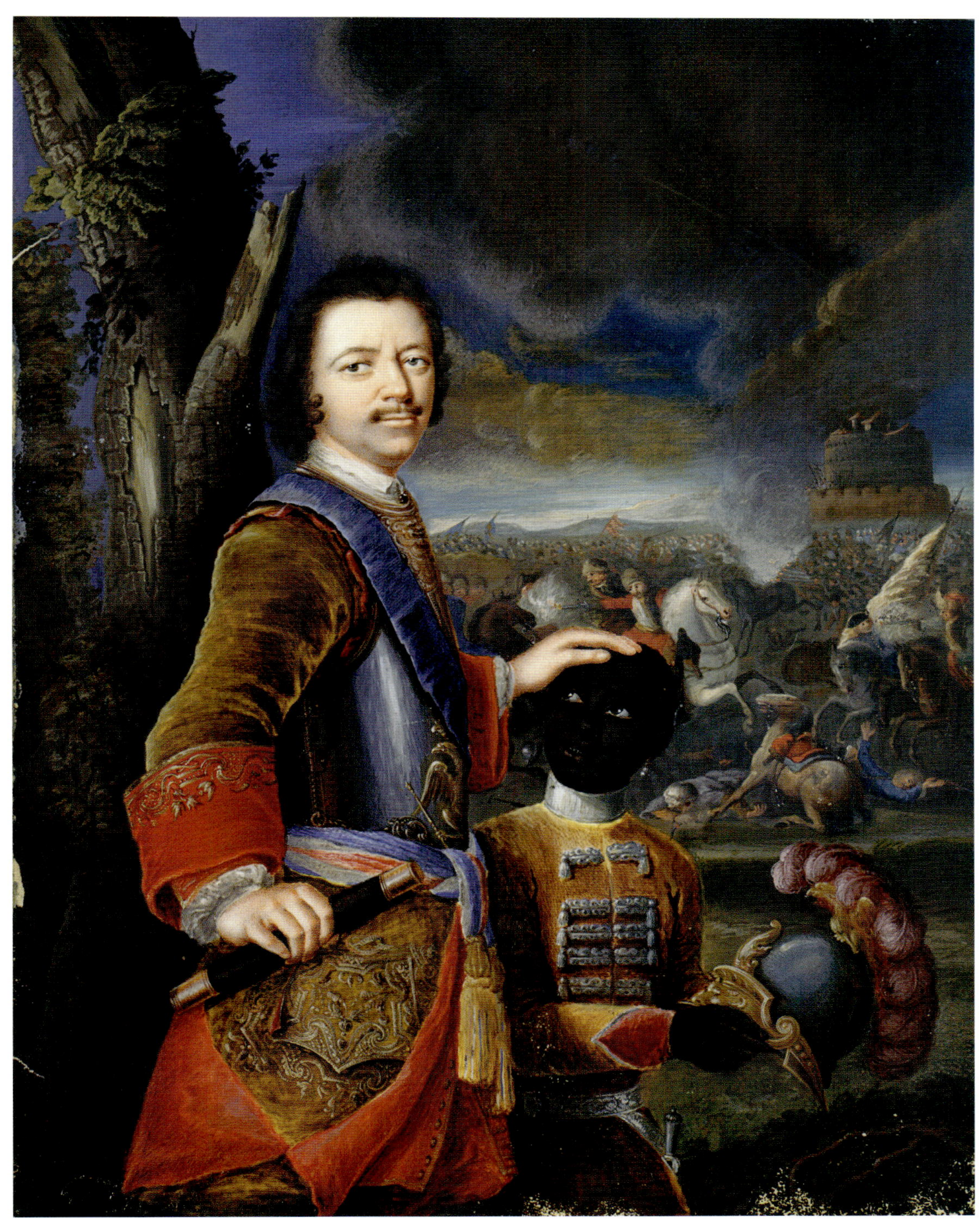

WOVEN SILK

Probably designed by Jean-Demosthène Dugourc
(1749–1825); manufactured by Camille Pernon et cie
Lyons; 1797–8
Silk brocaded with metal threads
V&A: T.69–1951; h. 297 cm, w. 75.5 cm,
h. pattern repeat 297 cm

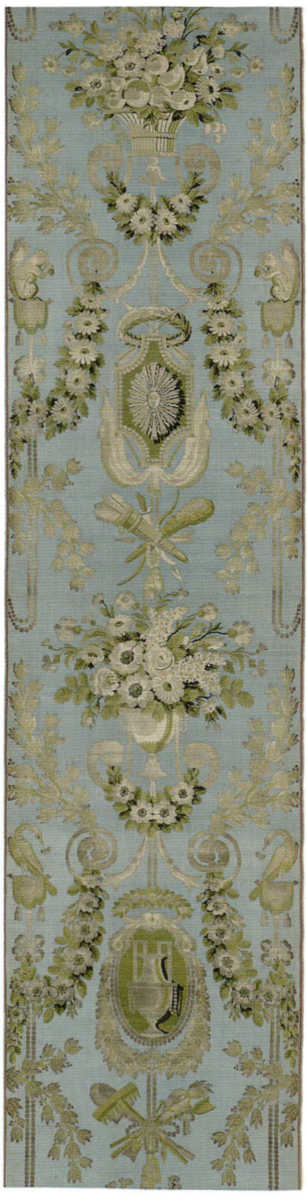

CARLOS IV (1748–1819) BECAME KING OF
Spain in December 1788, six months
before the French Revolution. A great
connoisseur of the arts, he spent twenty
years as heir to the throne amassing
collections of musical instruments, clocks
and paintings and indulging his passion for architecture. His
collections filled his apartments in the Spanish royal palaces
and in his newly built retreats, the Casita del Principe at the
Escorial and the Casita del Labrador at Aranjuez. Even
during the upheavals of the revolutionary wars outside Spain,
Carlos continued to decorate his palaces. He patronized not
only Spanish silk manufacturers, but also the pre-eminent
French silk-weaving partnership of Camille Pernon et cie,
from whom the Spanish royal family first commissioned
furnishing textiles in the late 1780s.

The French Revolution (1789) resulted in great
reversals of fortune for those involved in silk production. Yet
Pernon et cie, official supplier to the French royal household
until its suppression in 1797, managed to survive, weaving
silks for major clients outside France. An exceptional example
of the most technically complex of woven silks, this length
was probably designed for Carlos IV.

When acquired by the Museum in 1951, this silk was
thought to have come from the Doge's Palace in Venice.
However, an order book of the silk-weaving firm of Tassinari
et Chatel, successors to Pernon, contains a sketch of the
pattern in 1797, annotated as 'probably made for Carlos IV
of Spain'. Intriguingly, no trace of the delivery of this order
to Spain has yet been found in the Spanish Royal Archives.
However, it is very much in keeping with the designs by
Jean-Demosthène Dugourc for other Spanish commissions in
the period, the most notable being those still hanging in the
Billiard Room in the Casita del Labrador at Aranjuez. Both
the silver thread and the colours of the silk have survived in
a remarkable state of preservation, offering an unusually clear
impression of the impact that such grandiose neoclassical
colour schemes and motifs had in princely interiors.

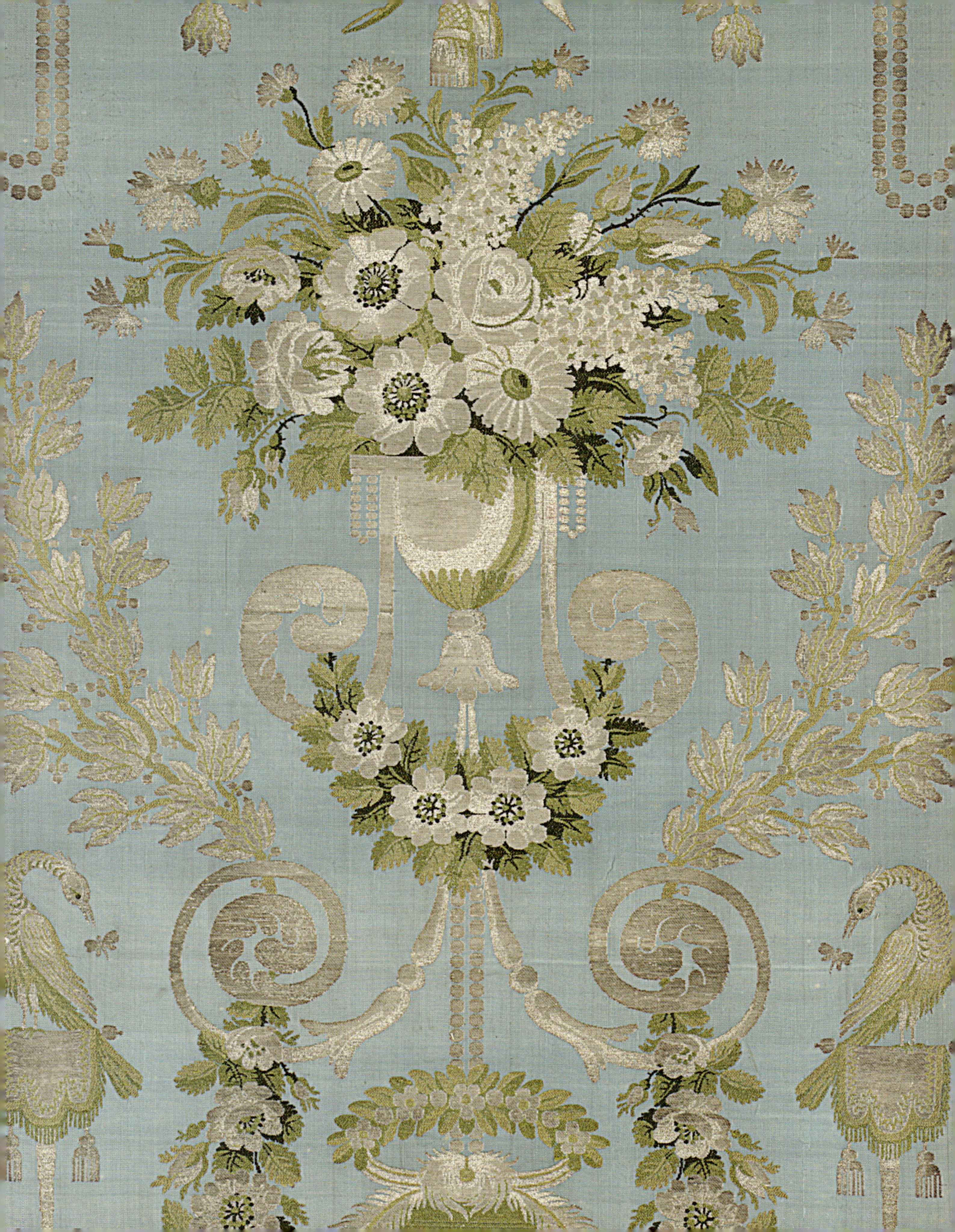

POWER AND GLORY

ANGUS PATTERSON

ETWEEN 1600 AND 1800 NOT A YEAR went by without parts of Europe either being at war or preparing for war. Princes and rulers were expected to take a personal role in such conflicts, and the objects in this section show how even warfare could offer an opportunity for the creation of luxury goods for personal use in war or to celebrate victories.

The period began with the Thirty Years War (1618–48), the first European-wide conflict, encompassed the Seven Years War (1756–63), often described as the first world war, and ended with the French Revolutionary and Napoleonic Wars (1792–1815), a cataclysm that redrew the map of Europe for the next 100 years. Wars became increasingly strategic, large-scale and motivated more by issues of state than by the religious divisions that had prompted earlier conflicts. The War of the Spanish Succession (1701–14) saw a wide-ranging coalition of the Holy Roman Empire, Britain, the Netherlands and Portugal resisting the unification of the French and Spanish crowns. More than a million people were killed.

While warfare remained a constant in European life, its conduct, cost and scale changed during the period. Participants in battle grew from the 19,000 per side average of the Thirty Years War to 45,000 by the 1790s. States took greater control over the recruiting, training, provisioning and deploying of their armed forces. The French Army was 350,000 strong by 1700. The British Navy grew from 50,000 in 1700 to 150,000 by the early nineteenth century. In Prussia, Frederick the Great (1712–86) aimed to professionalize warfare to the extent that civilians might be unaware that it was happening. Armies set off to war in spring, and conflicts were suspended during winter.

Contemporary accounts by those who experienced the Thirty Years War suggest that the arts suffered catastrophically as castles and cathedrals burned, and plundered communities starved or succumbed to disease. Destruction, like the storming of Magdeburg in Germany in 1631 – described by Jürgen Ackermann, a captain who took part, as 'such a thunder and crack of muskets, incendiary mortars and great cannon that no-one could either see or hear'[1] – was well documented, but rare. Germany, according to the art dealer Joachim Sandraert (1606–88), 'saw her palaces, decorated with beautiful paintings, and her churches, go up in flames, and her eyes were so clouded by smoke and tears, that she was unable to retain any desire or energy to look after the arts'.[2] Despite these grim reports, damage to the arts was actually localized and intermittent.

Artists and craftsmen, accustomed by their training to travelling as journeymen, sometimes moved in search of work because of war or persecution. After the Revocation of the Edict of Nantes in 1685, 250,000 French Protestants (Huguenots) emigrated, many of them silversmiths, pewterers and textile workers who revolutionized their trades in their new home cities, especially in London. Not only did artists relocate, broadening their inspirations and influence, but so did artworks. Looting, ransom demands and taxation were cultural and economic drains for towns in war zones. In 1631 the wealthy Simon Prinz of the German city of Augsburg bought protection for his house by handing over 'silver and gold goblets, bracelets and rings, together with a variety of other good things' and then, at his protecting officer's invitation, had to endure an army dinner at which toasts to the invading commanders were celebrated in his goblet.[3] Looting with official backing was not theft, but a gratuity. Queen Christina of Sweden (1626–89) is said to have ordered her army to attack Prague just before the signing of the Peace of Westphalia in 1648, in order to secure Rudolph II's art collection.[4]

War was a means to an end, and that end was not just territorial. War built reputations for both princes and artisans. It was an essential element of kingship, proclaiming power. Tapestries (page 54), sculpture (page 44), paintings (page 50) and medals celebrating great victories enabled royal images to be created, controlled and broadcast. The finest examples of firearms, long revered as luxury items, combined the skills of the gunsmith with those of the wood-carver, the goldsmith and the engraver to produce deadly weapons decorated in the same manner as furniture, ceramics or sculpture. So efficient did guns become that it was no longer sufficient to protect the individual with armour. Entire armies needed protecting in increasingly sophisticated fortifications, designed by the most imaginative engineers and architects. The use of artillery and the daring exploits of grenadiers – champions of this siege warfare – were commemorated in miniature on snuffboxes (page 58, 60) and on a heroic scale in tapestries.

Depictions of war were vital ingredients of a successful image-building campaign in the public arena of court and city. In around 1619 Don Baltasar de Zuñiga (1561–1622), who was in control of Spanish foreign policy, wrote, 'A monarchy that has lost its reputation, even if it has lost no territory, is a sky without a light, a sun without rays, a body without a soul.'[5] Later in the century a letter from Jean Chapelain to Louis XIV's finance minister, Jean-Baptiste Colbert, in 1662 outlined a programme to glorify war and monarchy using 'pyramids, columns, equestrian statues, colossuses, triumphal arches, marble and bronze busts, pedestals. To these historical monuments one can add our rich tapestries, fresco paintings and engravings.'[6]

This was art as political propaganda. It is epitomized in Louis's *Salon de Guerre* at Versailles by

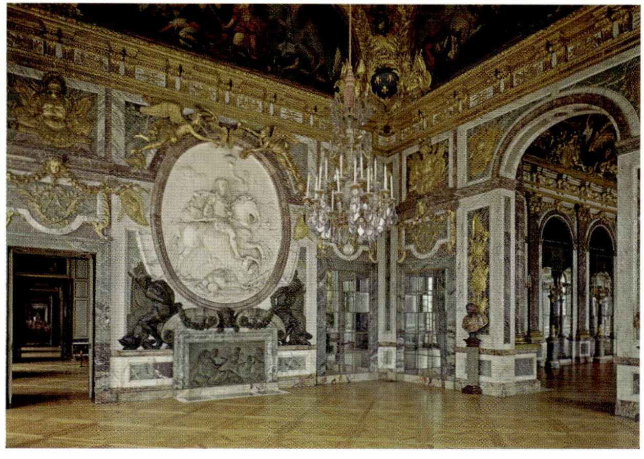

10 The *Salon de Guerre* at the Palace of Versailles, designed by Charles Lebrun, with a sculptural relief of *Louis XIV on Horseback riding in triumph over his enemies* by Antoine Coysevox. Paris, 1678–86

a relief sculpture of the King on horseback trampling his enemies. This stood below the ceiling frescoes by the King's painter, Charles Lebrun (1619–90), and showed the war goddess Bellona destroying the Spanish, the Dutch and the Germans, as well as rebels within France. Engraved prints of the scenes were sold far and wide (pl.10).

1 Geoff Mortimer, *Eyewitness Accounts of the Thirty Years War*, London, 2002, p.67

2 Sigrun Haude, 'Warfare and Artistic Production in the German Lands during the Thirty Years War (1618–48)', in Pia Cuneo (ed.), *Artful Armies, Beautiful Battles: Art and Warfare in Early Modern Europe*, History of Warfare Series, Vol.9, Brill, 2002, p.55

3 Mortimer, 2002, pp.68–9

4 Luca Mola, 'Arts and Society', in Beat Kumin (ed.), *The European World 1500–1600*, London and New York, 2009, p.155

5 Humphrey Butters, 'Dynastic Politics, Religious Conflict and Reason of State ca 1500–1650', in Kumin (ed.), 2009, p.297

6 Julie Anne Plax, 'Seventeenth-Century Images of French Warfare', in Cuneo (ed.), 2002, p.131

STATUE OF HENRY IV OF FRANCE (1553–1610)
ON HORSEBACK TRAMPLING HIS ENEMY

Attributed to Hubert Le Sueur
(about 1590–after 1658)
Paris; about 1620–25
Cast bronze
V&A: A.46–1951 and A.1–1992 (enemy figure
acquired separately and reunited); h. 96 cm,
w. 83.8 cm, d. 39.7 cm

THE DRAMA OF THIS STATUE, IN WHICH A contorted foot-soldier writhes under the flailing hooves of Henry IV's warhorse, contrasts with the serenity of its pair, an equestrian figure of Henry's successor, Louis XIII (1601–43). The statues together proclaim the stability of France after the tumultuous religious wars of the previous century. With the 1598 Edict of Nantes, Henry guaranteed freedom of worship to French Huguenots, ensuring that in 1610 Louis XIII inherited a kingdom at peace. In this statue Henry's calm attitude portrays a mixture of the righteous and the merciless. The horse is performing a *corvetto*, a prancing move that showed the great skill of its rider and the exceptional training of the horse. Thus Henry IV and his horse move as one, confidently symbolizing an implacable state that tamed unrest and marched on regardless.

Hubert Le Sueur's bronze-casting skills spread his reputation. After working for the French royal family, he was sent to London, where his life-size statue of Charles I (1600–1649) now stands in Trafalgar Square. His equestrian bronzes were inspired by classical prototypes. He also apparently drew inspiration from the workshop of the Florentine sculptor Giambologna (1529–1608) and his followers, including the practice of creating small-scale compositions from separately cast components.

As the son of a Parisian armourer, Le Sueur was well placed to create the accurate depiction of Henry's armour. This cuirassier's (cavalry soldier's) armour was heavier than armour of 50 years earlier, because by then it increasingly had to withstand gunfire on the battlefield. The cut of the short, square breastplate and the long, rounded tassets (thigh protectors) fastened below the knee compare closely with contemporary doublets and hose, and date the armour to the early seventeenth century. No cuirassier's helmet would be quite so open at the front. Le Sueur needed to identify the figure as Henry and, by equipping him with a classical Roman helmet, has transformed him into a mythological hero. Henry's armour gives him a modernity and authority that contrasts with the plain, old-fashioned half-armour of the defeated enemy.

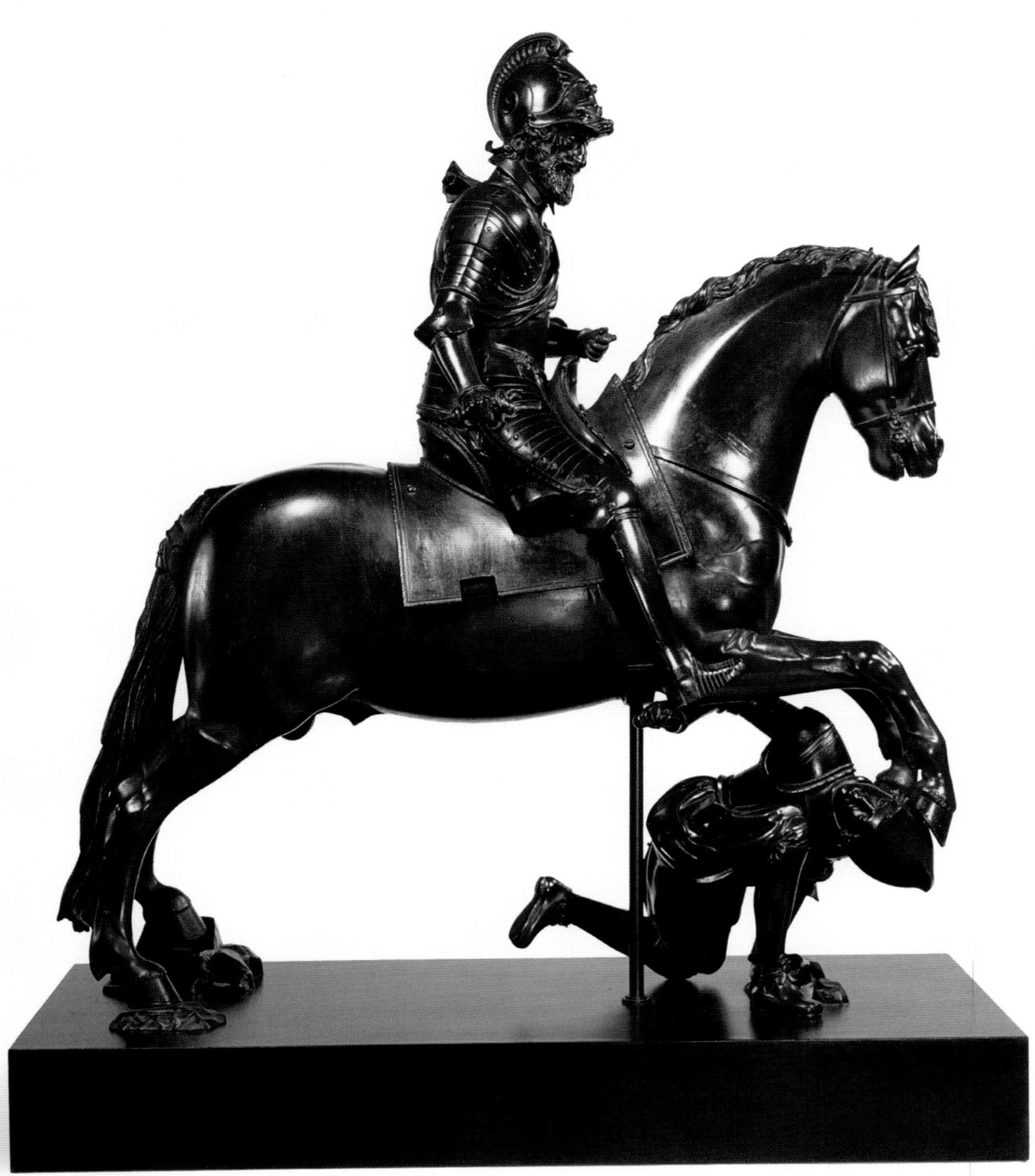

PAIR OF GAUNTLETS

Madrid; about 1614
Steel, parcel-gilt, gold, silver and silk
V&A: 1386&A–1888; h. 13.7 cm, l. 24.5 cm

THESE GAUNTLETS ARE DECORATED WITH palm banches, laurel wreaths, weapons and trophies symbolic of victory. They were not, however, designed to protect the hands, but to project an image. They probably come from one of three identically decorated parade armours commissioned for the sons of King Philip III of Spain (1568–1621) in around 1614, which survive in the Royal Armouries in Madrid.

The gauntlets are from the last great period of all-over body armours commissioned by noblemen for no purpose other than to impress. Modern art historians have tended to separate art from weapons and armour – and the violence and bloodletting with which they were associated were the antithesis of taste and style. Parade armour was ostentatious and showy, governed by the same aesthetics that shaped and adorned contemporary clothing. The armours associated with these gauntlets were designed to be worn with velvet hose and silk stockings; brightly coloured plumes atop the helmet completed the impression of magnificence. The crimson silk lining decorated with gold and silver thread is a rare survival. Its presence provides a soft contrast to the hard steel, and reminds us that the combination of rich fabrics and virtuoso metalworking turned the armoured body into a work of art.

The gauntlets are thoroughly international in their decoration and style. The gold and silver have been applied using 'damascening', a technique that European craftsmen imported from countries such as Syria (Damascus), Egypt and Turkey. This method, also used on other metalwork, involved inlaying gold and silver wire into engraved channels on the surface of the metal. In Europe the wire was often applied as an overlay, as on these gauntlets. Damascening came to Europe via Venice and was a particular favourite of the armourers of Milan. The Madrid armouries contain a number of damascened Milanese armours, which may have provided a source of inspiration for these gauntlets and their associated armours.

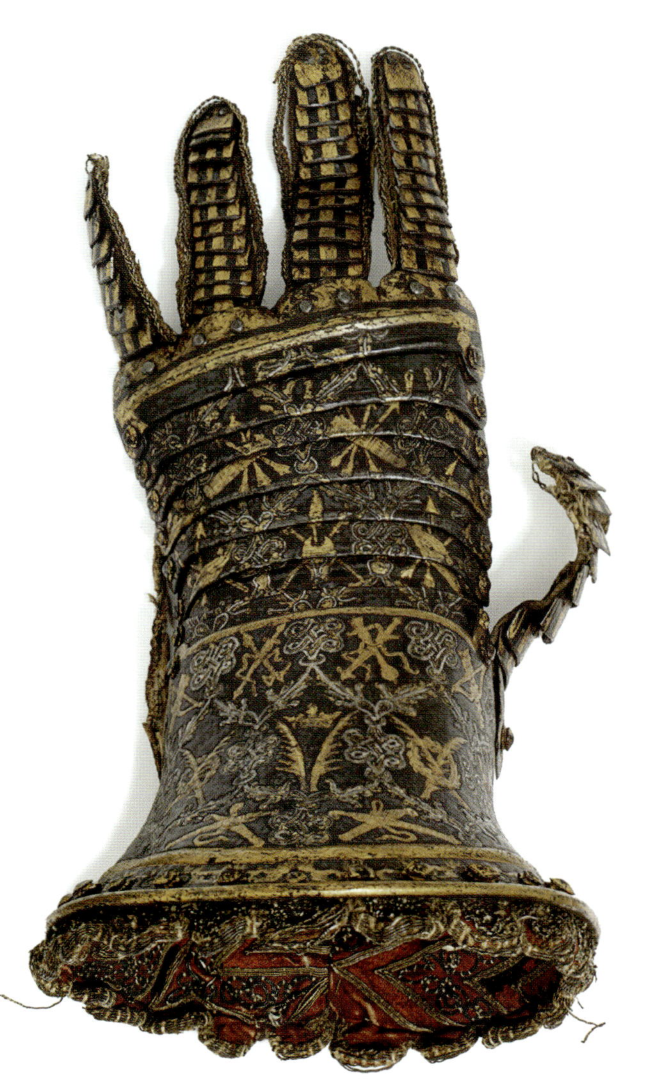
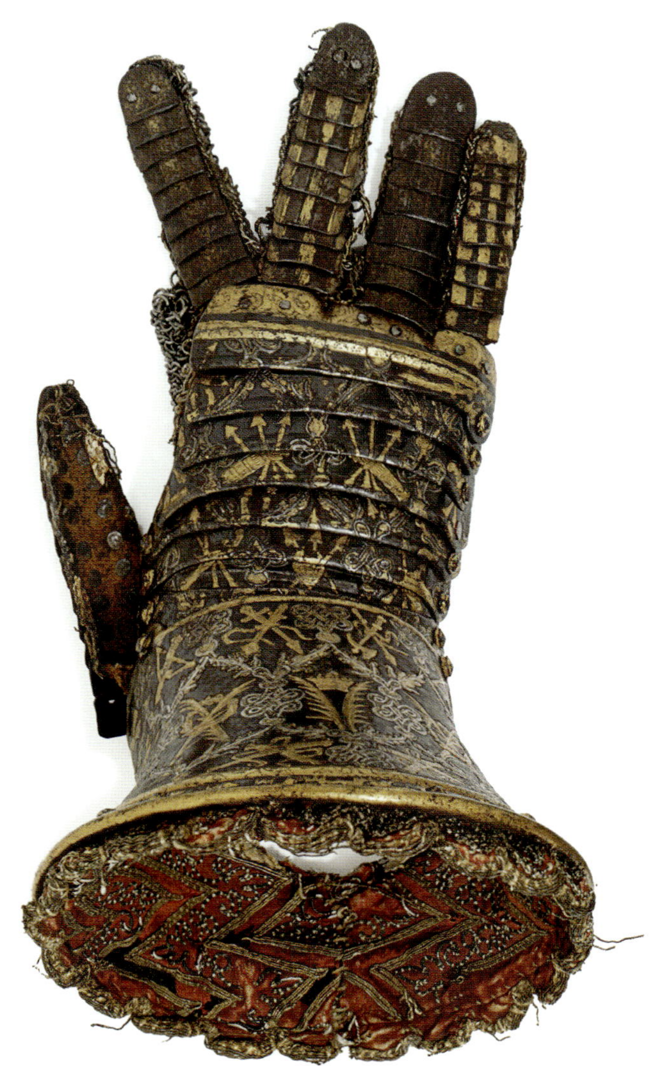

GORGET (ARMOURED COLLAR)

Probably Paris; 1600–25
Iron, brass rivets, remains of canvas lining
V&A: M.19&A–1976; l. 30.7 cm (frontplate),
30.4 cm (backplate)

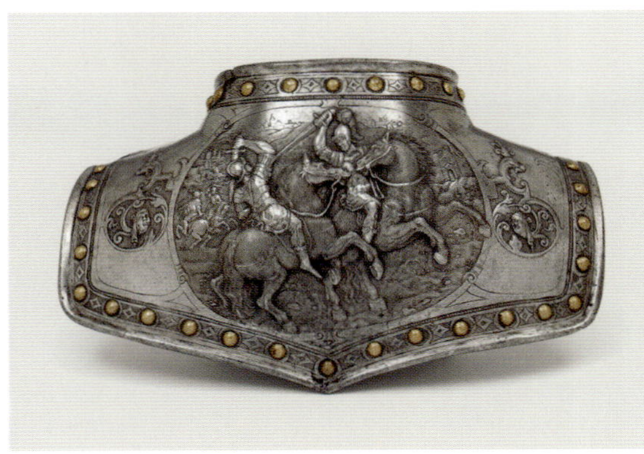

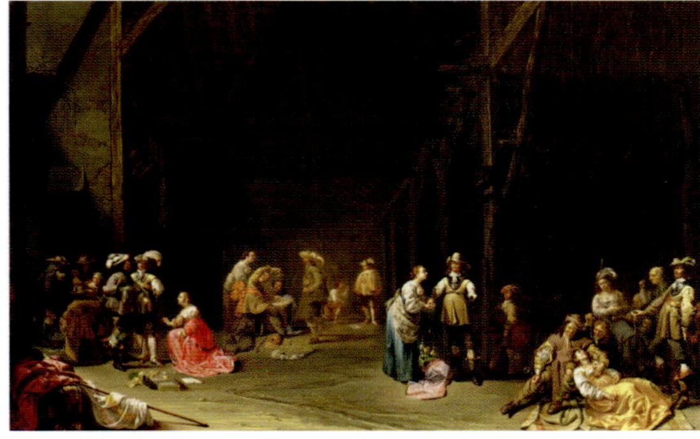

Dividing the Spoils (detail) by Jacob Duck. Oil on panel.
The Netherlands, *c*.1635 (Private Collection / Johnny Van
Haeften Ltd, London / Bridgeman Art Library)

THIS GORGET IS AN ITEM OF COSTUME armour rather than battle protection. By the early seventeenth century it was increasingly common for men to proclaim their military professions or aspirations in portraits by combining armour or weaponry with civilian clothing, with gorgets, spurs, swords and daggers taking on the role of dress accessories.

The early history of this armoured collar is unclear, although it is likely that it came from the French Royal Armouries. During the nineteenth century it was in the Armoury (*Cabinet d'Armes*) of the Emperor Napoleon III (1808–73) at the Château de Pierrefonds, where, in inventories of 1865 and 1867, the entry for it is annotated with the letters M.L., for 'Musée du Louvre'. The inventory makes clear that the gorget survived because it was a 'remarkable French work'.

Both front- and backplate are decorated with military scenes that suggest it was made for a cavalry leader. The frontplate shows a mounted officer controlling a rearing horse and addressing a troop of pikemen. On the backplate the battle is in full swing. The cavalry officer thrusts downwards, towards the body of his opponent, with a stiff, broad-bladed sword. The positioning of the scenes on the plates is appropriate: a cavalry officer faced his troops to organize and motivate them, but they followed him into action.

The scenes show the soldiers in classical armour. Military strategy in the seventeenth century was as much influenced by ancient Rome as architecture and sculpture were. While men did not go into battle dressed like Caesars, the use of large numbers of foot-soldiers arranged in grids was a conscious revival of ancient Roman battle formations.

The decoration on the gorget is embossed, chased and engraved. Embossing involves hammering the metal from behind into areas of high and low relief using shaped punches, while chasing uses a fine tool called a burin to work intricate details from the front. These techniques are more commonly the preserve of the goldsmith and brazier, as they would have interfered with the structural integrity of armour made for use in battle.

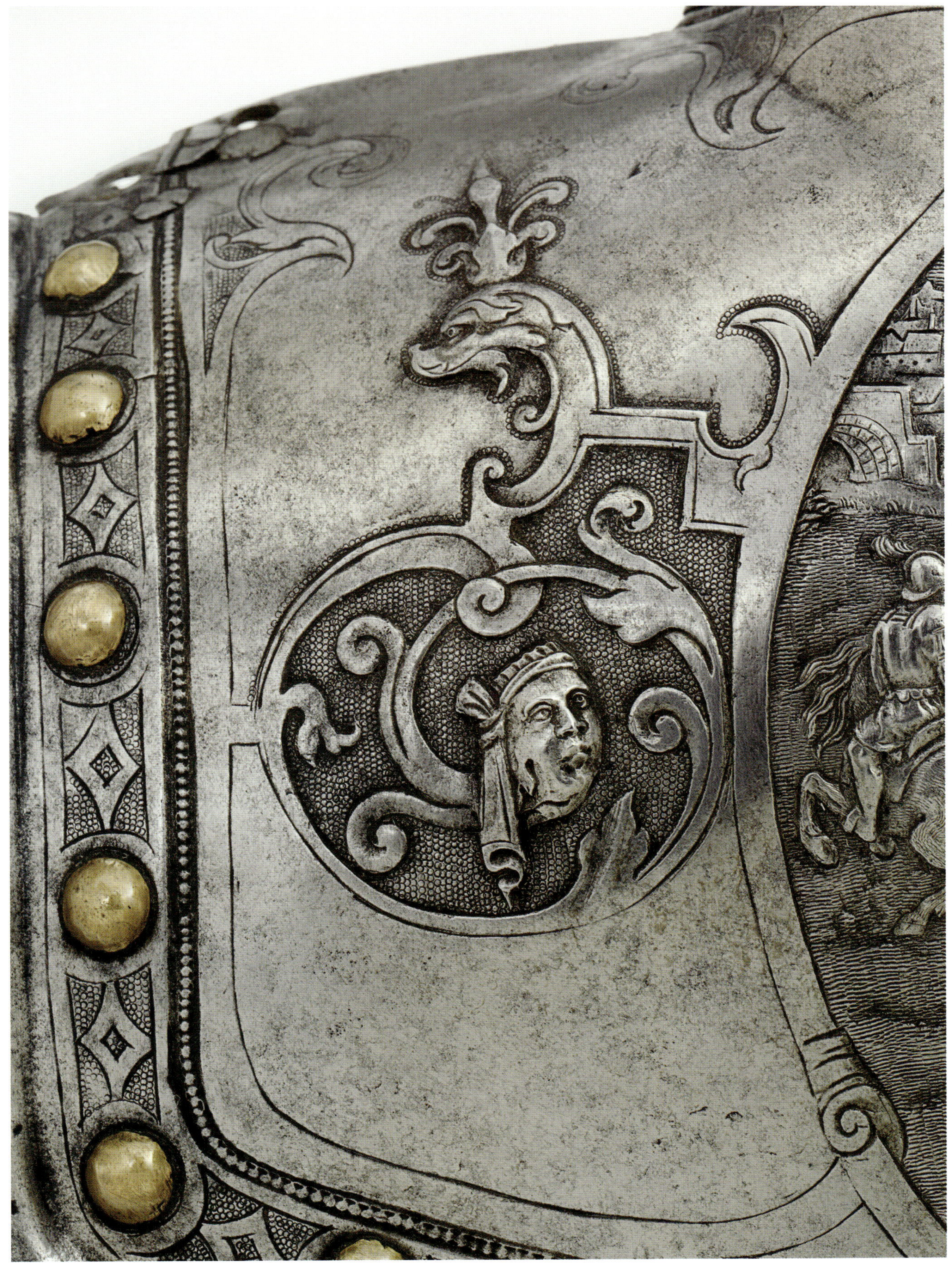

WAR AND VICTORY:
MODEL FOR A TITLE PAGE

Peter Paul Rubens (1577–1640)
Antwerp; 1634–5
Oil on panel
Painting: V&A: D.1399–1891; h. 16.8 cm, w. 13 cm
Frame: V&A: W.14–1915; h. 28 cm, w. 22.5 cm,
d. 3.6 cm

RUBENS'S PROPAGANDA PAINTINGS contradict the notion that the Thirty Years War prevented the development of the creative arts. He combined his work as a painter with his role as both courtier and diplomat, and his diplomatic career took him to Spain in 1628 and to London in 1629–30, where Charles I (1600–49) knighted him. He portrayed himself as a man of peace, yet his war art was grandiose, violent and triumphalist. He was a master of imperial Catholic propaganda.

This is his design for an engraved frontispiece for *El memorable y glorioso viage del infante Cardenal D. Fernando de Austria (The memorable and glorious journey of the Cardinal Infante Don Ferdinand of Austria)* (Antwerp, 1635), which recounts the journey of the Cardinal Infante Ferdinand (1609–41), the Spanish king's brother, from Spain to Brussels, where he had been appointed Governor of the Spanish Netherlands. It is one of 48 known title-pages by Rubens, for books ranging from poetry to archaeology, science and warfare. Rubens's designs also trumpeted Ferdinand's glorious entry into Antwerp in his street decorations for the *Pompa Introitus Ferdinandi (Entry celebrations of Ferdinand)*. Rubens was unusual in using oil paints for such sketches.

In the margin to the left are the remnants of Rubens's explanation of the design. An eighteenth-century collector, P.J. Mariette, trimmed the margins, but had the foresight to transcribe the notes onto a label still stuck to the back of the panel:

> *The arms of Cardinal Infante. The journey of his highness is compared to a flying eagle, with a serpent in its talons. The two Genii crowning [the arms of] His Serene Highness have butterfly wings, which denote the eternity of his glory. Victory holds a laurel wreath up to the eagle which signifies that Empire was restored through the victory at Nördlingen. The two palm trees supporting the arms of His Highness signify victory and strength for they hold the shield despite its weight. Mars is striding forward to indicate the victories worn by His Highness on his voyage.*

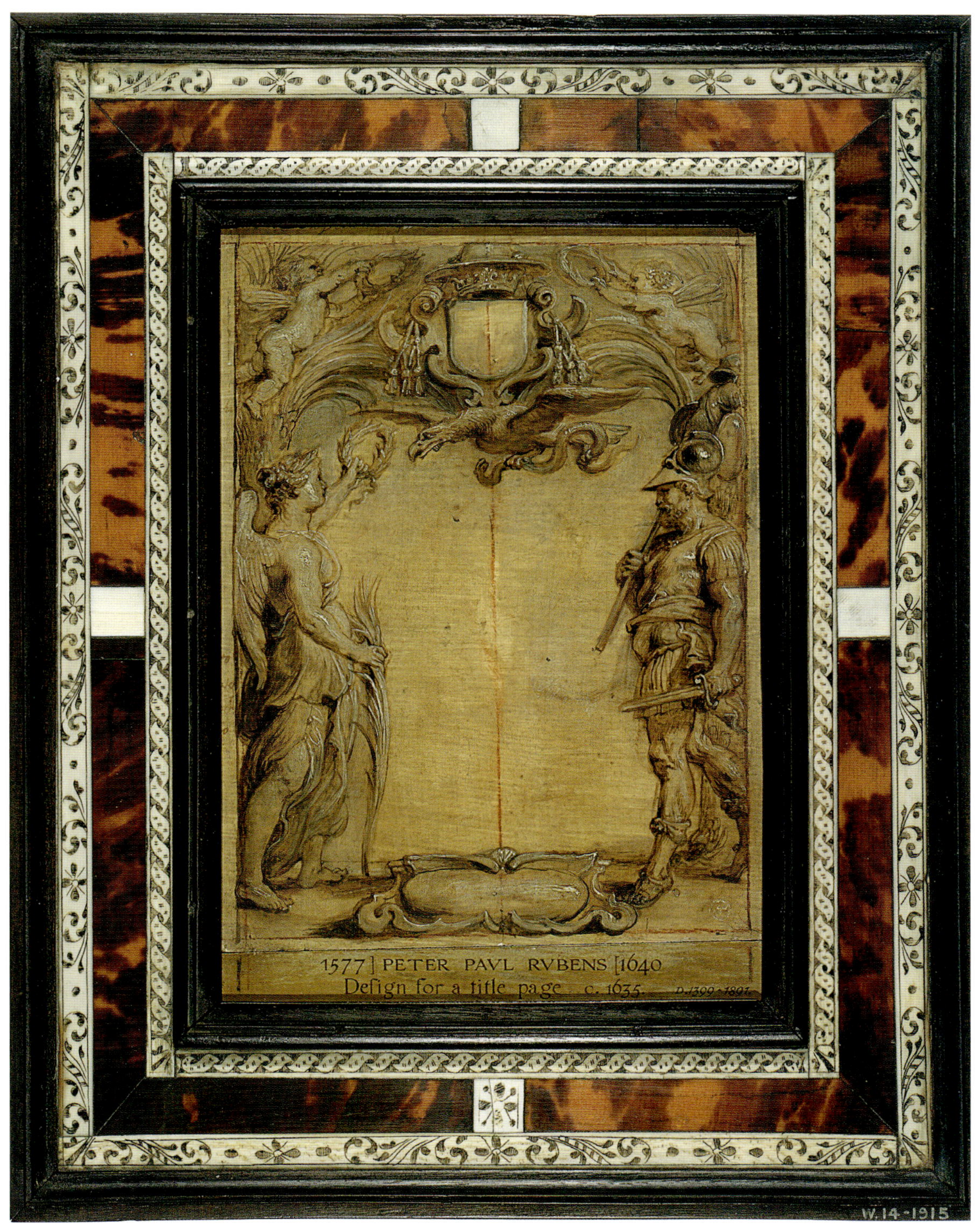

1577] PETER PAVL RVBENS [1640
Design for a title page c. 1635

THE HANGING

Designed by Jacques Callot (1592–1635);
published by Israel Henriet
Paris; 1633
Etching on paper
V&A: 21714:11; h. 8.8 cm, w. 19.2 cm

A SOBERING ANTIDOTE TO TRIUMPHALIST military art in the seventeenth century is a series of etchings called *The Miseries and Misfortunes of War* by Jacques Callot, published in 1633. *The Hanging* is one of 18 blood-curdling scenes depicting the sorry lot of the ordinary soldier. *The Miseries and Misfortunes of War* was published during a particularly violent phase of the Thirty Years War.

Callot's etchings introduced an exaggerated realism into the depiction of war. The rhyming couplets underneath were composed for the second printing, by Abbé Michel de Marolles, a seventeenth-century art dealer. They encourage us to see the soldiers as aggressors meeting a deserved fate. Irrespective of this later caption, it seems that Callot's aim – as his contemporary biographer, Filippo Baldinucci, explained – was to illustrate the 'hard life of the poor soldier'. The threadbare and malnourished soldiers on the right say a final prayer before being dragged up the ladder to swing with their comrades.

The soldier's hard life was one of long marches, interminable waits and haphazard payment, punctuated by occasional bouts of terrifying violence. In poorly disciplined troops, destruction, extortion, looting and rape marched with them, engendering panic as they approached. Other prints in Callot's series show soldiers pillaging towns, villages and convents, before community vengeance was meted out with lynchings and shootings. The lucky survivors lived on as deformed beggars. This was war with no winners.

Callot was an Italian-trained artist from Lorraine who worked at the Italian and French courts. He was an innovative etcher, developing a needle with an oval point (*échoppe*), which he turned as he drew, enabling him to vary line-widths to create a striking sense of depth. This technique has thrust the oak tree into the foreground, bringing the viewer nearer the action and adding to its immediacy.

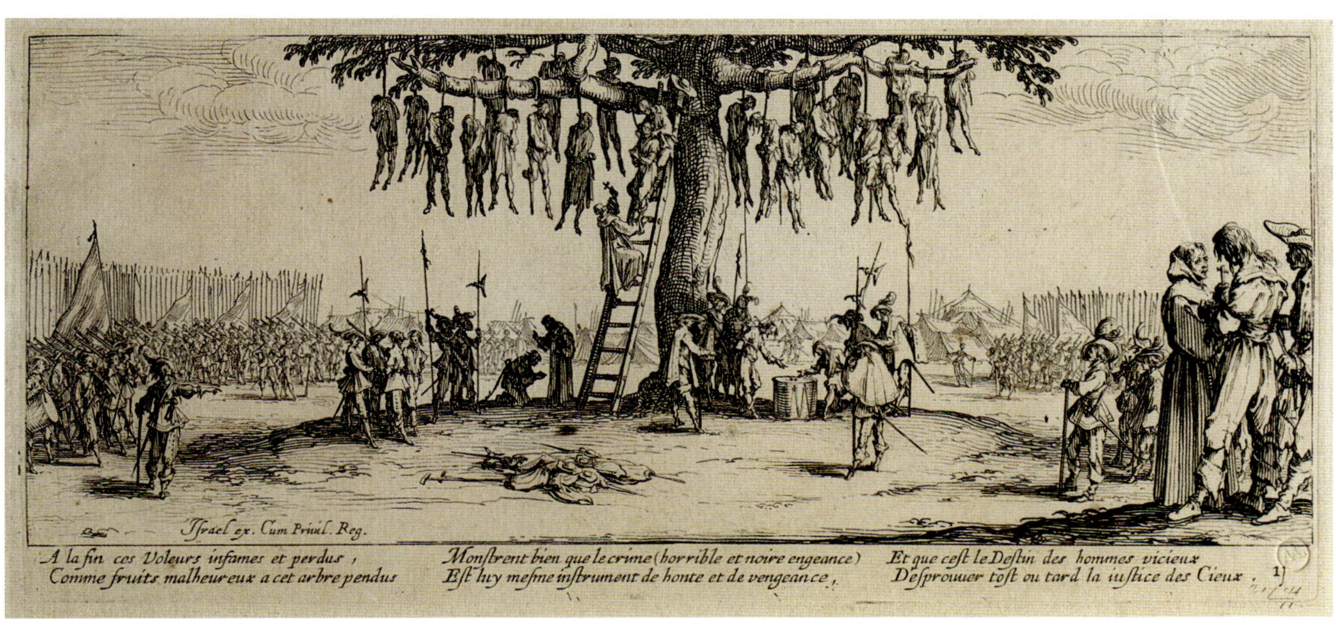

A la fin ces Voleurs infames et perdus , Monstrent bien que le crime (horrible et noire engeance) Et que cest le Destin des hommes vicieux
Comme fruits malheureux a cet arbre pendus Est luy mesme instrument de honte et de vengeance , Desprouuer tost ou tard la iustice des Cieux , 11

THE MARCH

Possibly designed by Philipp De Hondt
(1683–1741); made by Judocus de Vos (1661–1734)
Brussels; 1718–19
Tapestry woven in wool
V&A: T.283–1972; given, along with six others
from *The Art of War* series, by Mrs Josa Finney,
in memory of Oswald James Finney; h. 419.1 cm,
w. 616 cm

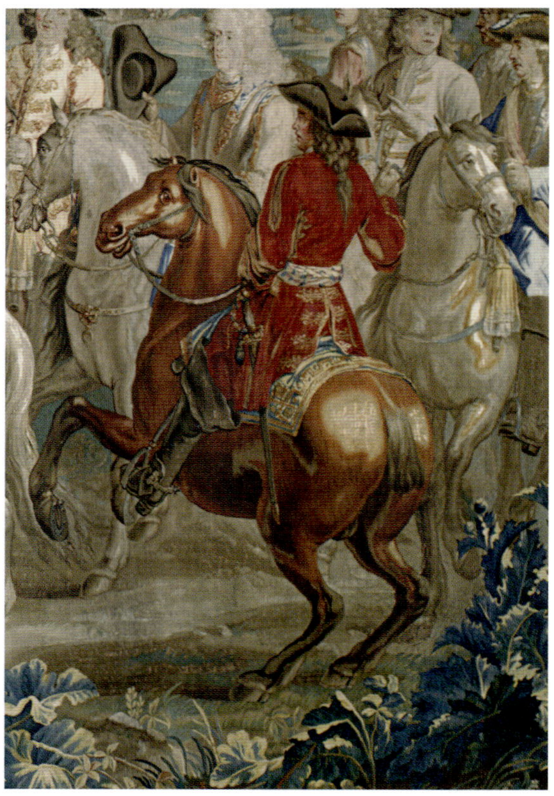

TAPESTRY WAS THE MOST EXPENSIVE AND
prestigious form of pictorial art between
1600 and 1800. As a medium for
commemorating military exploits it has a
long history. While fifteenth-century
tapestries placed the viewer in the centre
of the action, among the charging horses and slashing blades,
the baroque period saw the shift towards a more detached
celebration of the power of a glorious commander.

This tapestry is from a second version of a series
known as *The Art of War* and dates from the early eighteenth
century. The Museum owns seven tapestries in the series. The
scenes of military life shown in the series include *The Camp*,
The Siege and *The Ambush*. In the centre of this tapestry,
depicting *The March*, the commander, mounted on a white
horse, holds up his baton as if conducting an orchestra. His
officers, attended by messengers and servants (one a black
African), follow a long line of cavalry and foot-soldiers as
it winds into the distance across a plain. The tapestries are
framed with military trophies, and each has an emblem of
the subject that it depicts in the centre of the lower border –
in this case, saddles, harnesses, trunks and riding boots.

The tapestry scenes follow a format created by the
Flemish artist Adam Frans van der Meulen (1632–90) in his
famous *Histoire du Roi* series, first woven in the 1660s in
Louis XIV's Gobelins factory 'to render immortal the actions
of the King'. In these a rise in the foreground creates a stage
for the main players, while the vastness of the landscape
beyond hints at the massive scale of military operations.
The less edifying aspects of campaigning – the drudgery, the
hunger, the destruction – are kept in the distance. We view
the tapestries as detached observers of skilful leadership: all
is well organized and controlled.

The first *Art of War* series was woven for Elector
Maximilian Emanuel of Bavaria (1662–1726). This tapestry
is from the second series, woven for Augustus the Strong
(1670–1733), Elector of Saxony, King of Poland and Grand
Duke of Lithuania.

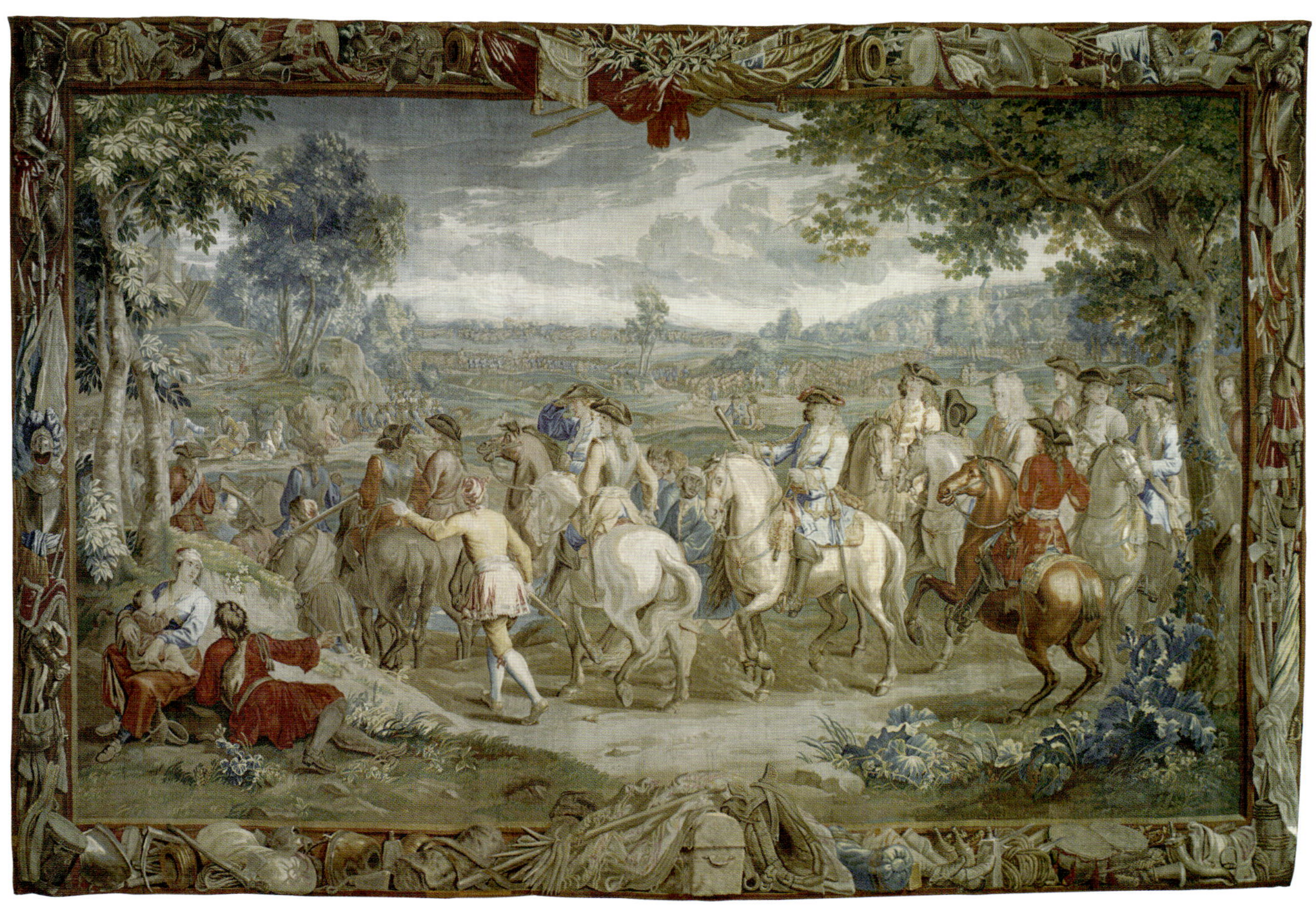

AIRGUN

Johann Gottfried Kolbe (active 1730–53)
London; 1730–43
Carved walnut with chased and engraved silver,
brass; the lock signed 'Kolbe'; the barrel signed
'*Kolbe Fecit Londini*' ('Kolbe made this in London')
V&A: 494–1894; l. 135.7 cm

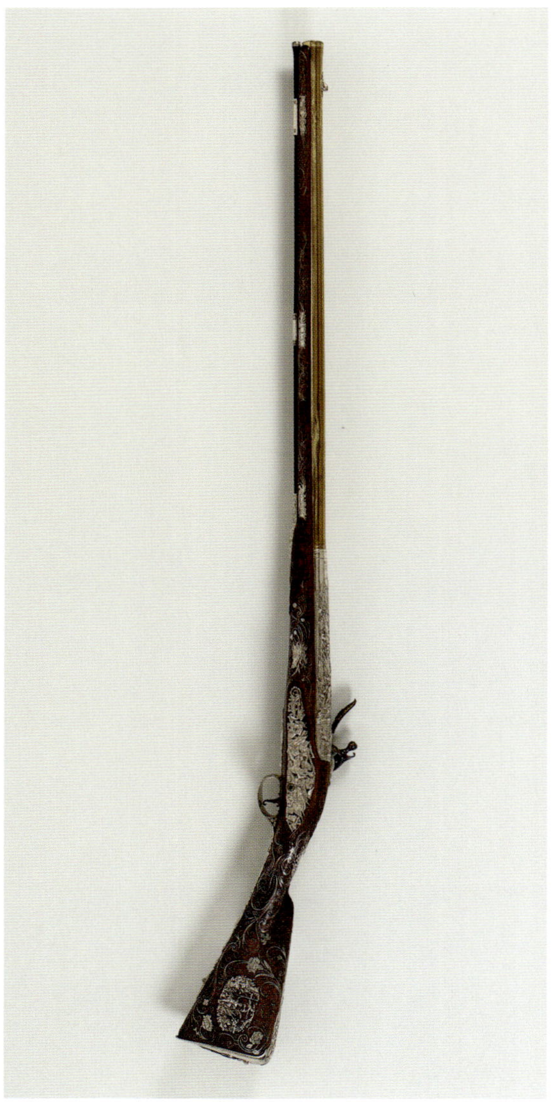

THE BEAUTY OF THE CARVED WALNUT STOCK, chased silver mounts and inlaid silver wirework on this airgun are certainly of royal quality, and when it was sold in 1817 its sale catalogue listed it as 'formerly in the possession of George II'. The gun is signed by Johann Gottfried Kolbe, a gun-maker from Suhl in eastern Germany. Kolbe was the son of Johann Christoph Kolbe, an engraver, and produced a number of delicately chiselled and engraved airguns, some disguised as walking sticks. He is known to have worked in London during the 1730s, and the fact that some of the designs of mounts on this gun relate to a book of engraved designs published in 1743 suggests that he was in London until at least that date.

Among the triumphalist trophies chased on the lock, stock and barrel are allegorical figures. The butt-plate shows a town surrendering its keys. On the left of the stock, Mercury, the messenger of the gods, flies above a figure of Minerva, the goddess of war. On the right, sitting next to a lion and holding laurels and palms of victory, is an eagle from whose beak darts a bolt of lightning, an attribute of Jupiter. Both turn to face a wilting lily. It is possible the group celebrates the alliance of Prussia and Britain against France during the War of the Austrian Succession (1740–48) and that Minerva may symbolize Britannia. In 1743 George II (1683–1760) led a British and Prussian army successfully against France at the Battle of Dettingen, the last time that a British monarch led his troops into battle.

Airguns had advantages over other firearms. The mechanism needed less protection from the weather, and misfires were rare. Compressed air provided the force for the shot, and one charge of air allowed multiple shots. There was no puff of smoke or loud bang to alert prey, but pumping too much air into the reservoir might cause the gun to explode.

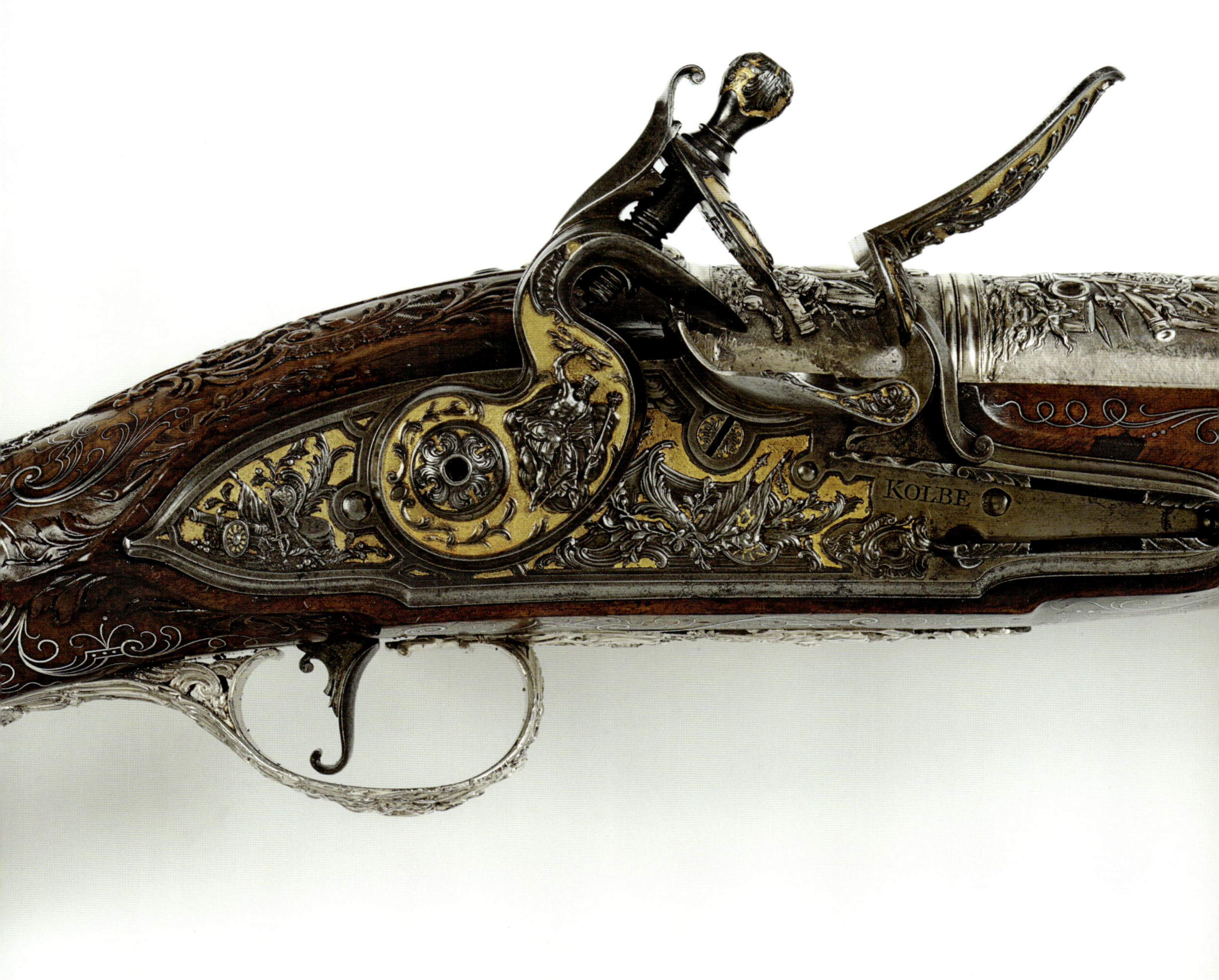
KOLBE

SNUFFBOX

Probably Germany; 1740–65
Turtle-shell overlaid with chased gold and piqué
in gold
V&A: 907–1882; bequeathed by John Jones;
h. 4.3 cm, w. 8.5 cm, d. 9.9 cm

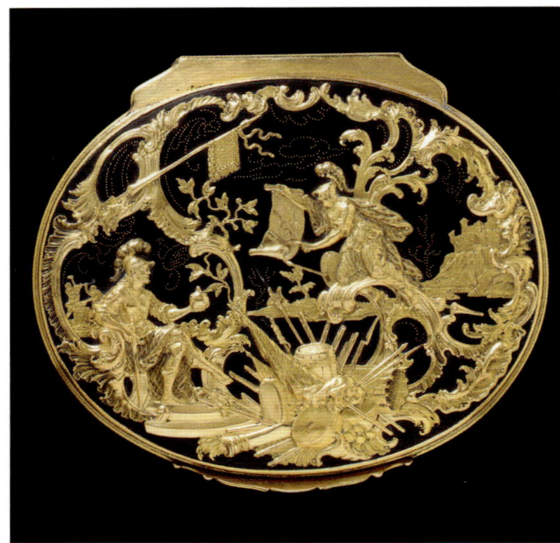

S NUFFBOXES WERE USED BY BOTH MEN AND WOMEN. They held powdered tobacco to be inhaled through the nose. A whole range of precious and natural materials went into their manufacture, and lavish silver and gold mounts made them objects to be collected as well as used. The exquisite goldwork on this box, in the style of engraved ornament prints published in Augsburg, makes it one of the finest turtle-shell boxes to survive from the eighteenth century. The piqué inlay was created by piercing the turtle-shell with a small, profiled gold or silver rod to give the surface this appearance.

On the lid of the box the gold is chased with a scene combining ancient Roman mythology with modern military practice. Bellona, goddess of war, reveals the plan of a fortification to a soldier in classical dress. The soldier sits facing a fortified town on a rocky outcrop, his right hand resting on his sword and his left raising the staple weapon of eighteenth-century siege warfare, the explosive grenade. Behind him, armourers hammer new weapons on anvils, while in the foreground and on the other surfaces of the box, trophy arrangements of muskets, bayonets, swords and hatchets, among banners and drums, commemorate the role of the grenadier. Baroque military art frequently looked to Bellona for inspiration.

Grenadiers were elite stealth-troops of strong, educated, athletic risk-takers. Among their weapons they carried a pouch of 12–15 iron grenades, to within throwing distance of an enemy's defences. Grenades, medieval in origin, came to be relied on during the late seventeenth century when hand-to-hand battles became rarer and fortifications reached their peak of sophistication under Louis XIV's military engineer, Marshal Vauban (1633–1707). The box may have been a gift to the commander of a company of grenadiers.

In 1882, when the Museum acquired the box by bequest from the military tailor John Jones, it came with a legend that it had been a present from Louis XIV (1638–1715) to Vauban, but its elegant, chased gold scroll- and shellwork date it to the mid-eighteenth century, making an association with the Seven Years War much more likely.

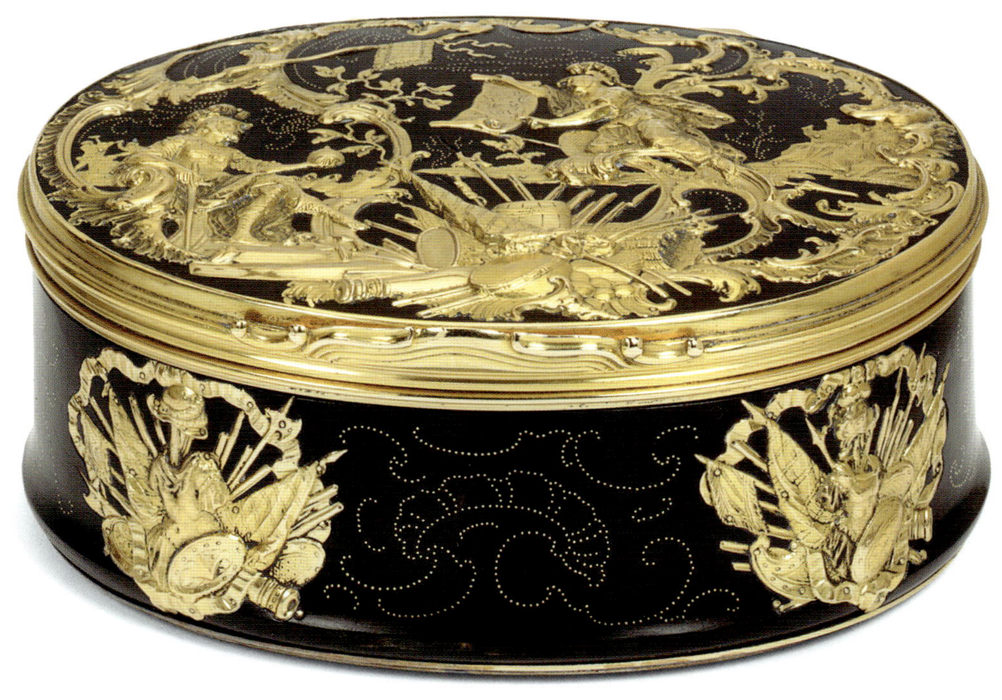

SNUFFBOX

Maker unknown; according to the inscription on
the box, the main map was taken from a design by
Charles Beduzzi and painted by Jordan Scheydl:
*'Tirée de la grand Carte Universelle et decinee en
petit par / Charles Beduzzi Ingenier et Architect
L'annèe 1757 / Peint par Jordan Scheydl'* [sic]
Berlin (probably); about 1757–8
Enamelled copper and engraved gilt-metal
V&A: LOAN:GILBERT.503–2007; The Rosalinde and
Arthur Gilbert Collection on loan to the Victoria
and Albert Museum, London; l. 8.2 cm, h. 4 cm,
d. 6.3 cm

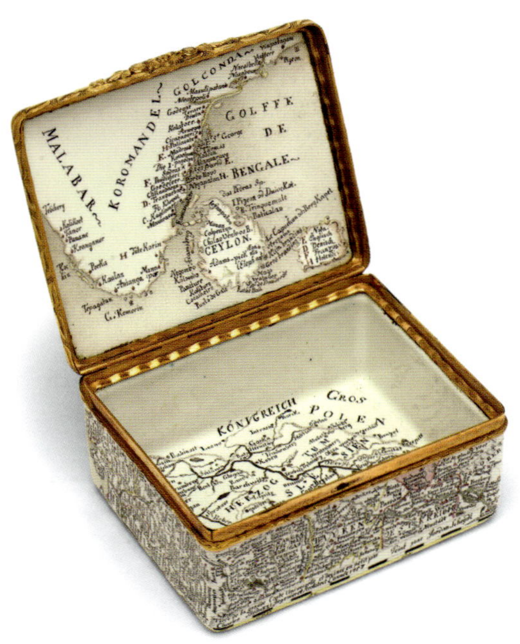

THIS BOX IS AN EXAMPLE OF POLITICAL
propaganda during the Seven Years War
(1756–63), with the major areas of the
conflict in central Europe mapped on the
outside. The disputed sovereignty of
Silesia, which is also depicted on a
separate map inside, triggered this war. The duchy had
become Prussian territory during the War of the Austrian
Succession (1740–48) when King Frederick the Great of
Prussia (1712–86) defeated Empress Maria Theresa of
Austria. All major European powers of the time became
involved: Prussia, Great Britain and Hanover opposed
Austria and its main allies, France, Russia, Sweden and Spain.
Colonial interests outside Europe led to an escalation of the
war into what might be considered the first global conflict.

The allies around Prussia, including Hanover, are
prominently placed on the top, while Austria is shown
fragmented at the margins. The inside of the lid is painted
with a map of the Indian subcontinent, and a map of North
America decorates the base. In these parts of the world,
British and French colonial interests also culminated in
military conflict at this time.

Such white enamel boxes were an inexpensive
alternative to porcelain boxes. Similar boxes are known,
and depict either maps or a portrait of Frederick the Great
in celebration of Prussian supremacy in 1757, when the
Prussian Army won two important battles at Rossbach
and Leuthen. The date 1757 is also given on this box; it is
therefore likely that it was made in Berlin, a centre of the
production of enamel boxes, as a souvenir of the successful
military campaigns of that year.

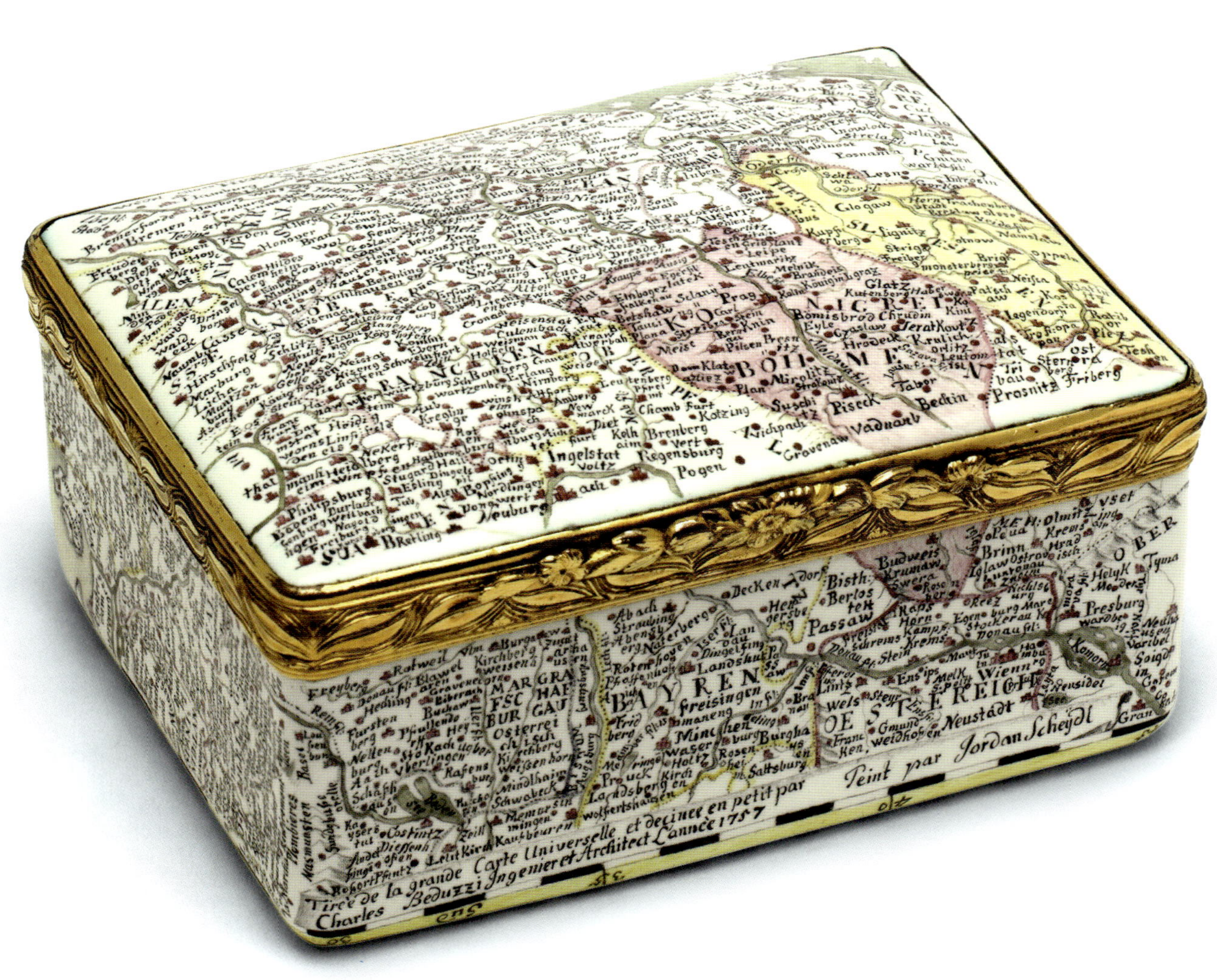
BÖHM
KÖ PRAG
BAYREN
MARGRAF
BURGAU
OESTEREICH
Passau
Budweis
Krumaw
Brinn
Regensburg
Ingelstat
Neuburg
München
Saltzburg
Presburg
Wienn
Prasnitz Friberg
Tiree de la grande Carte Universelle et deßiner en petit par
Charles Beduzzi Ingenier et Architect l'année 1757
Peint par Jordan Scheydl

PAIR OF FLINTLOCK PISTOLS

Jean-Baptiste La Roche (d. 1769)
Paris; about 1760
Carved walnut, blued steel, chased gold and silver,
silver inlay; signed '*Les La Roches aux Galeries du
Louvre*'
V&A: 2243&A–1855; l. 48.7 cm

THESE PISTOLS WERE PROBABLY MADE FOR Louis XV (1710–74), King of France. They bear the royal arms of France and Louis's monogram and portrait. As sophisticated technical devices, guns held great attraction for princely collectors. Louis's grandfather, Louis XIII (1601–43), is regarded as the first systematic firearms collector. Guns that survive from his *Cabinet d'Armes*, of which there are several examples in the V&A, are all marked behind the trigger with his inventory numbers. Louis XV was less systematic, but knew the value of exquisitely crafted firearms as diplomatic gifts. A similar pair in the Palace of Capodimonte in Naples retains its original red morocco case lined with blue silk, possibly a gift from Louis to Prince Ferdinand (1751–1825), King of the Two Sicilies from 1759.

The pistols are of exceptional quality. Although they were designed to work, they have never been fired and were probably never intended to be used. On more restrained working guns, the mounts combined functionality with decorative detailing, but for these pistols their whole purpose was decorative. The stocks are so lavishly inlaid with scrollwork in gold wire that the walnut bases are almost covered. The locks and steel mounts are chiselled in high relief against a rich gold background with scenes from classical mythology, including Jason with the Golden Fleece and Hercules slaying the monster Geryones. The fire-blued barrels retain their original deep colour and are profusely mounted with chiselled-gold war trophies.

The barrels are signed '*Les La Roches aux Galeries du Louvre*'. Jean-Baptiste La Roche of Paris was one of the best gun-makers of the eighteenth century. He was *Archebusier du Roi* (Gun-Maker to the King) during Louis's reign, and from 1740 to 1742 was head of the Paris Gun-Makers' Guild. In 1743 he was given an official residence in the Louvre, where during his later career he worked with his son. Their workshop was renowned for its presentation firearms, whose intended destination was the collector's cabinet rather than the hunting armoury.

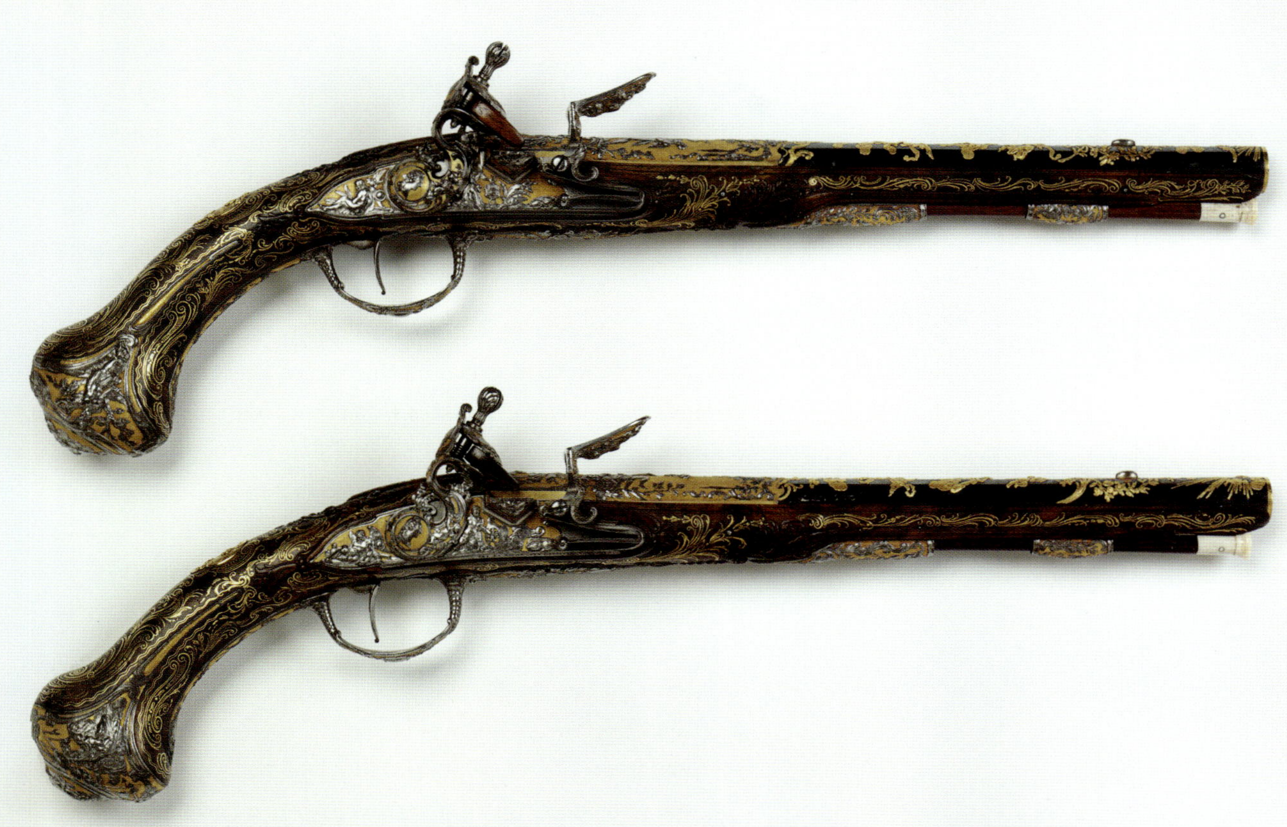

TABLE TOP

Possibly designed by Jean-François Oeben
(1721–63); probably made by Jean-Henri Riesener
(1734–1806)
Paris; designed about 1760–63, made in 1776
Various woods, including purplewood, tulipwood,
sycamore, boxwood and satinwood on a carcase
of oak
V&A: 138:1–1865; h. 53.5 cm, w. 108.2 cm

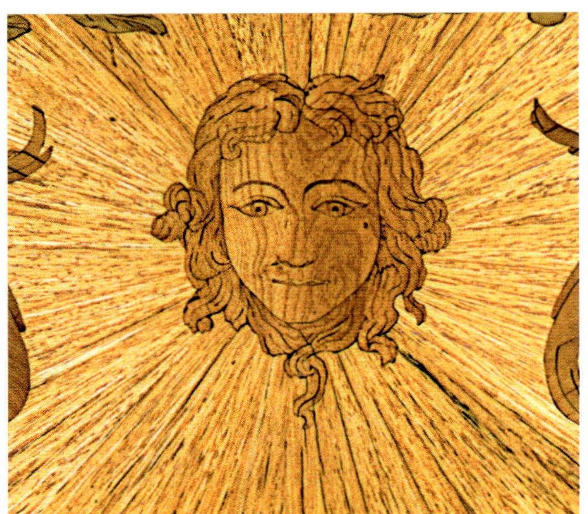

THIS PANEL ONCE FORMED THE TOP OF ONE of two mechanical tables used by Queen Marie Antoinette of France (1755–93) in her apartment at the Petit Trianon, her personal retreat in Versailles. The table is described in detail in an inventory of the French royal wardrobe. Its decorative top slid back to reveal luxurious fittings, probably equipped with silver or gold reading and writing materials or her personal toilet service.

The panel is of oak, veneered with a panel of marquetry, giving a remarkable sense of light, shade and depth to the scene. In the centre at the top is the head of the sun god Apollo, representing France, whose radiating beams light up a water fountain surrounded by trophies of naval banners and weapons. Flanking the arrangement are two globes on pedestals, one depicting the Earth, the other the Heavens. The composition celebrates France's claim to mastery of the universe.

Despite this fine workmanship, the table was relatively old-fashioned when it was delivered to the Queen in July 1776 by the royal cabinet-maker, Jean-Henri Riesener. It was of a form invented by his predecessor, Jean-François Oeben, in the mid-1750s. Oeben had been particularly interested in mechanical furniture, developing a spring mechanism that enabled table tops to move smoothly backwards and forwards, revealing the fitted compartments underneath. The marquetry is also of a style associated with Oeben. It is possible that Riesener, who took over the workshop of Oeben and married his widow, incorporated a surviving Oeben tabletop into one of his own tables.

The naval prowess depicted in the marquetry is not a theme normally associated with furniture made for a woman. It is possible that the panel was originally intended for another royal patron and it was the sheer quality of the craftsmanship that made it appropriate for the Queen.

During the reign of William IV (1765–1837) an English cabinet-maker incorporated the panel into a new desk, from which it has now been detached for display. This was in the collection of the Earl of Cadogan, before it was purchased by the Museum in 1865.

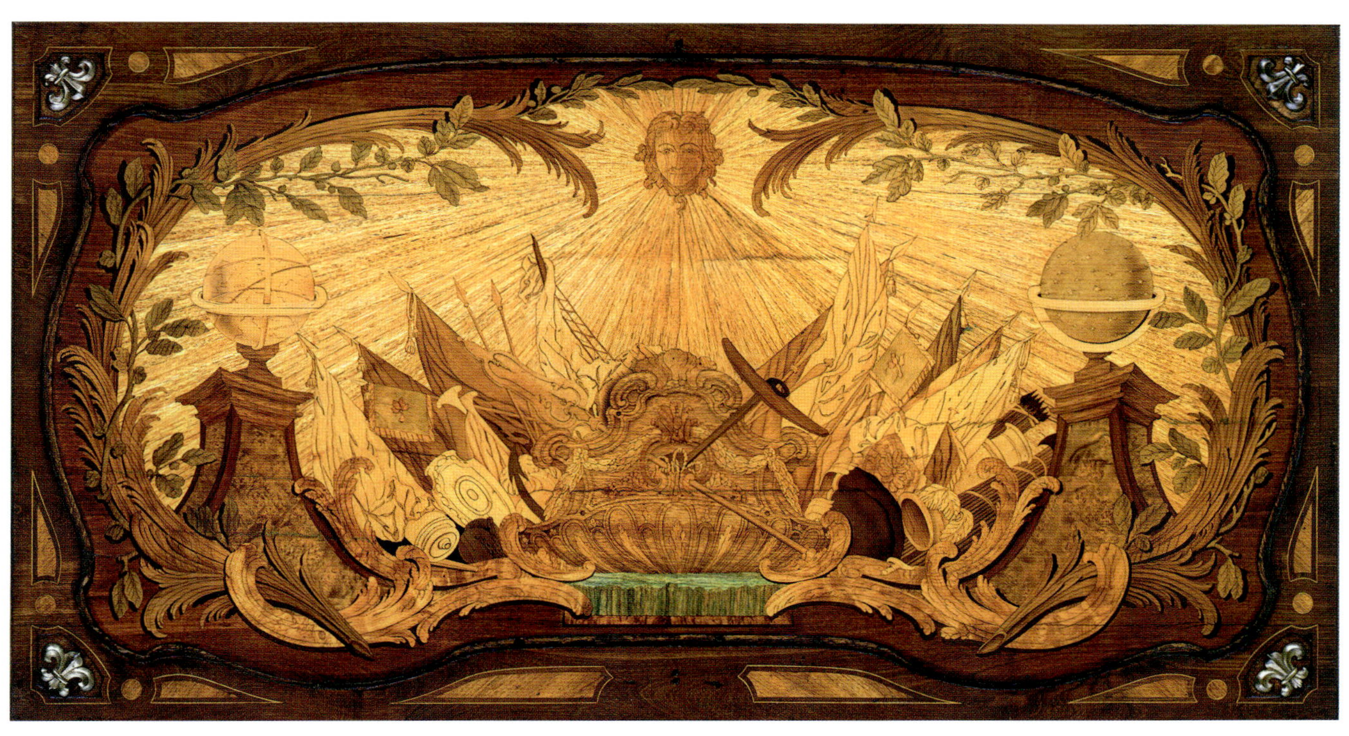

RELIGIOUS SPLENDOUR

JOANNA NORMAN

THE RELIGIOUS MAP OF EUROPE AT the beginning of the seventeenth century was one still riven by the divisive effects of the Protestant Reformation, which had split the previously unified western Christian Church. Across Europe, Protestant, Catholic and Orthodox nations fought for religious as well as political dominance. Although Christianity in all its guises was by far the predominant religion in Europe during this period, it was not the only faith. Islam was present, although largely unwelcome. The Muslim inhabitants of eastern Europe continued as a minority under the Holy Roman Emperor, providing a reminder of the threat of the Ottoman Empire. Judaism, the largest minority faith, was tolerated to a certain degree in some parts of Europe.

Religious differences, whether between Christianity and other faiths or within Christianity itself, created tension across different countries. In France, a desire for religious conformity led to the Revocation of the Edict of Nantes in 1685 and the subsequent flight of French Protestants (Huguenots) to safety in Protestant countries. In Britain, the Catholic sympathies of the restored Stuart monarchs ultimately led to the abdication of James II (1633–1701) and to the Glorious Revolution of the Protestant William III (1650–1702) in 1688.

At both Protestant and Catholic courts, religion played an integral role in daily life, court ritual often being dictated by the liturgical calendar. In Catholic countries, saints' days occurred every two to three days, while festivals such as Christmas and Easter could turn into week-long events. In 1726 the powerful French aristocrat the Duc de Richelieu complained that he had spent more than 100 hours in church with the Habsburg emperor during Holy Week (the week before Easter). A nation's sense of identity was often bound up with the notion of *pietas* (piety), which might be reinforced through the complex painted decoration of royal churches and palace chapels. Absolutist regimes also employed religious imagery and language in order to underline the divine right of kings, whereby a monarch's authority over his subjects came directly from God and was therefore absolute and indisputable. Although Church and state were inextricably linked in this way, the relationship between them, which had in earlier centuries been strongly weighted in favour of the former, was already shifting. From the beginning of the seventeenth century the papacy increasingly lost its hold as an effective, or even relevant, temporal power.

The Catholic response to the Protestant Reformation was to direct all its efforts towards reclaiming its flocks. Under the leadership of the papacy, the Catholic Church placed its faith in the power of the senses, promoting the grand and magnificent baroque style pioneered by the sculptor, architect and painter Gian Lorenzo Bernini (1598–1680) and the architect Francesco Borromini (1599–1667) in Rome. Dynamic architecture, illusionistic decoration, glittering textiles and altar vessels, emotional sculptures and highly theatrical religious festivities and celebrations were intended to overawe and impress people of all social levels. The Mass, the religious service at the very heart of Counter-Reformation theology, was an elaborate ritual during which the congregation experienced rich and intricate vestments (page 74), jewel-encrusted altar candlesticks and chalices to hold the wine. Incense, candlelight and music heightened the whole sensory effect (pl.11).

A wave of church-rebuilding, refurbishment and decoration took place, coinciding with the flowering of the baroque style. Italian historian Lodovico Antonio Muratori (1672–1750) expressed the significance of

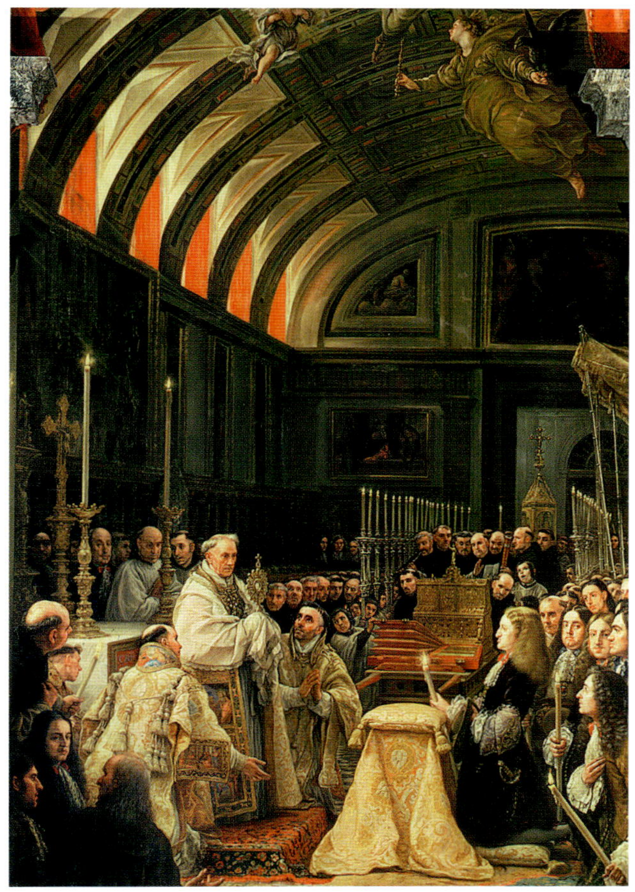

11 *Charles II in Adoration of the Holy Sacrament*, by Claudio
Coello. Oil on canvas. Madrid, 1685–90 (Monasterio de El
Escorial, Madrid / Giraudon / Bridgeman Art Library)

such building in 1749: 'an infallible sign of the
opulence of a town are its beautiful and magnificent
sacred buildings which one can admire'.[1] This building
programme was perhaps most evident in Rome itself,
where a series of popes sought to magnify the glory of
God, and of their own pontificates, through their
commissions in the papal basilica of St Peter's. Beyond
Rome, lavishly decorated pilgrimage churches and
monasteries sprang up in southern Germany and
central Europe, while in Protestant Britain the steeples
of the city churches and the dome of St Paul's Cathedral,
designed by the architect Christopher Wren (1632–
1723), enriched the urban landscape of London after
the ravages of the Great Fire in 1666.

If the Catholic Church placed its emphasis on
spectacle and magnificence, focusing particularly on

the celebration of Mass, the Protestant Church was
in complete contrast, generally suspicious of lavish
decoration and concentrated on preaching and reading
of the Bible, both in public and in private. The
Catholic Church promoted the concept of the cult
of saints acting as intercessors with Christ on behalf
of the faithful, and canonizations provided occasions
for public demonstrations of piety, as well as the
adornment of churches. The Protestant churches
granted less importance to saints and religious imagery,
and as a result their places of worship were generally
plainer than their Catholic counterparts. The Jewish
approach varied from place to place; the size and
opulence of the exterior decoration of synagogues
was often restricted by law, meaning that patrons
could only show their wealth and artistry through the
richness of works commissioned to decorate the inside
of their synagogues (pages 102, 104).

By 1800 the religious balance of Europe had
shifted considerably. The conflicts between different
Protestant and Catholic factions had largely been
settled, but the secularization of society that was
already in evidence from the early seventeenth century
had firmly taken hold, partly as a result of the influence
of Enlightenment ideas. The religious and monastic
orders that had held such influence across Catholic
European courts during the seventeenth century lost
support and were disbanded. The papacy lost any last
semblance of political power during the second half of
the eighteenth century, the final humiliating blow being
Pope Pius VII's capture in 1809 by Napoleon's troops.
While 200 years earlier the Church had still believed
that it held authority over the court or state, by 1800 it
was absolutely undeniable that the state had triumphed
over the Church.

1 Lodovico Antonio Muratori, *Della Pubblica Felicità, oggetto
de' buoni principi, trattato*, Lucca, 1749

DESIGN FOR A PROJECTED CHURCH OF THE ORDRE DU SAINT-ESPRIT, PARIS

Juste-Aurèle Meissonnier (1695–1750)

Paris; 1726–31

Pen and watercolour, heightened with white

V&A: D.372–1887; h. 33 cm, w. 46 cm

THIS DRAWING AND AN EXTERIOR ELEVATION (V&A: 9085) relate to the architect and goldsmith Meissonnier's unexecuted project for a church for the Order of the Holy Spirit in Paris. Founded by Henry III (1551–89) in 1578, this order was predominantly composed of high-ranking nobles at the French court, with the King as its Sovereign and Grand Master. When Louis XV (1710–74) took on this role, he proposed the building of a new church for the order, for which several architects, including Meissonnier, submitted designs. Uniquely, Meissonnier's designs also included a palace attached to the church, both buildings being crowned with monumental domes surmounted with a Maltese cross, the symbol of this order. The architect was clearly influenced in his design by the location of the proposed site, opposite the Palais du Louvre. He employed a colossal order of columns, which seems to respond to the colonnade of the palace building, designed by the architect Claude Perrault (1613–88).

The interior design demonstrates the intended sumptuousness and grandeur of the church decoration, with massive orders of Corinthian columns, sculptural reliefs and a tall double-dome decorated with illusionistic painting and rococo shell motifs. Although no scale is marked, the size of the people shown in the design gives an indication of the monumental scale of the church and of the extremely tall baldaquin, or canopy, underneath the dome.

Meissonnier revisited his project in the 1740s when, inspired by his experience of Rome, he proposed to unify the architecture of central Paris through a series of grand domes. An illustration of his *Parallèle Général des Edifices* shows a perspective view of the church and palace in relation to other domed buildings, including Les Invalides, the home for elderly or wounded soldiers, and the Collège des Quatres Nations (College of the Four Nations), part of the University of Paris. The view suggests that the proposed height of the domes depicted here would have matched that of Les Invalides, at 107 m.

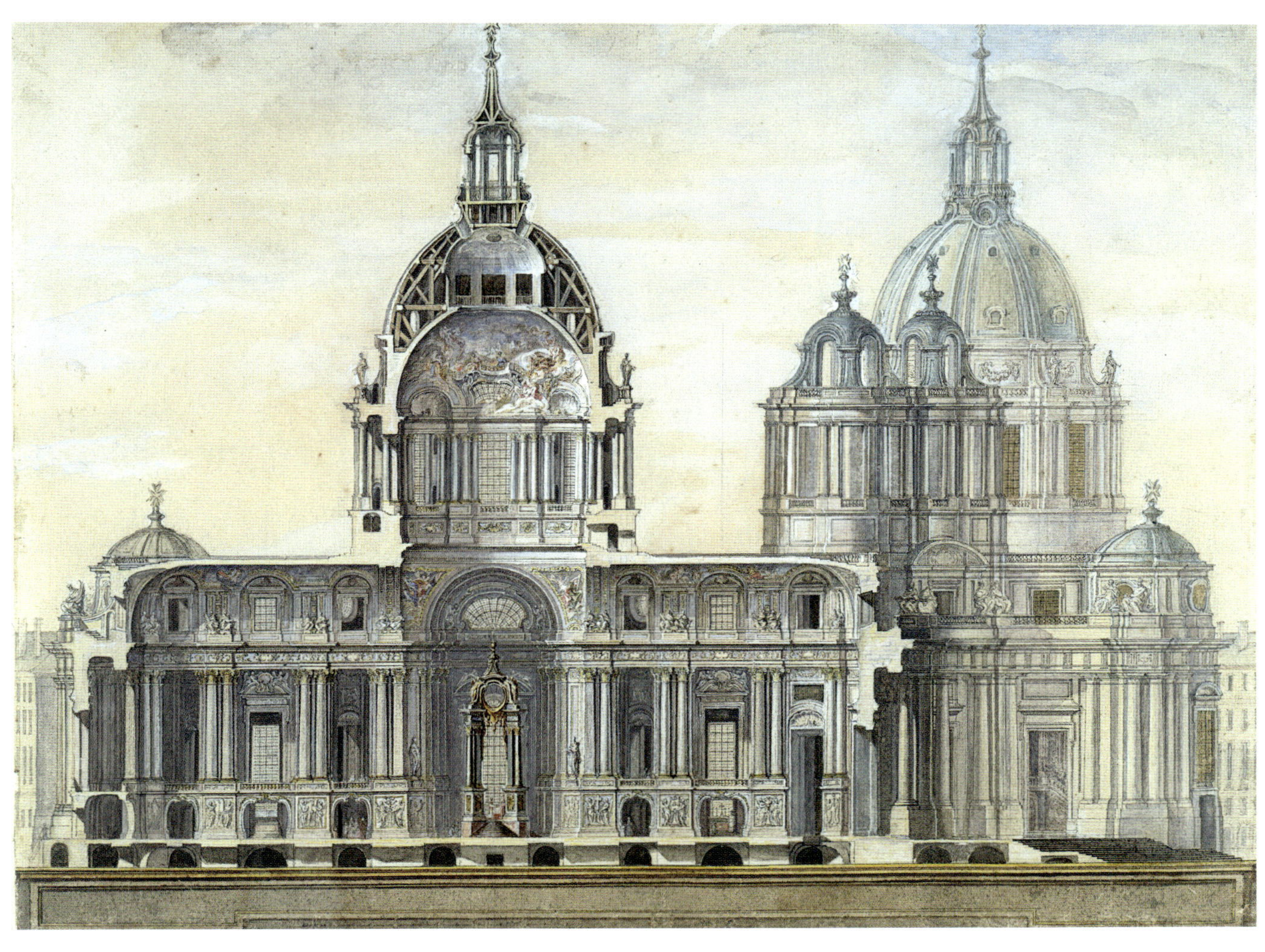

PAIR OF ALTAR BALUSTRADES

Naples; 1700–50
White and coloured marbles
V&A: LOAN:GILBERT.1083–2008 and 1084–2008;
The Rosalinde and Arthur Gilbert Collection on
loan to the Victoria and Albert Museum, London;
h. 74.9 cm, w. 189.2 cm, d. 20.3 cm

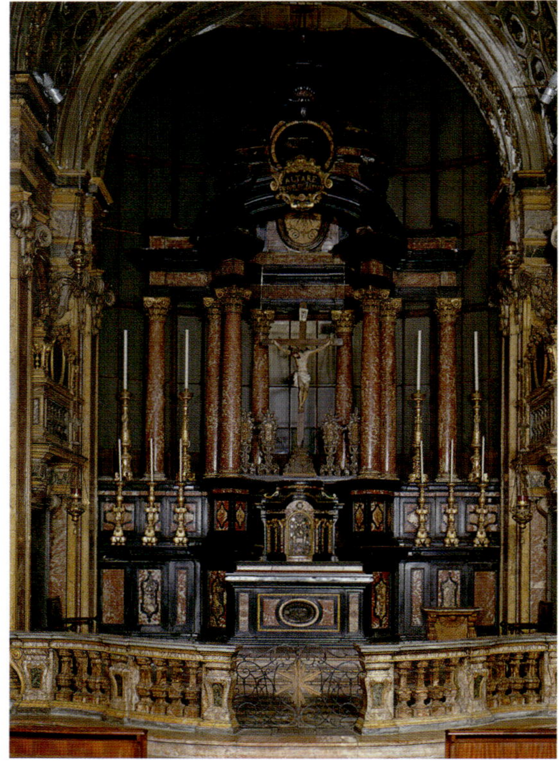

Altar in the Church of Santissima Trinita, Turin. Filippo
Juvarra, 1717 (Photo: Scala, Florence)

ALTHOUGH THERE WAS NO SINGLE RULE FOR the design of churches in the seventeenth and eighteenth centuries, Catholic churches often followed a similar model. While the main body of the church (the nave) was occupied by the congregation, the area at the east end of the church was reserved for priests for the celebration of the Mass. This (the chancel) was the holiest part of the church because it was where the altar was situated. Altar balustrades, such as this pair, often stood in churches as both a physical and symbolic demarcation of this division of space. Because the balustrades were low, they divided the church space, while still allowing members of the congregation to observe the priest performing the Mass. Balustrades could also be used to mark the entrance to individual side chapels, which are often recessed into the walls of the nave, additionally serving as a rail at which the faithful could kneel in prayer and for communion.

These particular balustrades are carved from white marble, with red and yellow marbles inlaid on the sides and on the top of the altar rails. Marble was used for both the exterior and interior decoration of churches from the medieval period onwards. It was used particularly in Italy, as the Apuan Alps were rich in marble quarries, most famously that of the white marble at Carrara. However, the considerable expense of transporting marble (in flat-bottomed boats from La Spezia, on the Ligurian coast) meant that, even within Italy, only locations near the sea, or with large funds at their disposal, could afford it. Coloured marbles became particularly popular in the later sixteenth and seventeenth centuries as patrons sought to emulate the polychrome marble floors and walls of ancient Roman buildings.

In seventeenth-century Naples, the technique was employed to a particularly fine level by the architect and sculptor Cosimo Fanzago (1591–1678). His work adorns many Neapolitan churches, such as that of the Certosa di San Martino. His legacy lasted well into the eighteenth century, and balustrades such as this pair testify to his continuing influence in works produced for churches in Naples.

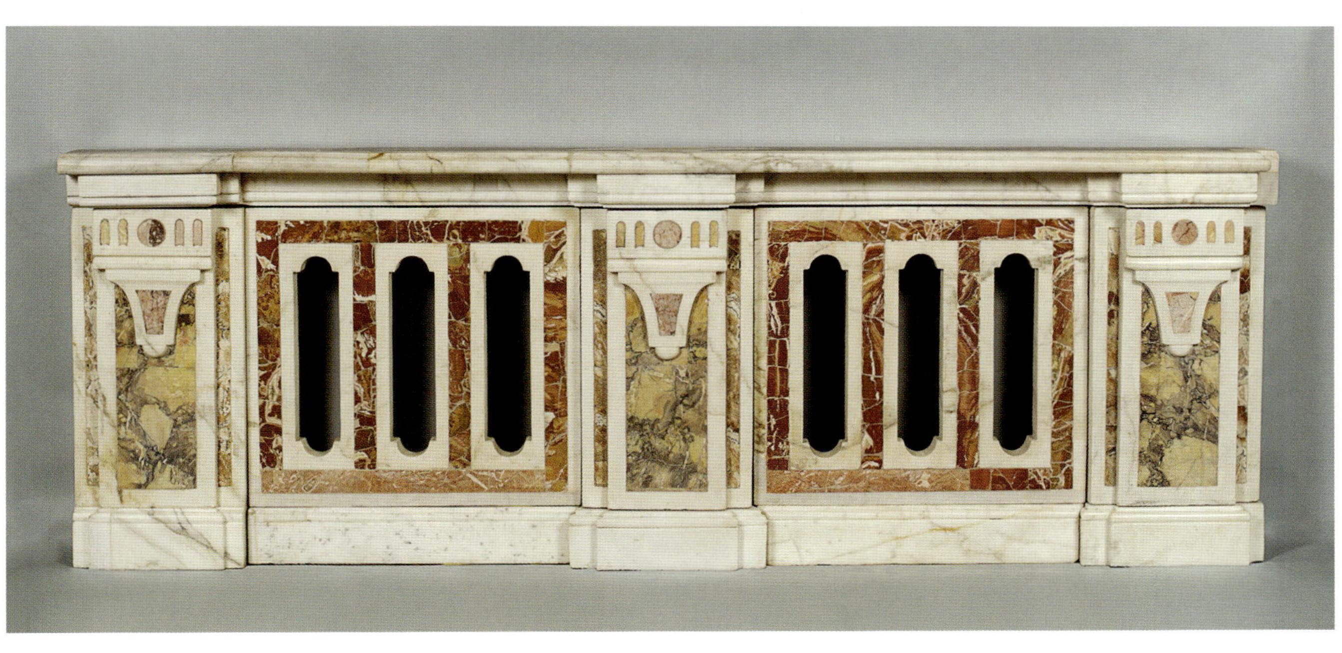

THE DESCENT FROM THE CROSS

By Charles Lebrun (1619–90)
France; 1642–5
Oil on canvas
V&A: 9103–1863; h. 78.7 cm, w. 63.5 cm

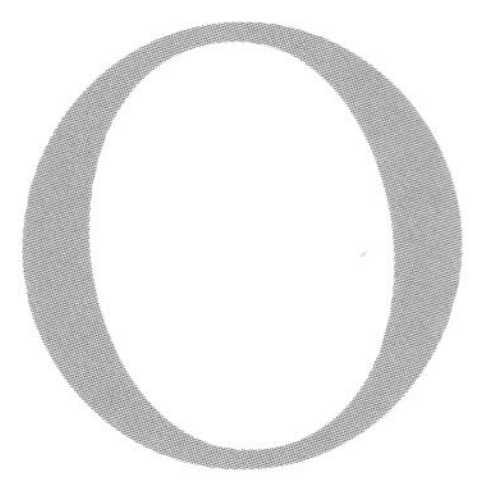

RIGINALLY ACQUIRED AS A WORK BY Sébastien Bourdon (1616–71), this painting is now known to be the work of Charles Lebrun. An engraving of it in reverse by François de Poilly (1623–93) identified the artist. Although much of Lebrun's career was spent in France as *Premier peintre* (First Painter) to Louis XIV (1638–1715), this particular work was painted during the time that he spent, early on in his career, in Rome, where he would have come under the influence of the dramatic baroque style.

The Descent from the Cross was a popular subject for altarpieces, particularly with baroque painters, who exploited its emotional content to the full in depicting the ashen flesh tones and contorted body of the dead Christ. The dramatic intensity of this work shows the clear influence of works by Peter Paul Rubens (1577–1640) and Annibale Carracci (1560–1609) and offers a marked contrast to the more academic and restrained classicism of Lebrun's later works, such as a painting of the same subject in the Nationalmuseum, Stockholm. It also shows the influence of Rome in the experimentation with a diagonal composition and sharp contrasts of lighting.

Two other versions of this painting exist. They differ in the omission of the tree and ladder on the left. Another smaller version was sold from the collection of the French collector Cardinal Fesch in 1845, but has since disappeared. The extent to which the three paintings are autograph works by Lebrun is not clear. They may instead be workshop replicas of a lost original, as it was usual practice for an artist to head a studio that might include several assistants, who undertook varying amounts of work on paintings that were produced by the artist or to his design. Although some of the original brilliance of the painting has been lost by paint wearing through to the brown ground beneath, the red cloaks of the soldier and St John, and in particular the blue robes of the swooning Virgin, give an indication of the vibrancy and contrast of the original colouring.

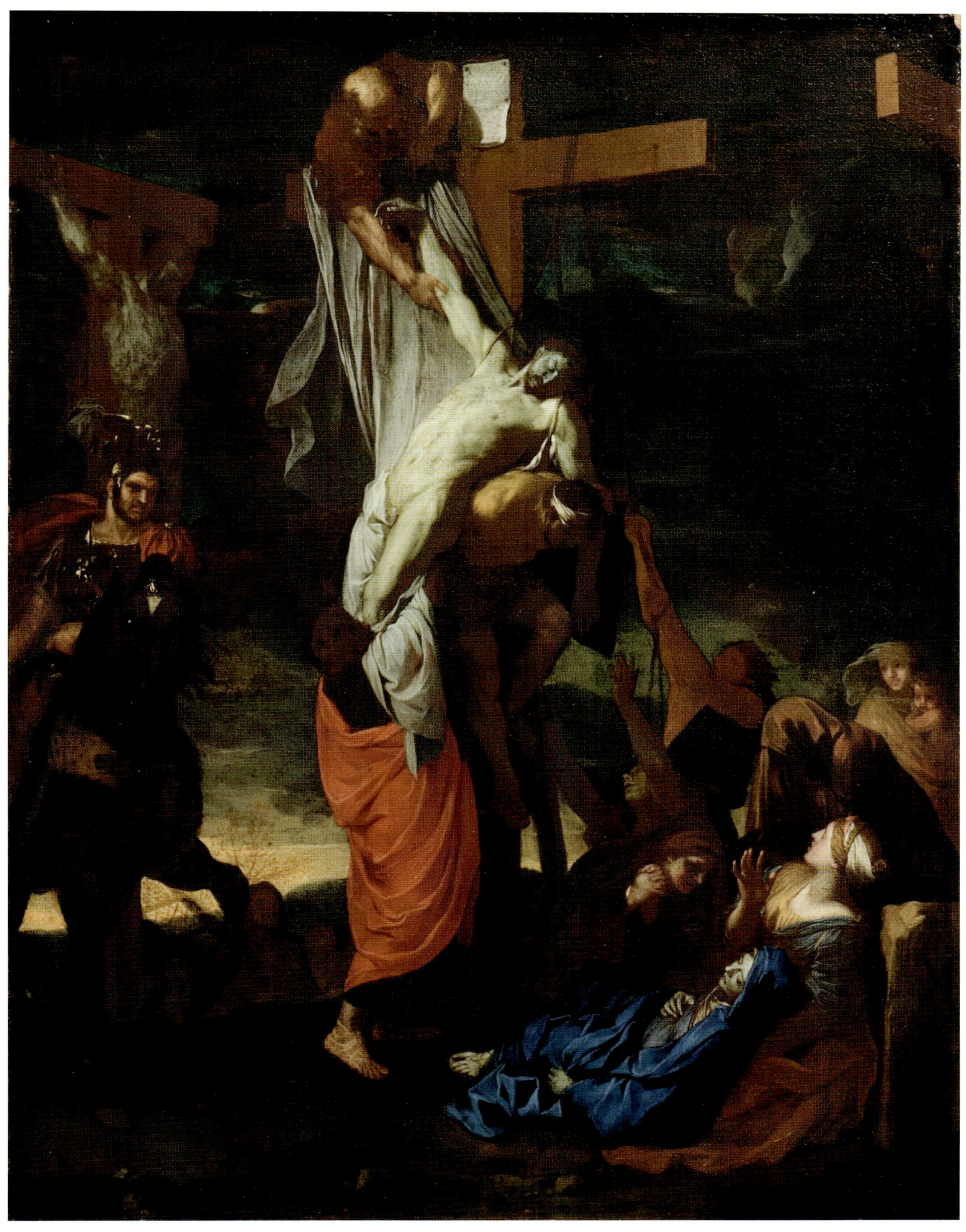

CHASUBLE AND MANIPLE

Venice; 1670–95
Needle lace worked in linen thread and mounted
on silk
Chasuble: V&A: 743–1870; h. 106 cm, w. 69 cm
Maniple: V&A: 745–1870; h. 94 cm, w. 23 cm
(max., at ends)

THIS SET OF ECCLESIASTICAL VESTMENTS, which aso includes a stole and chalice veil, was made at the height of Venice's power as a centre of production of high-quality needle lace. From the 1660s onwards it was this kind of three-dimensional Venetian needle lace (rather than Flemish bobbin lace, which had been fashionable in the previous generation) that was most sought-after. It was used to decorate both male and female fashionable dress as well as church vestments. The economic significance of the Venetian lace industry, which expanded during this period under the patronage of the Catholic Church, can be judged by Louis XIV's establishment in 1665 of state-sponsored French lace manufactories, a deliberate attempt to halt the importation of expensive Venetian lace into France. He also encouraged Venetian lace-makers to settle and work in France.

These vestments were worn by a priest officiating at Mass, the most important sacramental ceremony of the Catholic Church. The chasuble was worn over a white linen alb or gown, which was edged with lace and reached to the feet. A stole hung around the priest's neck and the maniple over his left wrist. Such vestments were often produced to match other church fittings, including altar frontals and missal cushions, in order to create an overall effect of luxury and magnificence that was both fitting for the service of God and representative of the wealth of the commissioning patron.

In the 1660s Venetian lace-makers adapted their designs to the baroque style, creating a form of raised needle lace that was strongly three-dimensional, its bold motifs and rich weight well adapted to baroque interest in mass and movement. They were skilful in producing such complex designs in sections, which could be joined to build up whole garments, vestments or furnishing pieces. In the nineteenth century there was a great vogue for collecting antique lace. These pieces, like many that were sold at that time, were remounted onto red silk, probably shortly before their acquisition by the Museum in 1870. The narrow outer edging on all the pieces of the set is also likely to date from this period.

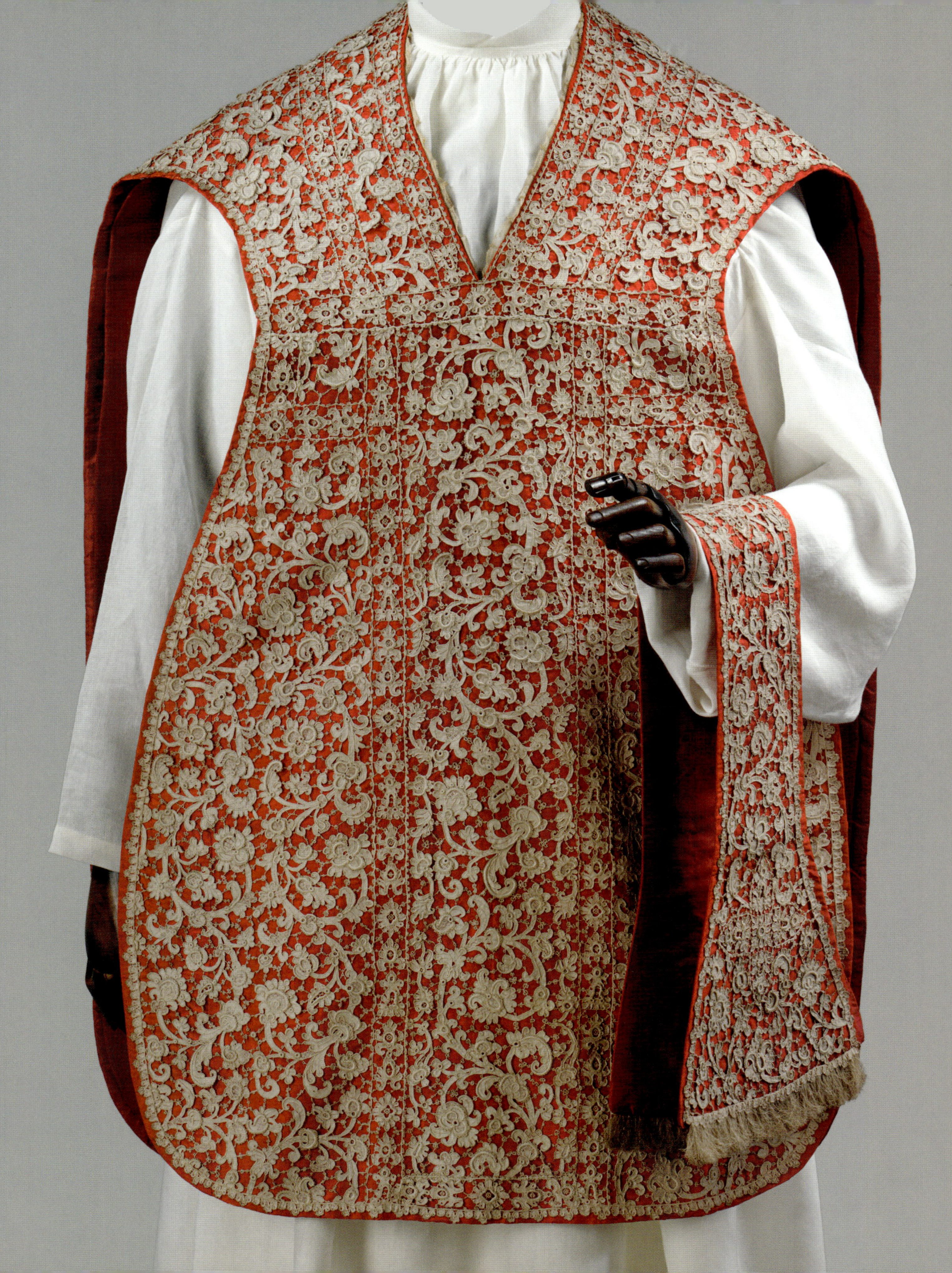

MONSTRANCE

Johannes Zeckel (d. 1728)
Augsburg; 1705
Silver and silver-gilt
V&A: M.3–1952; given by Dr W. L. Hildburgh, FSA,
1952; h. 84.6 cm, w. 45.2 cm, d. 19.8 cm

A MONSTRANCE IS USED TO HOLD AND display the Host, the wafer of unleavened bread that Catholics believe becomes the body of Christ at the moment of the consecration during the Mass. Monstrances were first made and used after the institution of the Feast of Corpus Christi (the Body of Christ) in 1264, but they took on particular prominence with the Counter-Reformation, when the Catholic Church placed a greater emphasis on the Eucharist and especially on the display of the sacrament.

This monstrance was made in Augsburg, southern Germany, one of the most renowned centres of silver production in the eighteenth century. It is decorated in a typically baroque style. A silver relief at its centre depicts the Last Supper, with the Apostles (the first followers of Christ) seated around a table. The scene commemorates the occasion when, as Christians believe, Christ instituted the sacrament of the Eucharist that is celebrated in the Mass. Only the figure of Christ is absent, his presence being added when the Host is presented in the central window, its sacred glory represented through the sunburst of silver-gilt rays emanating from it. This central scene is flanked by cornucopiae, with ears of wheat and vine tendrils referring to the bread and wine used for the Eucharist. Two angels support a crowned canopy above the dove of the Holy Spirit, while below the central plaque is a figure of the Lamb of God, one of the titles given to Christ in the gospels. The stem of the monstrance is composed of personifications of Faith, Hope and Charity, while the base is decorated with reliefs of the Crucifixion and with other episodes from the Old and New Testaments of the Bible.

Such richly decorated pieces of altarware were designed both to glorify God in their magnificence and to provide a visual focus for the prayers and devotions of Catholic congregations. The monstrance would have been placed on the altar during the service of Benediction, or would have been carried in procession, when its silver and silver-gilt would have glittered in the church candlelight.

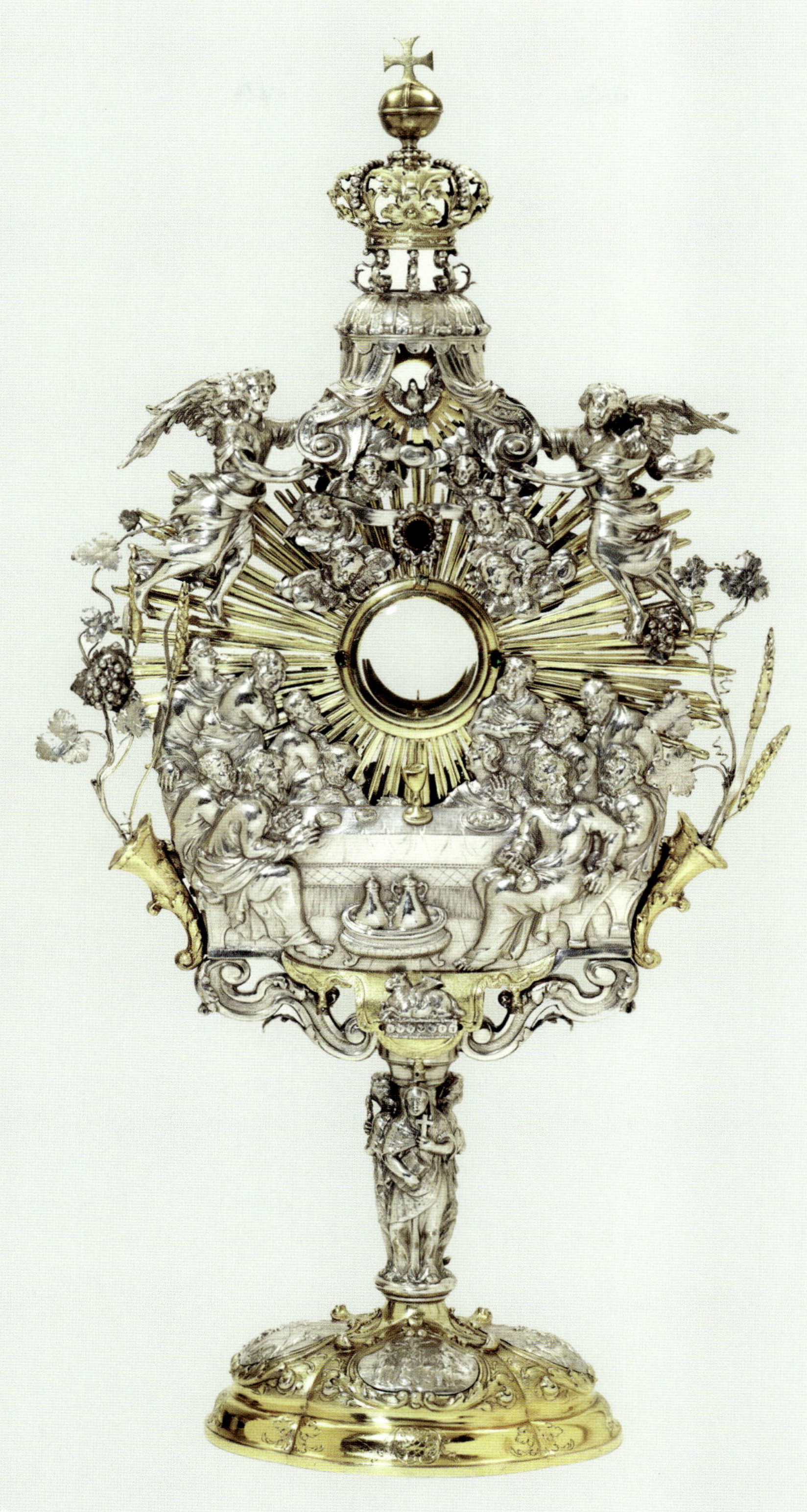

CHALICE

Naples; about 1700

Silver-gilt

V&A: M.42–1951; given by Dr W. L. Hildburgh, FSA, 1951; h. 26.5 cm, diam. 13 cm

THE CHALICE IS ONE OF THE MOST IMPORTANT items of sacred metalwork, used to hold the Eucharistic wine, which, Catholics believe, becomes the blood of Christ at the moment of consecration during the Mass. Its decorative nature relates to its function as a visual focus for the congregation during the Mass, when it is held up by the officiating priest.

This chalice was made in Naples, and its decoration is typical of the Italian baroque of the late seventeenth and early eighteenth century, showing a lightening of earlier, more monumental forms towards what would become known as the *barochetto* style. The stem of the chalice is made up of figures of Christ, the Virgin and St John the Divine, interspersed with cherubic heads, while the base shows seated demi-figures of St Peter (holding keys), St Paul (with a sword) and St Andrew in scrolls of acanthus ornament. The plainness of the bowl of the chalice contrasts with the decorative edging around it, again composed of acanthus and floral ornament, separately cast and applied. The bowl is supported on the heads of cherubs and figures of angels. The chalice is unusually heavy for its size, as a result of its manufacture from a series of cast elements: the figures would have been made separately and soldered onto the body of the chalice.

Naples was renowned as a centre for the production of silver work in the seventeenth and early eighteenth centuries, and a number of monumental silver sculptures, such as reliquary busts and figures of saints by such artists as Lorenzo Vaccaro (1655–1706), survive in Neapolitan collections.

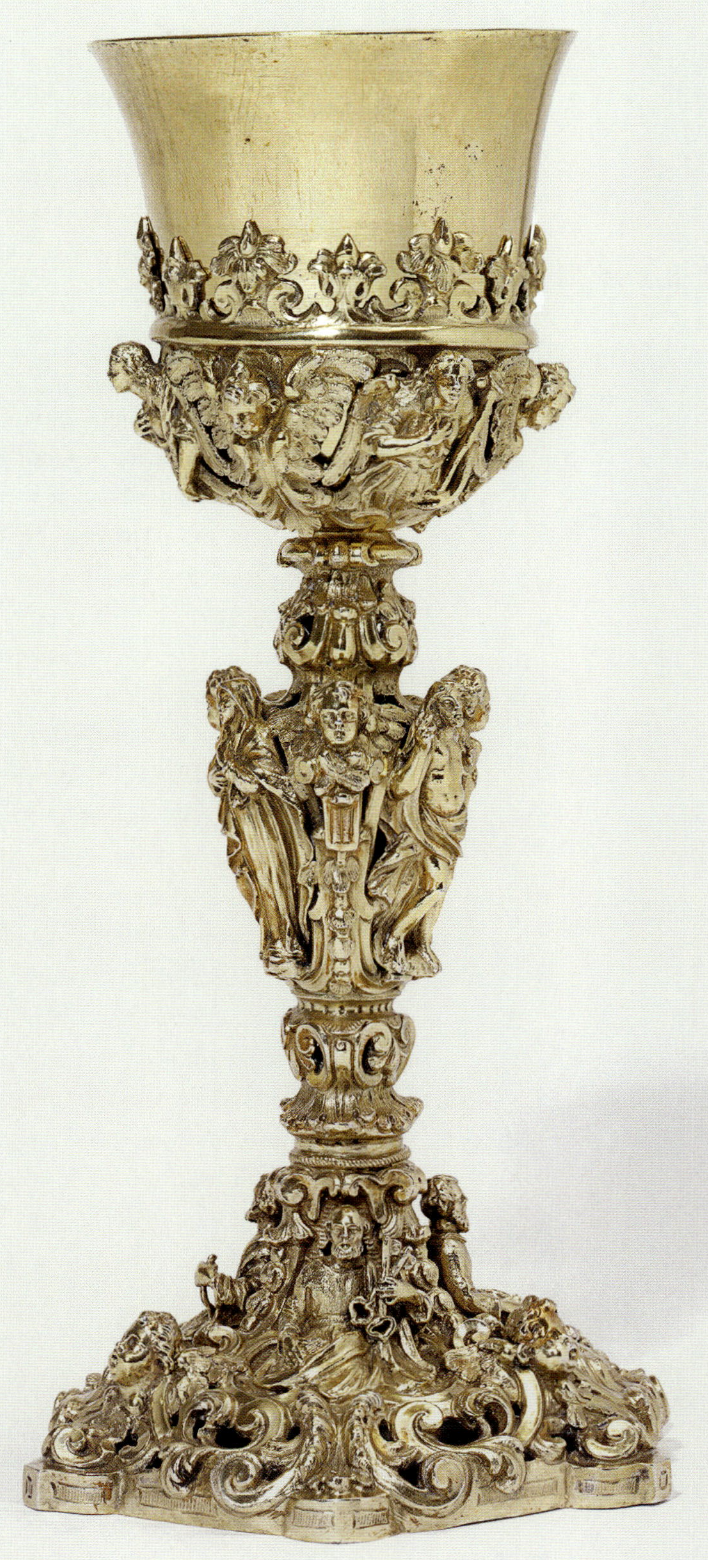

CHALICE

Probably Kremlin workshops, Moscow; 1702
Raised, chased silver and silver-gilt, with applied
gold and polychrome enamel plaques and reliefs
V&A: LOAN:GILBERT.93–2008; The Rosalinde and
Arthur Gilbert Collection on loan to the Victoria
and Albert Museum, London; h. 40 cm,
diam. 20.7 cm

THIS RICHLY DECORATED CHALICE HAS BEEN attributed to the Kremlin workshops on the grounds of stylistic similarities with documented cups from the same workshops. It is relatively large, compared with Catholic examples of the same period, and this is in keeping with the style of chalice commonly in use in the Russian Orthodox Eucharistic rite (called the Divine Liturgy) because in the Orthodox rite the whole congregation partakes of communion, whereas in the Catholic Church only the priests do. The Orthodox Church, like the Catholic Church, believes that the wine becomes the blood of Christ through the operation of the Holy Spirit at the moment of consecration.

Both the bowl and base of this chalice are decorated with polychromed enamel plaques: those on the base show scenes from the Passion of Christ, while those on the bowl show individual figures of Christ, the Virgin, St John the Baptist and the Archangels Michael and Gabriel, who are considered particularly significant saints in the Orthodox Church. The plaques are linked by scrolling acanthus and floral ornament in silver, and are interspersed with enamel cartouches (four of six survive) containing scriptural inscriptions in Old Church Slavonic, referring to the mystery of the Eucharist and its importance in the Orthodox faith as the path to salvation.

An inscription on the base suggests that the chalice was commissioned by Sampson, Metropolitan (Bishop) of Astrakhan and Tersk, for the Cathedral of the Dormition of the Mother of God in Astrakhan. The date of 1702 would coincide with Sampson's tenure as Metropolitan (1697–1714) and with the busiest phase of the planning of the cathedral, which was begun in 1698 and dedicated to the 'pure Virgin Mother of God'. It would be entirely fitting that only vessels of such richness and fine goldsmith's work would have been deemed appropriate for such an important cathedral dedicated to the Virgin, the most significant of all the saints in the Orthodox faith.

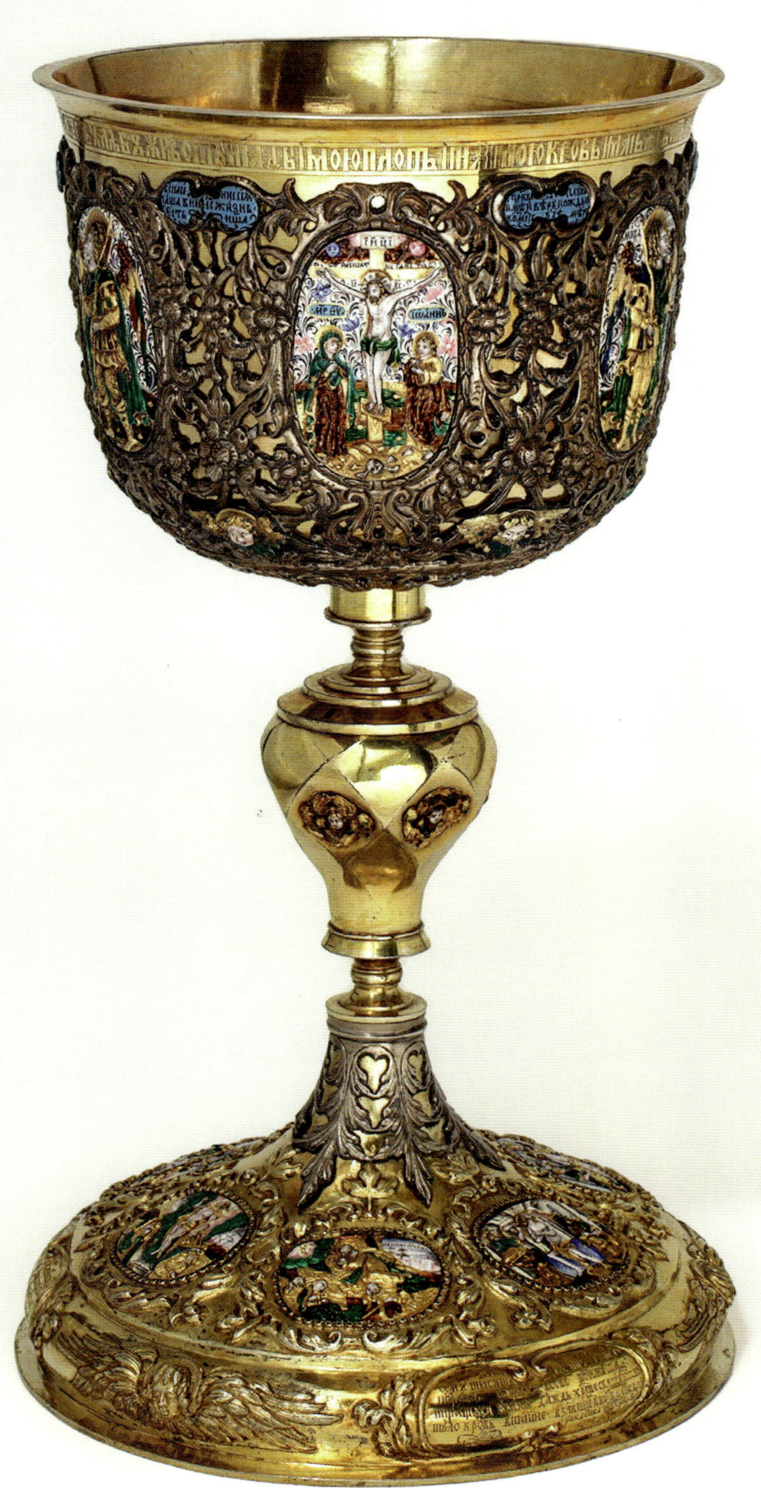

BUST OF THE VIRGIN OF SORROWS

José de Mora (1642–1724)
Granada; about 1680–1700
Carved and painted pine set, with ivory and glass
V&A: 1284–1871; h. 48.35 cm, w. 49 cm, d. 29 cm

FIGURES OF THE VIRGIN OF SORROWS WERE produced in considerable numbers in Spain in the seventeenth century. They were often paired with busts of Christ as the Man of Sorrows (*Ecce Homo*) and sometimes placed on side altars, where they aided the faithful in their devotions by focusing their thoughts on the suffering and death of Christ, witnessed by his mother, the Virgin Mary. As a type, they recall the traditions of Netherlandish devotional paintings and reliquary busts, while the half-length form, often virtually life-size, creates an unprecedented level of intimacy and heightened emotional intensity between sculpture and viewer.

The tradition of polychromed wood sculpture is particularly associated with Spain, most commonly with the *paso* figures taken out of churches during Holy Week (*Semana Santa*), the week before Easter. Such figures were set on floats and paraded through the streets, a practice that still continues today. Belief in their miracle-working powers was very strong. When the sculptor of this bust supplied a full-length figure of the Virgin of Sorrows for the church of St Ana in Granada in 1671 it was taken to the church in procession, and a contemporary chronicler recorded that it cured a sick woman as it passed by the house where she lay.

Sculptures of this kind were often produced in workshops where the named artist oversaw several assistants carrying out his designs. José de Mora came from a family of sculptors and was active in both Granada and Madrid in the late seventeenth and early eighteenth centuries. He specialized in wood sculpture of devotional subjects, and in 1672 was appointed as court sculptor to the last Habsburg King of Spain, Charles II (1661–1700). The ingenuity of his sculpture is evident in the intricacy of the carving of this bust, despite its apparent simplicity: the Virgin's curls are made from corkscrews of wood shavings, while the luminosity of her eyes indicates that they may be made from painted ivory or glass. Like other similar works, she may originally also have had glass tears on her cheeks. Although some of the original colouring of the bust has been lost, the vibrancy and power of this style of heightened emotional realism remain strong.

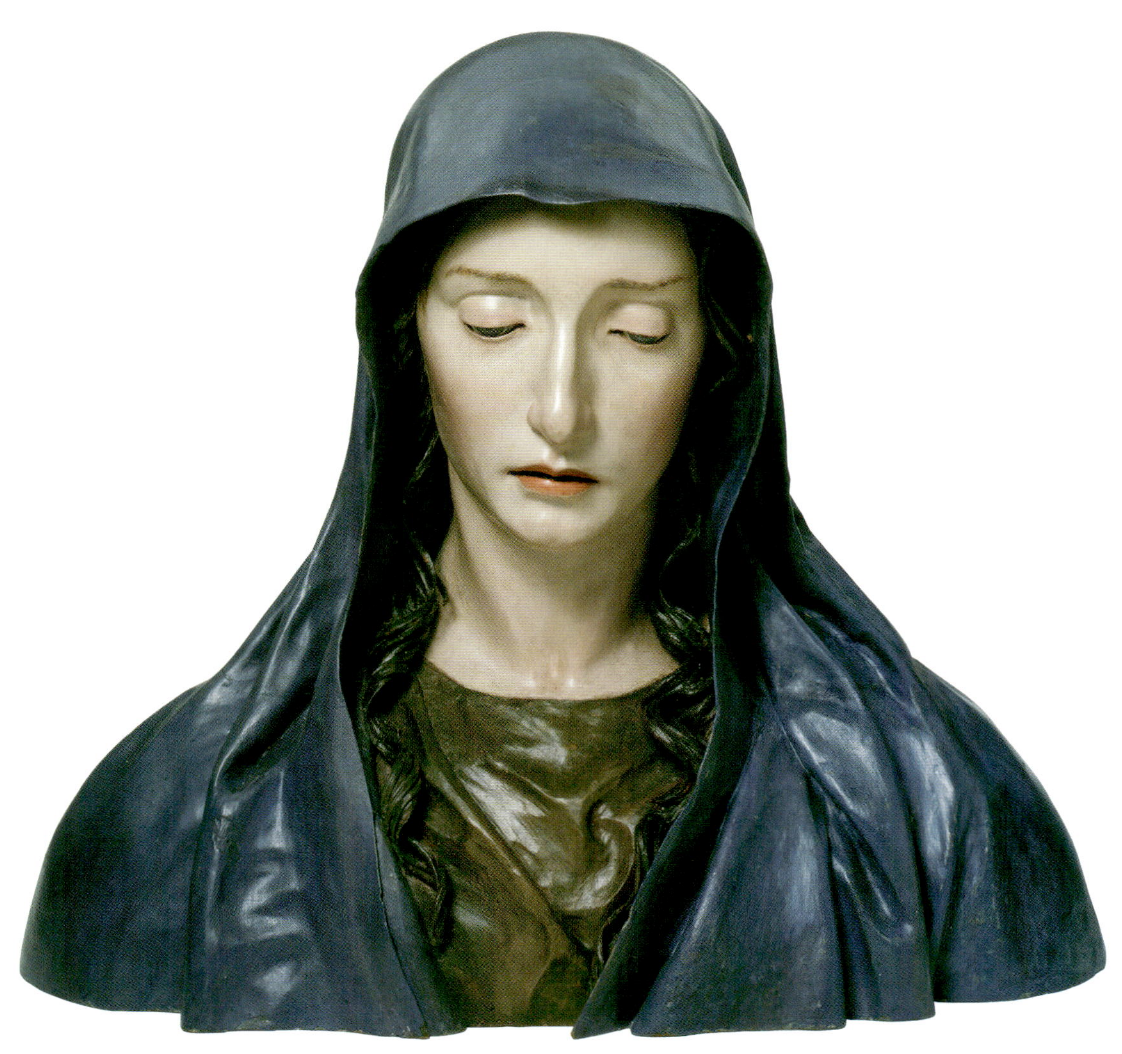

RELIEF OF THE VIRGIN AND CHILD

After Alessandro Algardi (1598–1654)
Bologna; about 1750, the relief possibly earlier
Gilt-bronze and ebony
V&A: A.5–1966; h. 55.9 cm, w. 43.2 cm, without
frame

THIS GILT-BRONZE RELIEF IS KNOWN TO HAVE come from the Palazzo Lambertini in Bologna, the family home of Pope Benedict XIV, who ruled as pope from 1740 to 1758. It represents the Virgin and Child against rays of light and cherubic heads, and was probably made for devotional use in this palace. The Lambertini arms appear on the base of the elaborate gilt and ebony frame, which may have been produced at a later date than the relief itself; the marble ground is modern, added when the work entered the Museum's collection.

This relief, together with two others (in the Musée des Arts Décoratifs, Paris, and the Museum für Kunst und Gewerbe, Hamburg), is derived from the marble sculpture on the high altar of the church of San Nicola da Tolentino at Capo le Case, Rome, designed in about 1651 by Alessandro Algardi. It was quite usual for sculpture (or elements of it) to be reproduced for use in other contexts. Sculptural workshops consisted of teams of workers, under the direction of the sculptor, some serving as assistants as a step in their own training as sculptors. The sculpture on which this relief is based is likely to have been designed by Algardi, but was probably made by his assistants Domenico Guidi (1625–1701) and Ercole Ferrata (1610–86).

The marble prototype also depicts figures of St Augustine – one of the most celebrated thinkers of the early Church – his mother St Monica and St Nicholas. As a terracotta *bozzetto* or model for the marble figure of St Nicholas survives in the Museo di Palazzo Venezia in Rome, it has been suggested that a similar model, since lost, may also have been made for the Virgin and Child group, from which the bronze figures of all three reliefs could subsequently have been cast. If so, it is possible this relief was made earlier than 1750, the date hitherto assigned to it, because of its association with Pope Benedict XIV. He is known to have been a keen patron of the work of his Bolognese compatriots, both living and dead, so it is not surprising that he owned a work derived from an altar designed by one of the most renowned Bolognese sculptors of the previous century.

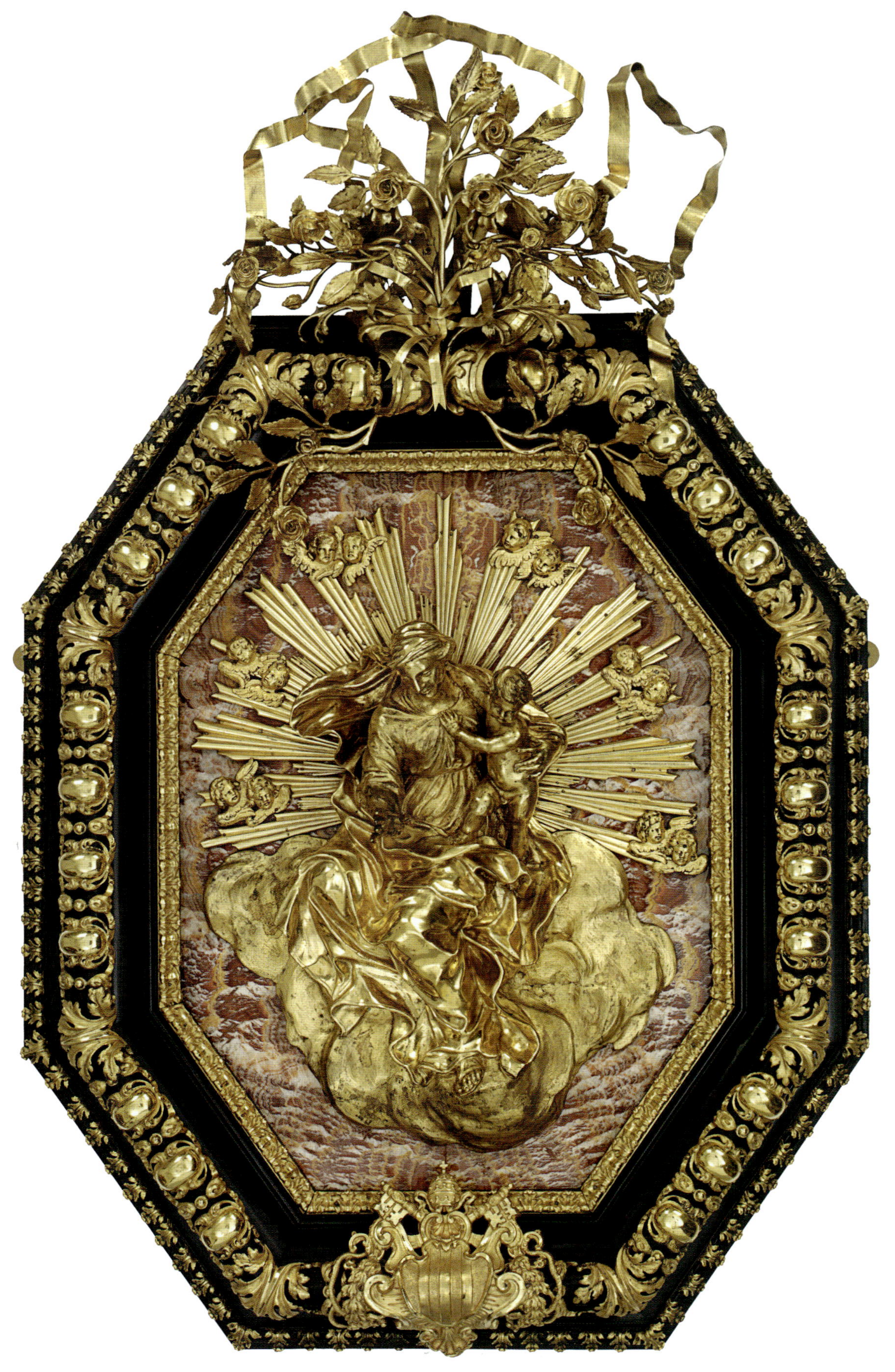

HOUSE SHRINE WITH THE *PIETÀ*

Christoph Lencker (d. 1613)

Augsburg; 1600–13

Ebony veneer on oak, with silver-gilt and applied
silver figures and decoration

V&A: M.1–1953; given by Dr W. L. Hildburgh, FSA;
h. 38.5 cm, w. 28 cm, d. 11 cm

HOUSE SHRINES WERE PRIMARILY USED by Catholics, for private devotion, either in a bedchamber or when travelling. For wealthy Catholics, the commissioning or purchase of such richly decorated items for personal use was as important as the commissioning of larger pieces for use in public churches. They sought to apply to both large- and small-scale religious art all the wealth of materials and workmanship they would seek in secular works of art. The central figure group on this shrine depicts the *Pietà*, the name traditionally given to this grouping of the sorrowing (usually seated) Virgin supporting the figure of Christ, her dead son.

The group is here flanked by two kneeling angels, and two standing angels behind holding instruments of the Passion, the group of objects that include the pillar at which Christ was whipped and the spear with which his side was pierced while on the cross.

The *Pietà* was a popular subject in art, particularly sculpture, from the fourteenth century onwards. Its iconography developed out of that of larger Lamentation groups, which portrayed the Apostles grieving with the Virgin Mary after the death of Christ. It was an appropriate subject for private devotion, the Virgin's sorrow being seen as a conduit for focusing the attention of the faithful on their own grief at the sacrifice of Christ's death.

This ebony shrine shows the influence of Mannerism in its architectural form, similar to that of many large-scale altarpieces. It is also decorated with silver cherub heads as well as small ornamental elements, and with a central silver-gilt niche forming a frame to the figures of the Virgin and Christ. By Christ's feet the silver bears the mark of Christoph Lencker (apprenticed 1575, master 1584), one of the most renowned Augsburg goldsmiths of his generation, employed by both the Habsburg court and the Wittelsbach dukes in Bavaria. He specialized in embossed and chased silver sculpture, and in 1596 was commissioned by Duke William V of Bavaria to make a silver altar for the church of the Holy Cross in Augsburg, southern Germany.

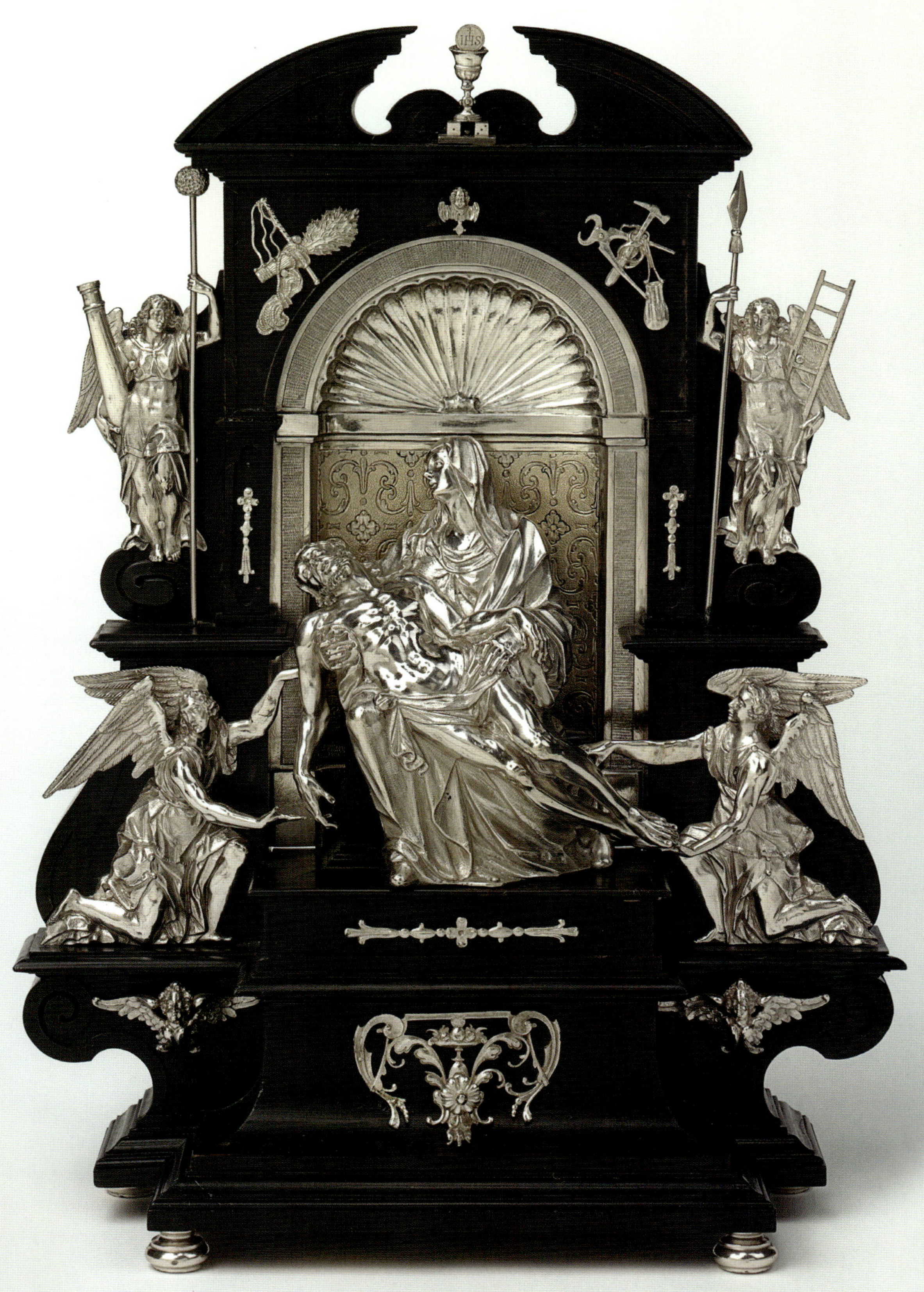

SHRINE

Trapani workshop, Sicily; after 1624
Gilt-copper, set with enamel and coral
V&A: M.157–1956; bequeathed by Dr W. L.
Hildburgh, FSA; h. 46.6 cm, w. 30.2 cm

THE SICILIAN TOWN OF TRAPANI WAS FAMED from the sixteenth century onwards for its coral-work, whose virtuoso carving and decoration were so highly prized that pieces were often given as diplomatic gifts. In 1605 there were already 25 coral workshops in Trapani, producing works for *gran principi* (grand princes) at *grandissimo prezzo* (the highest price) and being sent to *lontani paesi* (distant lands). By the end of the seventeenth century the number of workshops had increased to more than 40.

The technique of insetting small pieces of coral into gilded bronze, silver or, as in this case, copper is typical of Trapani work of this period, as is the combination of coral and enamel in the elaborate floral frame. A number of very similar shrines, of this form and with this kind of frame, exist in Italian private collections. The V&A holds several other devotional pieces of Trapani work, including another shrine, a plaque showing the Assumption of the Virgin into Heaven after her death, and a small figure of St Michael the Archangel. The same technique could be used for dishes, boxes, frames and other small trinkets for a secular market.

The shrine is clearly designed to be hung on a wall, as can be seen from the ring at the top. It shows a figure of the twelfth-century hermit St Rosalia at its centre, the patron saint of Palermo. Her cult developed wide popularity after 1624, when the discovery of her bones on Mount Pellegrino coincided with the liberation of Sicily from the plague. She is shown wearing a crown of roses, holding a crucifix and rosary in her hands, and wearing a nun's habit. The figures that flank her seem to represent St Anthony of Padua to the right, holding the Christ child and a lily, and St Michael, vanquishing Satan, to the left. In the frame of white-enamelled leaves, cherub heads alternate with coral flowers, and some heads have been replaced with flowers. Given St Rosalia's association with Palermo, the shrine was probably made for a Palermo family for domestic devotional use.

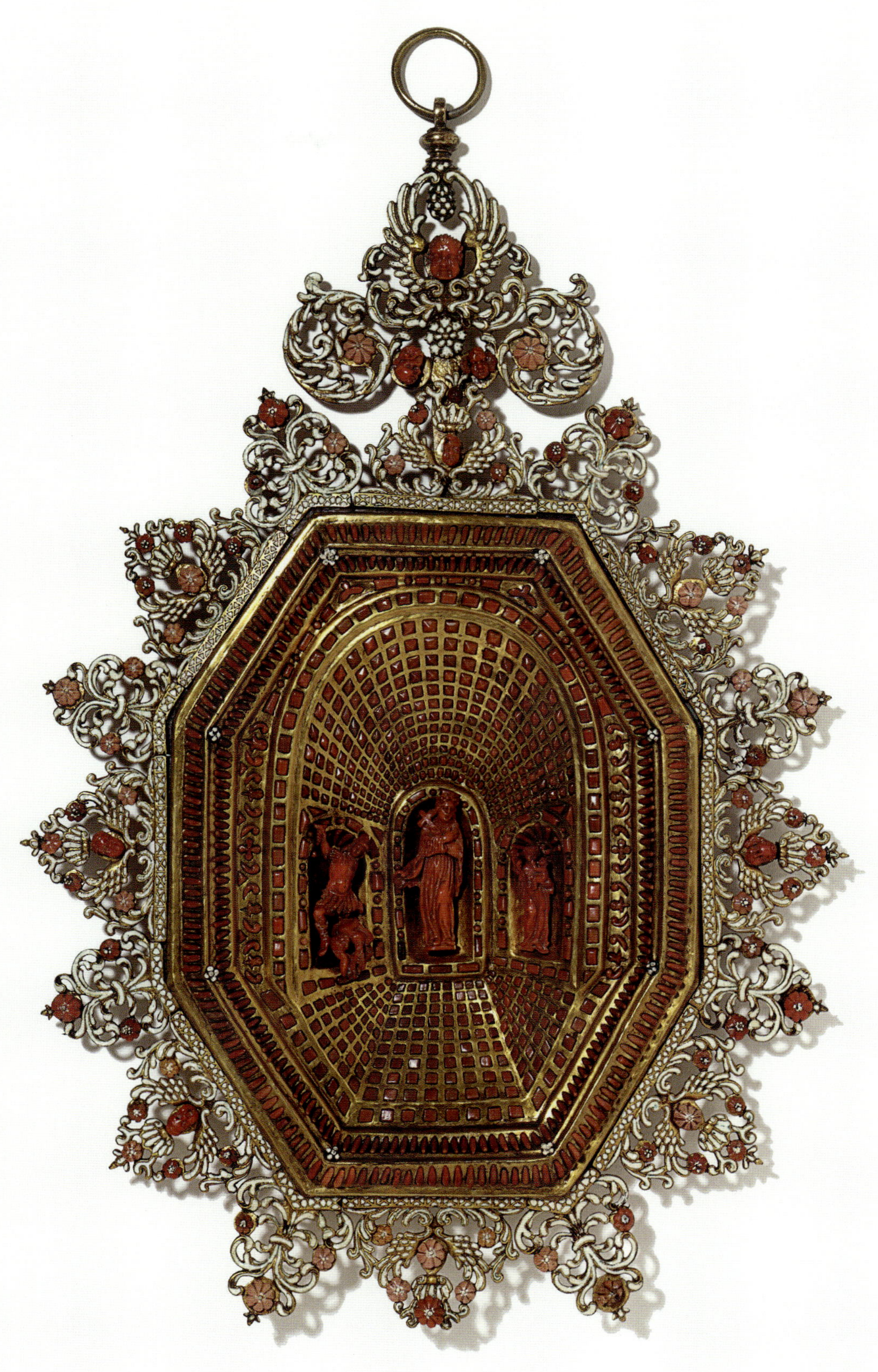

COMMEMORATIVE BEAKER

Maker's mark of Sigmund Dockler
(b. 1667, active 1696/7–1753)
Nuremberg; 1717
Silver-gilt
V&A: 260–1864; h. 17.8 cm, w. 11.4 cm, d. 11.4 cm

THIS BEAKER IS PART OF A GROUP OF OBJECTS, including cups, plates, engravings and medals, made to commemorate the Protestant Reformation and the role of Martin Luther (1483–1546) in that great religious controversy that had divided Europe in the sixteenth century. Many such beakers were made to record particular anniversaries related to the Reformation. This beaker bears the date of 1717. It commemorates the bicentenary of Luther's nailing of his 95 Theses (suggested reforms for Catholic theology) to the door of the church-castle at Wittenberg in eastern Germany in 1517, which sparked the beginning of the Reformation.

The beaker is set with five medals, all relating to Luther and all produced in 1717. Their iconography and inscriptions show a particular focus on light, perhaps interpreting Luther's act as shining the light of criticism and reform on the Catholic Church. The lid is set with a medal with a profile bust of Luther, the base with a medal whose inscription gives the date of the anniversary being commemorated. The sides are set with a medal showing Luther in the act of nailing his 95 Theses to the door, and another showing Luther and an angel at an altar. A half-thaler (a German coin) bears an inscription referring to Luther. The medals are from Nuremberg, Frankfurt and Augsburg. Their inscriptions all celebrate the reformed Protestant Church in these centres.

The practice of setting coins and medals into cups was long established by the eighteenth century, being particularly fashionable during the sixteenth century as a means of showing one's taste and erudition, at a time when the collecting of medals became one of the popular interests of educated people. The beaker itself, raised from a single sheet of metal, is simply decorated with engraved ornament in the early eighteenth-century Régence style. Such ornament contrasts with the decoration of the medals, and it draws attention to the commemorative nature of the object. It seems likely that the production of such numbers of commemorative objects may reflect an attempt to create a Protestant iconography to parallel that which formed such a vital visual element in the Catholic Church.

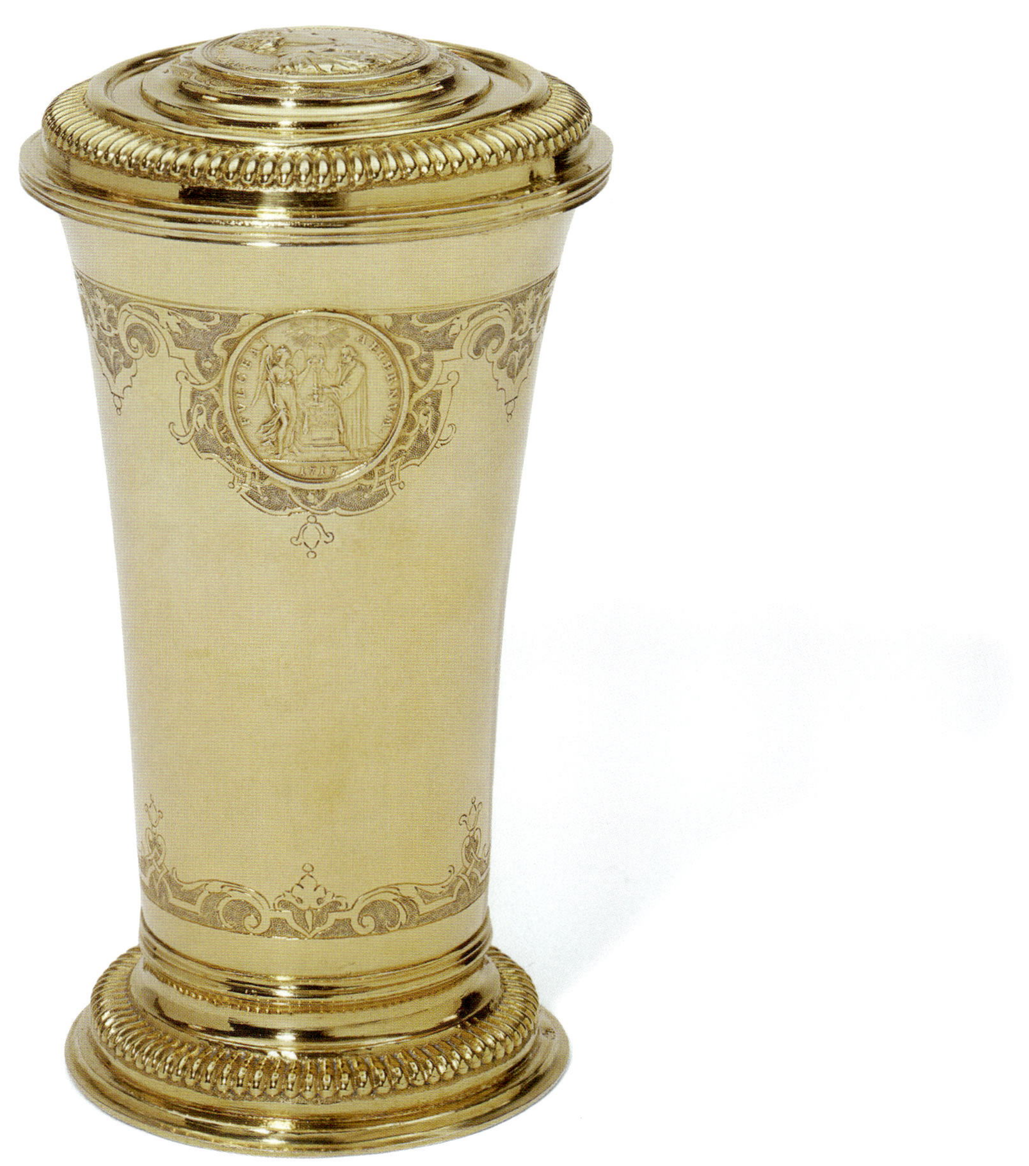

PRAYER-BOOK BINDING

France; about 1623

Gold, with enamel and emeralds

V&A: M.255–1984; h. 5.3 cm, w. 4.2 cm, d. 1.8 cm

DESPITE ITS DIMINUTIVE SIZE, THIS PRAYER book is of a level of splendour which implies that it must have been made for a wealthy and fashionable Catholic client, whose identity, however, remains unknown. The richness of the materials used and the similarity between the small, white-enamelled leaves on the cover and those on the frames of cameos formerly in the *Cabinet du Roi* (now in the Bibliothèque Nationale, Paris) and objects formerly in the *Galerie d'Apollon* in the Louvre, suggest both the expense of such a prayer book and the likely high rank of its owner.

The prayer book contains several sequences of prayers bound together, as was common practice, and includes an Office of the Virgin (published in 1623 and dedicated to the Queen, Anne of Austria (1601–66) wife of Louis XIII of France). It also includes other devotional prayers, including prayers on the Passion, published in 1623. As suggested by its small size, such a prayer book could easily be carried around for personal devotional use, as well as serving as a jewelled and possibly talismanic accessory.

The decoration of the binding is in the *cosse de pois* (pea-pod) style made fashionable in France during the reign of Louis XIII (1601–43), primarily by goldsmiths working in the royal workshops in the Galeries du Louvre in Paris. As a style, it was particularly suited to enamellers and jewellers, enabling them to display the breadth of their technical virtuosity as well as their inventiveness in design. In addition to pieces of jewellery and exquisite small accessories such as this book, these goldsmiths published sets of ornament prints, sometimes called *bouquets d'orfèvrerie* and often with titles specifically referring to their relevance to goldsmiths' work. The earliest such sheets in *cosse de pois* style were published in 1612 and the latest-known were published in 1642.

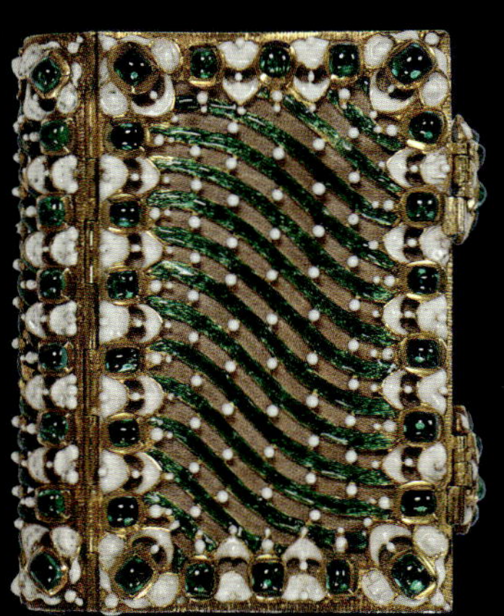

PATENT OF NOBILITY

Granada; 1626
Miniatures painted by Jerónimo Rodriguez de
Espinosa (1562–about 1638)
Illuminated manuscript on parchment; binding of
red velvet over wooden boards, with gilt-metal
corner pieces and clasps, and original lead seal
V&A: MSL/1981/11; h. 65 cm, w. 30 cm, d. 40.5 cm;
seal diam. 9 cm

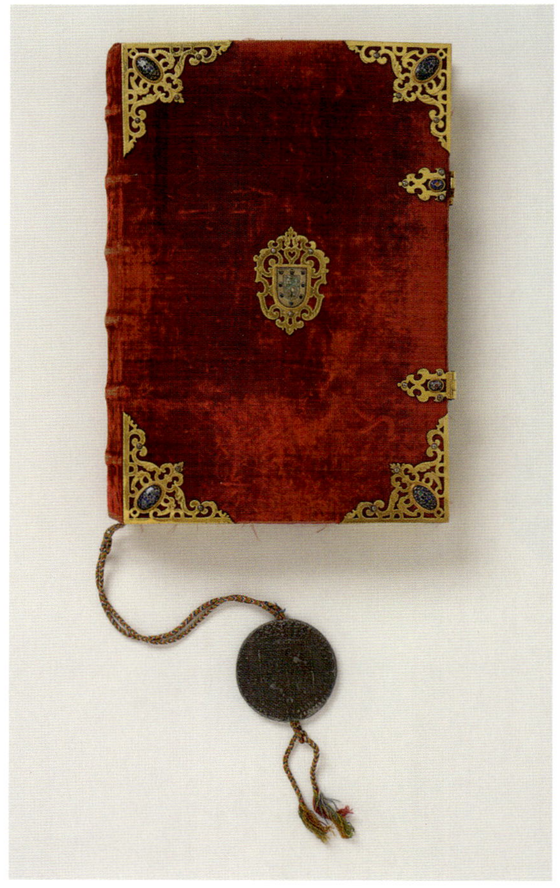

IN THIS MAGNIFICENT PATENT, ISSUED IN GRANADA, King Philip IV of Spain (1605–65) granted noble status to three brothers from Seville: Diego de Almonte, Juan de la Fuente Almonte and Hernando de Almonte. The text records the brothers' lineage, rights and coats of arms. It is bound between velvet-covered wooden boards, whose corner and centre pieces are made of gilt-metal; its original seal is still attached. One of the brothers probably commissioned the elaborate binding and illumination.

The illuminations were painted by the artist Jerónimo Rodriguez de Espinosa and refer to Catholic doctrine and the continuing conflict in Spain between Christians and Muslims. The Muslims had occupied large parts of Spain in the eighth century, and the Moriscos (Muslims forced to convert to Christianity) had only finally been expelled from the country in 1609. The left-hand page depicts Hernando de Almonte, kneeling with his wife before a vision of the Virgin of the Immaculate Conception – an extremely important figure of Catholic devotion, whose doctrine states that the Virgin Mary, mother of Jesus Christ, had been conceived without the stain of original sin. Between the kneeling figures are images of a fountain, a well, a rose bush and temples, all symbols of the Virgin Mary. The colourful borders show the Archangel Michael killing the Devil, and St Joseph, Mary's husband (a carpenter by trade), holding a flowering rod and leading the child Jesus. The name of the Spanish king, Philip IV, is inscribed at the bottom of the page.

The right-hand page, in contrast, shows a battle scene in which St James, patron saint of Spain, surrounded by dead or fleeing Muslims, rides a white horse and brandishes a sword. According to Spanish legend, St James is sometimes called 'the Moor-slayer', because he was said to appear during critical battles between the Christians and the Muslims, his presence ensuring a Christian victory. In the context of the patent, this imagery refers to the role played by the brothers' great-grandfather, Diego García de Almonte, when Granada was conquered from the Nasrids, the last dynasty to rule Islamic Spain, by the Catholic monarchs.

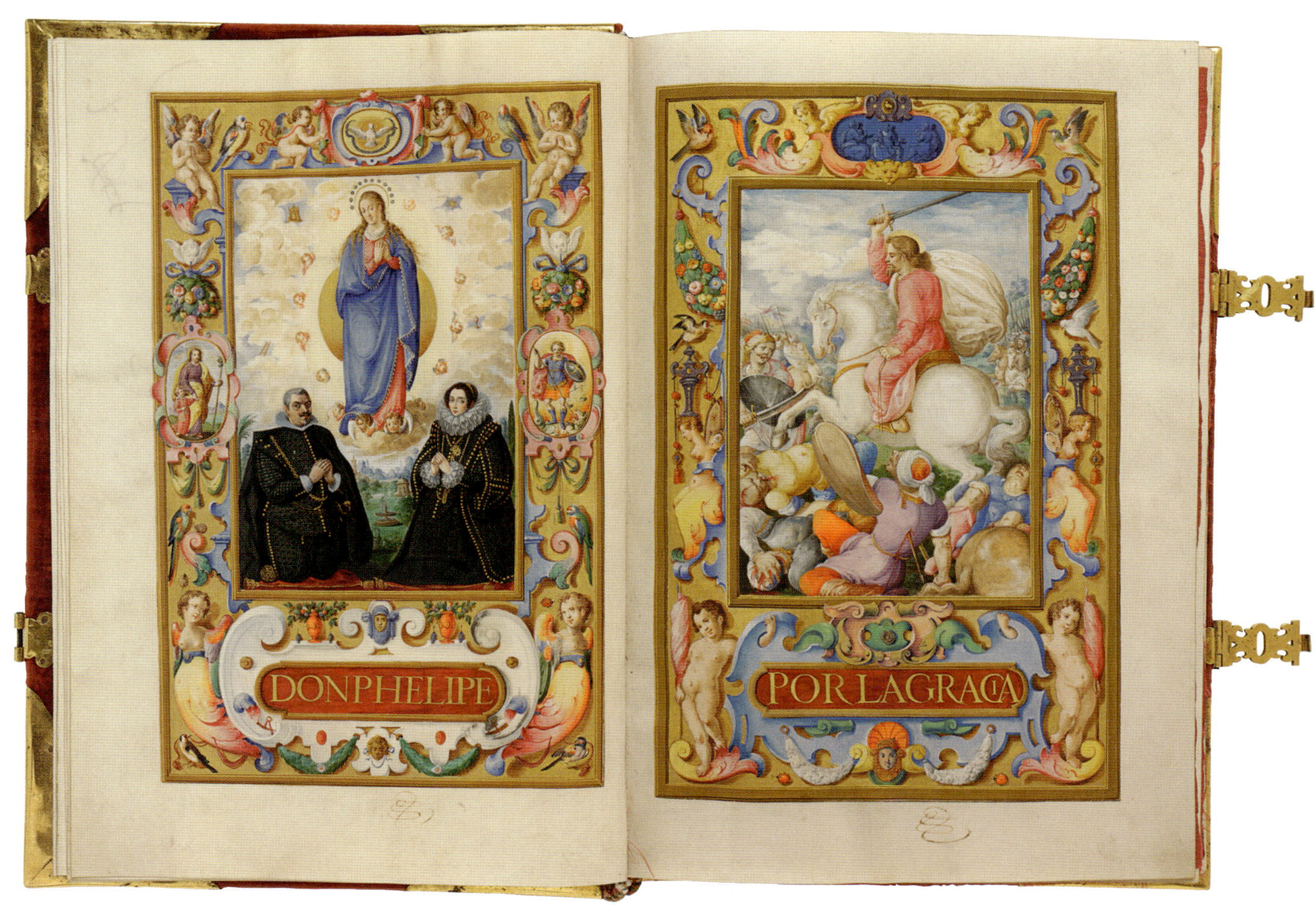
DONPHELIPE
PORLAGRACIA

COMMUNION BOOK

Texts: Augsburg and Nuremberg/Leipzig;
binding: Augsburg; 1731
Embossed silver (binding)
V&A: A.M.4506–1856; h. 16 cm, w. 8 cm, d. 3.5 cm

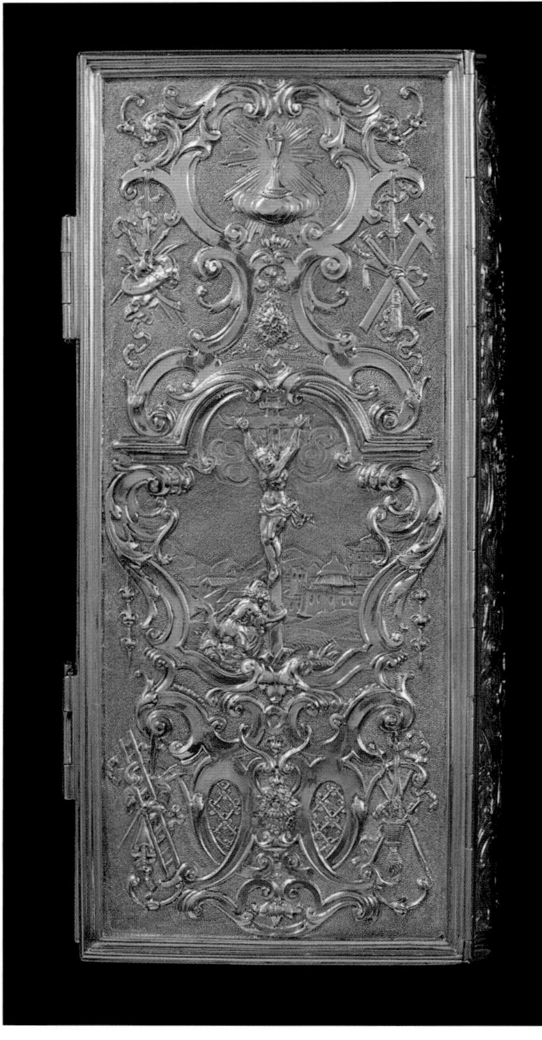

THIS SILVER BINDING CONTAINS A SMALL, portable communion book, which is composed of selections of texts from at least two printed books. Protestant lay people used such books in order to participate in the most important Church rite of communion, the taking of bread and wine, which for Protestants symbolize Christ's body and blood; unlike Catholics, Protestants do not believe in transubstantiation. The first part of the book contains communion prayers, which encouraged the faithful to reflect on how to follow the true path of sanctity. The second part of the book contains hymns, which were sung during church services.

The book's elaborate silver binding derives its subject matter from the texts that it contains. The front cover depicts the Old Testament story of the Sacrifice of Isaac, in which Abraham prepared to sacrifice his son Isaac to God, but was spared this through divine intervention. For Christians, Abraham's voluntary sacrifice foreshadows God's willingness to sacrifice his own son, Jesus Christ, on the cross, for the sake of humankind. Here, an angel prevents Abraham from killing Isaac. Above this scene is the figure of the Lamb of God (Jesus Christ), surrounded by rays of glory. The book's spine shows a crown with palm fronds emerging from it and a serpent being crushed by an altar. The crown may refer to Christ as King, while the palm frond is a symbol of martyrdom, and is closely associated with Christ's journey to his crucifixion. The serpent is a traditional Christian symbol of evil. The back cover shows the scene of the crucifixion, with the Virgin Mary kneeling at the foot of the cross to which Christ is nailed. Images of the instruments of the Passion surround this scene, which is surmounted by a chalice with a wafer above it and is surrounded by rays of glory. The wafer and chalice represent the bread and wine of the communion. Thus the whole decoration of the binding refers in some way to the subject of the communion rite.

The strapwork ornament in which these scenes are set suggests that the binding was made in the 1730s–40s in southern Germany, possibly in Augsburg, where at least one of the texts that it contains was published.

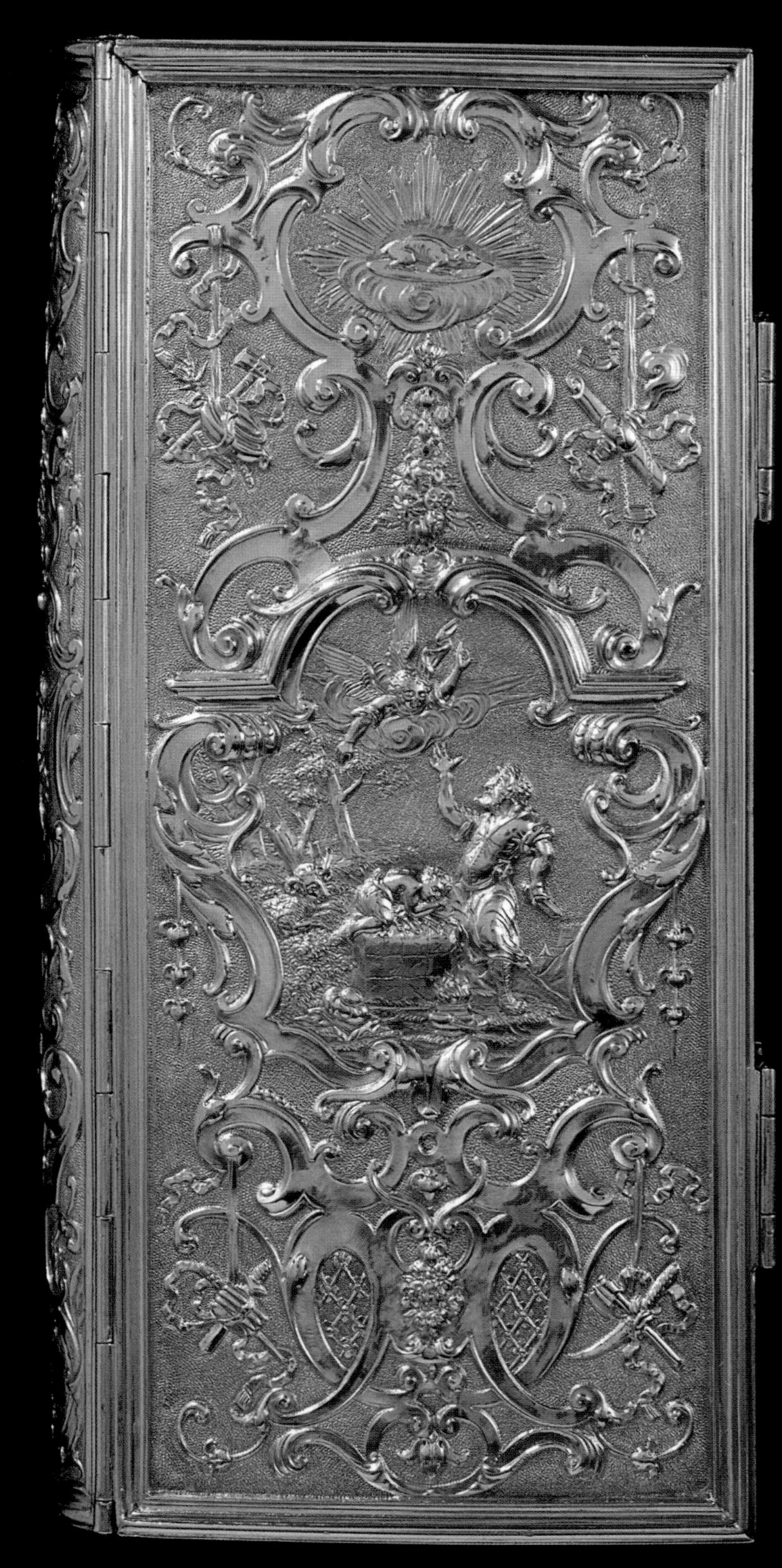

RELIQUARY

Naples; 1640–80
Cast silver and silver-gilt, Corsican green jasper,
chalcedony, cast gilt-bronze, paper, wood
V&A: LOAN:GILBERT.100–2008; The Rosalinde and
Arthur Gilbert Collection on loan to the Victoria
and Albert Museum, London: h. 61.6 cm, w. 21 cm,
d. 16.8 cm

THE CATHOLIC CHURCH PROMOTED THE cult of saints, the mortal remains of saints or holy objects associated with them being venerated. Reliquaries were the recipients designed to hold and display such relics. The design of reliquaries was often similar to that of monstrances (page 76). Unusually, this reliquary's original leather case survives, and is embossed with the initials and coat of arms of a later, nineteenth-century owner, Cavaliere Agostino Rem-Picci.

The reliquary is particularly rich in colour because of the combination of materials used: silver, gilt-bronze and Corsican green jasper, a combination that is characteristic of Neapolitan work. These costly materials enhance its status as a sacred object designed to be seen from afar, as well as close to. The silver plaque bears a narrative scene, which shows the Adoration of the Shepherds, the first witnesses of the birth of Jesus Christ. The infant Christ is seen lying in a manger at the centre of the composition, his mother the Virgin Mary kneeling over him and his father St Joseph standing on the left looking on, as two shepherds on the right offer their devotions and a gift of a lamb to the newborn child. It is a particularly appropriate scene for this relic, which is a fragment of the manger in which Christ was laid. The relic itself is housed in a clear glass opening at the centre of the silver plaque – in other words, at the very centre of the manger. The viewer's attention is drawn immediately to the relic. A piece of paper is wrapped around the relic itself, inscribed 'the sacred birthplace of our Lord Jesus Christ' in Latin.

The form and imagery of the reliquary appear to be loosely related to engraved designs by Orazio Scoppa (active first half of the seventeenth century), who, in 1642–3, published a set of engravings for metalwork, including an elaborate design for a monstrance, which served as the principal sourcebook for Neapolitan silversmiths. This reliquary seems to be a simplification and synthesis of some of his ideas, such as the combination of gilt-bronze C-scrolls, pea-pod elements, angel heads and festoons of fruit and flowers, but with the additional incorporation of auricular forms on the gilt-bronze base.

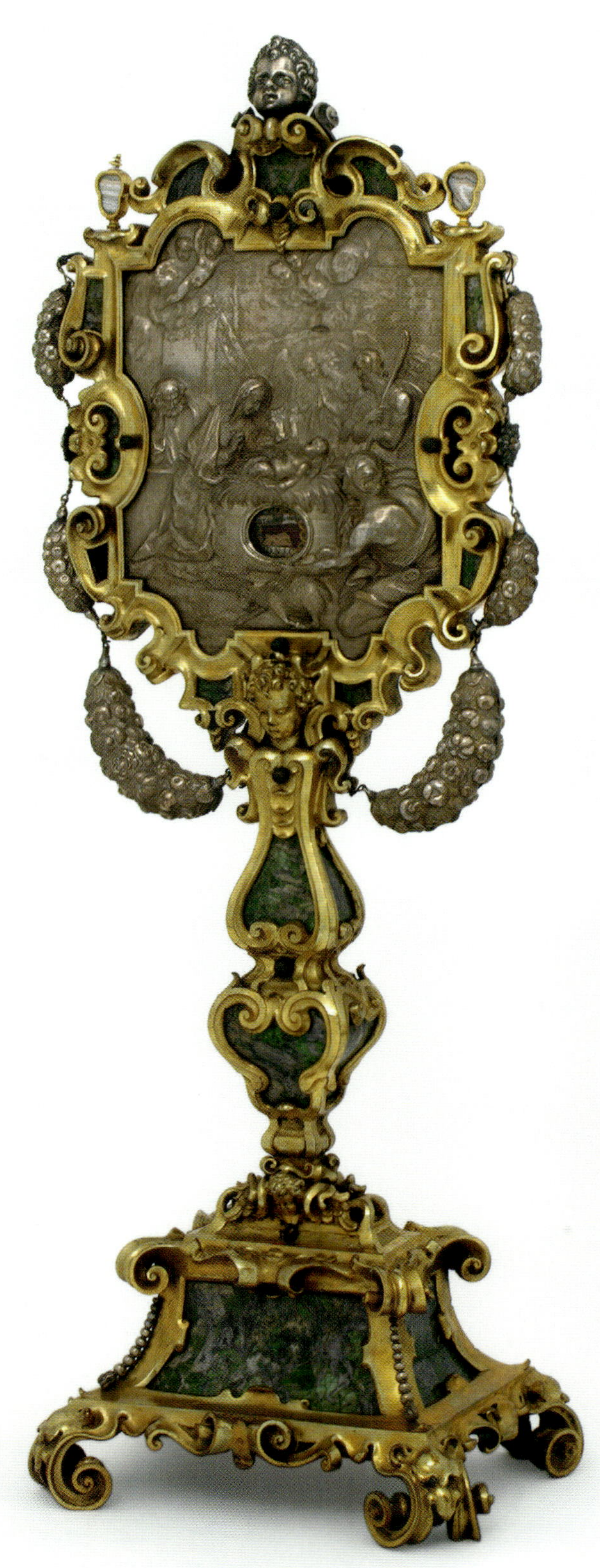

TABERNACLE

Rome; 1700–50
Pietre dure (agate, alabaster, jasper, lapis lazuli),
gilt-bronze, gilt-copper
V&A: LOAN:GILBERT.938–2008; The Rosalinde and
Arthur Gilbert Collection on loan to the Victoria
and Albert Museum, London; h. 57 cm, w. 34.7 cm,
d. 29 cm

IN CATHOLIC CHURCHES TABERNACLES, SUCH AS THIS one, were usually fixed, lockable boxes, designed to store the Eucharistic Host, once it had been blessed during the Mass. The Eucharist could then be taken from there and carried to the sick who were unable to participate in the Mass. While tabernacles had been used since the Edict of Milan in 313, they were not placed on the altar until the seventeenth century. In 1614 Pope Paul V (Pope 1605–21) led the move to place the tabernacle on the main or a side altar, by imposing that practice on the churches in his diocese of Rome. By the eighteenth century the tabernacle, whether on the main altar of the church or on the altar in a special chapel, was often a large and ornate object. Its dominant position on the altar served as a focus for prayers both during and outside church services.

This tabernacle is designed in the architectural form of a church façade, with a curved broken pediment above a central doorway flanked by coupled pilasters on either side. The doorway opens to reveal the sacred objects stored within. It is likely that a (now lost) crucifix would have stood on top of the tabernacle; the base is also lost. The precious materials used for this example indicate the significance of the object, and the preciousness of its contents.

Italy is particularly renowned for the technique used to make this tabernacle. Often called *pietre dure* (literally 'hard stones' in Italian), it had developed from a type of inlay used from antiquity. In this technique, a sheet of stone acted as the background. Recesses were chiselled into its surface, ready for the insertion of pieces of opaque coloured stones, such as jasper, bloodstone, cornelian, lapis lazuli, malachite and *rosso antico*. Once these stones had been cut and inserted, the surface was polished. The patterns could be purely ornamental or pictorial. This particular tabernacle is typical of the Roman style of hardstone work, as it is purely decorative, with no figurative elements. In contrast, Florentine work often used inlaid flowers or birds. The gilt-bronze cherub heads that adorn the top and sides are also typical of late Roman baroque sculpture.

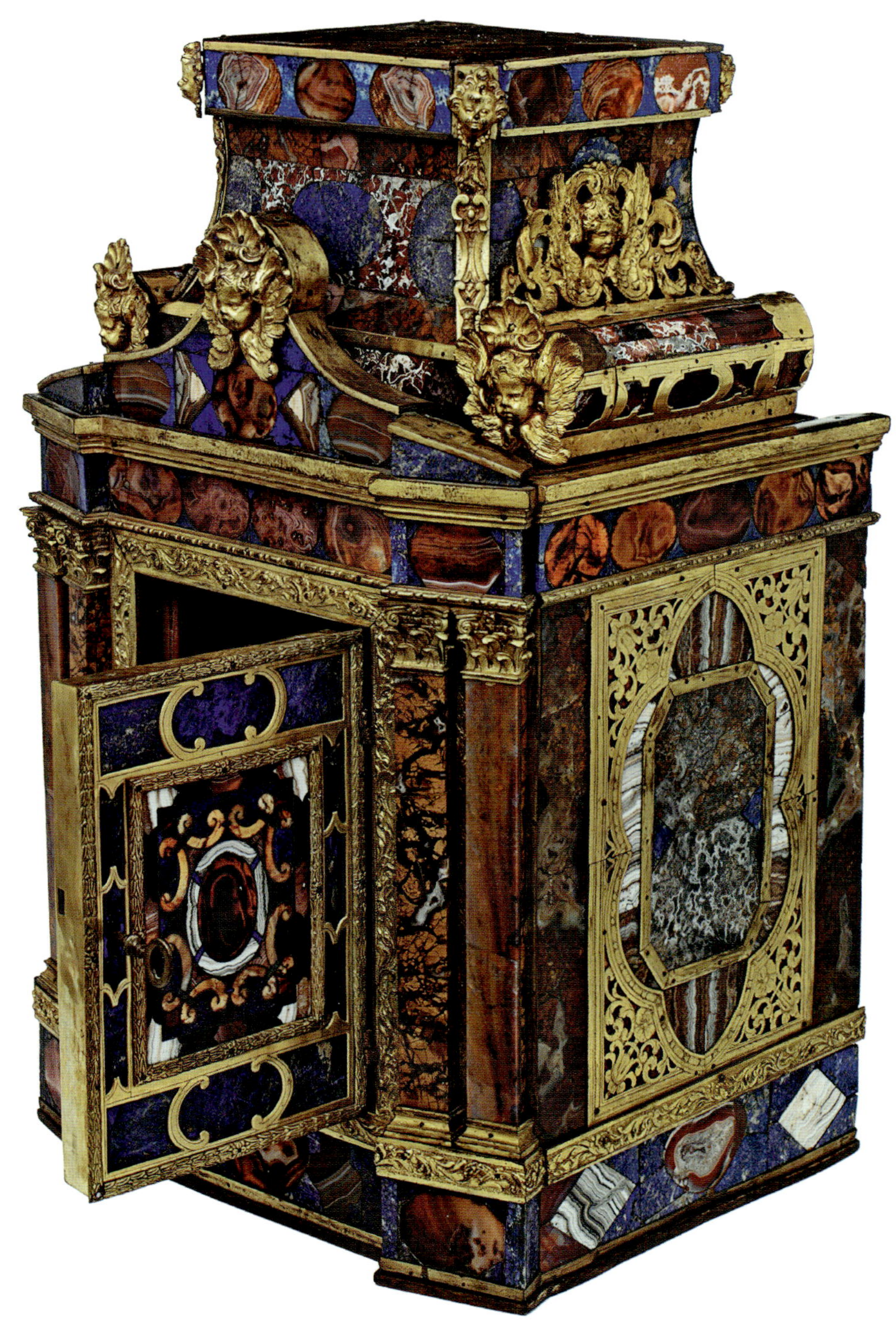

PAROCHET OR TORAH ARK CURTAIN

Probably Venice; 1676
Linen embroidered with silk and silver-gilt thread
and bordered with silver-gilt fringe
V&A: 511–1877; h. 190.5 cm, w. 165 cm

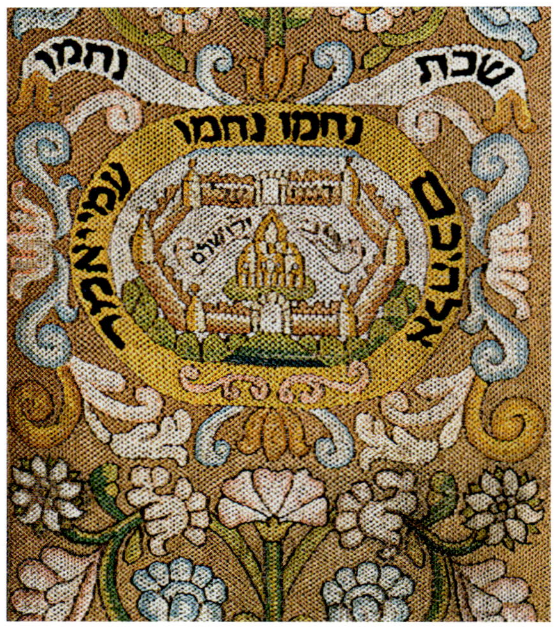

A *PAROCHET* IS THE CURTAIN THAT COVERS the doors of the Ark containing the Torah scrolls in a synagogue. This splendid example is dated twice by inscriptions following the Hebrew calendar. One inscription records that the embroidery was finished in August/September 1676, the other that it was presented to a synagogue by Joseph bar Haim Segal Polacko in 1711. It is likely to have been embroidered by a woman, but may have been designed by a professional artist, perhaps one who illuminated marriage certificates (*ketubahs*), which used a similar kind of artistic style of decoration. The embroiderer may have been Rikah Polacko, who, in 1662, signed her work on a binder for Torah scrolls, now in the Jewish Museum, New York. It is possible that she was the mother of Joseph, who presented the *parochet* to his synagogue.

The decoration of this particular *parochet* centres on the Decalogue, the two stone tablets of the law, which, according to both Jewish and Christian teaching, were given to Moses on Mount Sinai, by divine dictation; 12 further scenes or symbols depicted in the wide borders represent important festivals and Sabbaths, which commemorate particular events or on which special readings are heard in the synagogue. Each scene is accompanied by a relevant Hebrew quotation. The scenes are grouped together by theme, rather than reflecting the order of the festivals in the Jewish year, and seem to relate in particular to the identification of the Jewish community in Venice with the people of Israel, expressing their longing for the end of their exile and their return to the Promised Land.

In many parts of Europe restrictions were imposed on the size and external decoration of synagogues. Therefore the only way for Jewish worshippers to use their own wealth to declare their religious devotion through objects was for them to commission richly decorated ceremonial works such as these, which would only be seen by members of the community in the course of religious ceremonies within the synagogue.

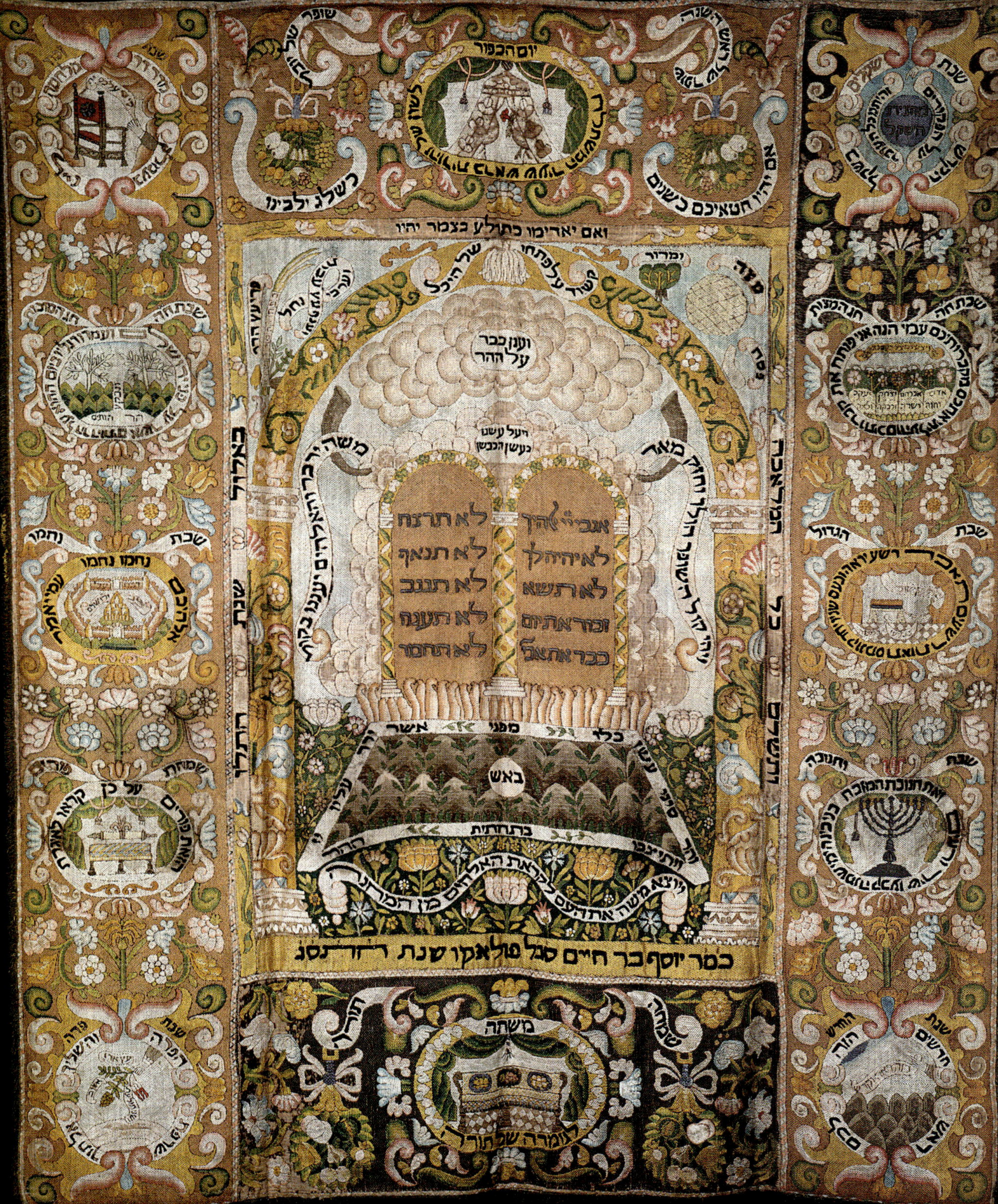

אנכי יי אלהיך
לא יהיה לך
לא תשא
זכור את יום
כבד את
לא תרצח
לא תנאף
לא תגנב
לא תענה
לא תחמד
כמר יוסף בר חיים סג"ל פולאקו שנת רחד"נסב

PAIR OF *RIMMONIM*

The Netherlands; about 1780
Silver-gilt and filigree
V&A: M.27&28–2009; presented by Lady Marjorie
Gilbert through the American Friends of The Art
Fund; h. 39 cm, w. 10 cm

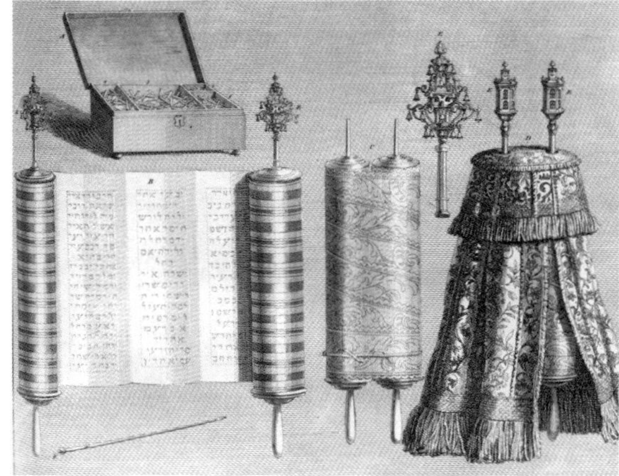

Illustration of *rimmonim*, from Bernard Picart, *Histoire
générale des ceremonies, moeurs et coutumes religieuses
de tous les peoples du monde*, 1741, National Art
Library (24.G.148–153)

R IMMONIM ARE THE DECORATIVE FINIALS generally placed on the rollers (known as 'Trees of Life' or *Atzei Hayyim*) holding the scroll of the Torah, the most sacred object in Judaism, which contains the first five books of the Hebrew Bible, the Pentateuch. The public reading of these texts in the synagogue is central to Jewish worship. Torah finials generally take the form of a pair of *rimmonim* or a crown, symbolizing majesty and the Law of the Torah. In this case the *rimmonim* are surmounted by a crown, to reinforce the symbolism. The word *rimmonim* comes from the Hebrew for 'pomegranates', which explains their bulbous shape. The bells on the *rimmonim* evoke those on the High Priest's robe as described in the Book of Exodus, and their tinkling would have announced to the congregation the bringing of the Torah scroll from the Ark to the desk for the reading of the Torah. The decoration of this pair of *rimmonim* is in intricate filigree work, while the engraved decoration on the staves mirrors the floral ornament of the filigree.

Judaism was the largest minority religion in Europe during the seventeenth and eighteenth centuries, treated with greater or lesser degrees of tolerance in different locations and at different times. By the eighteenth century many small communities of Jews had become established in the Netherlands, often making names for themselves as traders and diamond-cutters and protected under successive Stadtholders, as important contributors to the economic success of the state. As the richness of these *rimmonim* shows, although it was a minority religion, Judaism was nonetheless responsible for significant arts patronage during this period, albeit on a smaller scale than was permitted for Christian patrons of similar status.

This pair of *rimmonim* was owned by the Sassoon family and was displayed in the Anglo-Jewish Historical Exhibition in London in 1887.

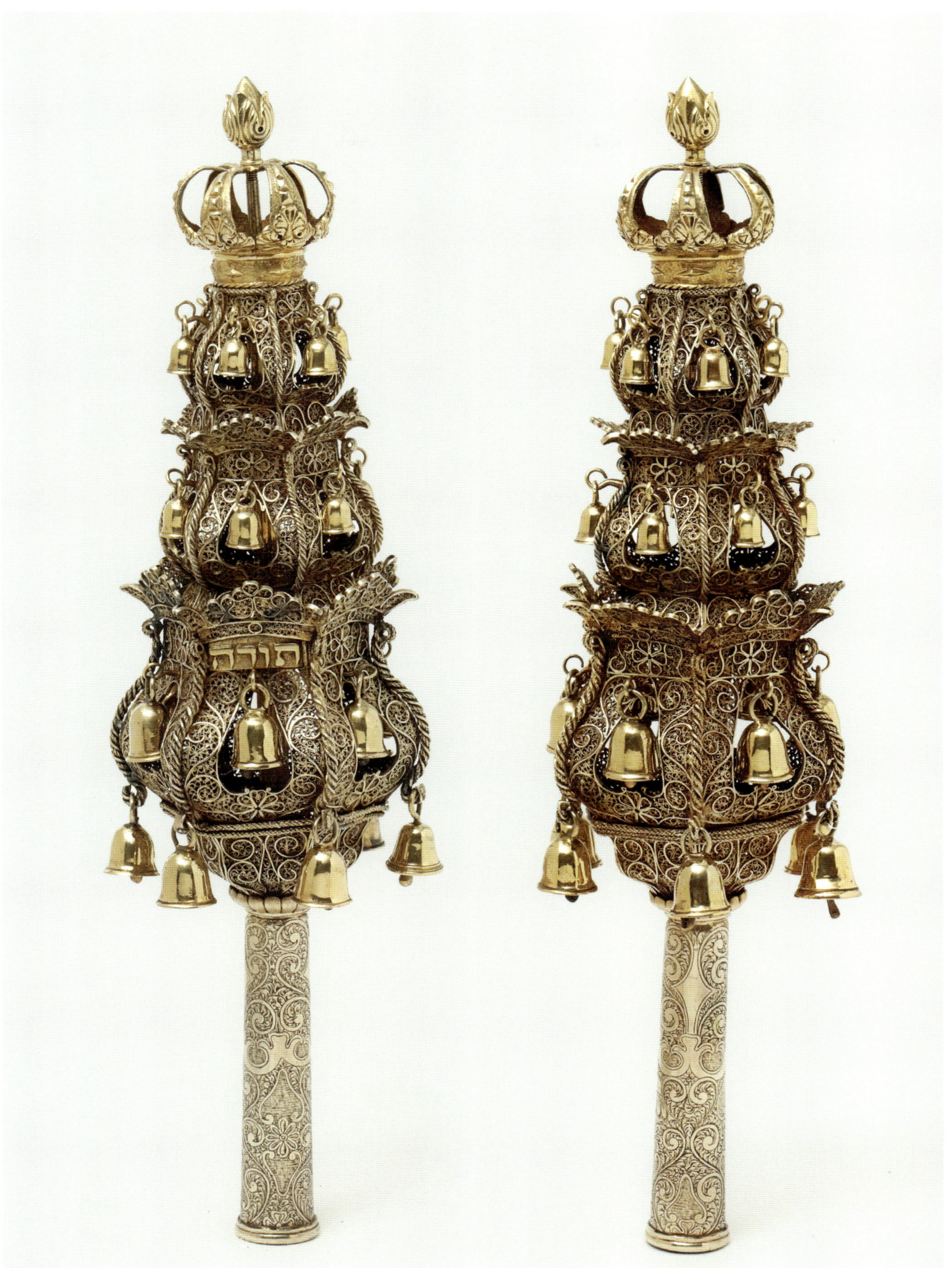

DISPLAY IN THE INTERIOR

ANTONIA BRODIE

ETWEEN 1600 AND 1800 THE HOMES of the wealthy across Europe continued to serve both as public arenas and private refuges in which to work and entertain, enjoy food and drink, play music, gamble, dance, do needlework, write letters and read books. Changing ideals of comfort and convenience, coupled with rising standards of luxury, meant that the interior became much more significant both as a theatre for fashionable display and as a place for personal indulgence.

Vast and lavish new palaces continued to proclaim the power and splendour of their princes. Such buildings were frequently surrounded by spectacular formal gardens, often incorporating highly engineered fountains or waterfalls, manicured hedging and paths, or exotic specimen plants from areas of the world newly trading with Europe. Both buildings and landscapes were designed to represent the domination of the ruler over the natural world. Individual princely projects could take years to complete. Versailles, outside Paris, the model for many other palaces across Europe, became Louis XIV's official residence in 1682. Building work following plans by the architect Jules Hardouin-Mansart (1646–1708) had, however, begun in 1669. Its main grand reception hall (now known as the *Galerie des Glaces* or Hall of Mirrors), decorated under the guidance of the painter Charles Lebrun (1619–90), took no fewer than eight years to complete (1678–86) and was copied by many monarchs in Europe. Between 1752 and 1780, Caserta in southern Italy followed the French example, becoming a palace with 1,200 rooms, a seemingly infinite façade and a cascade to outdo even Versailles, while the less ostentatious but nonetheless grand retreat of Sanssouci near Berlin had been designed and built for Frederick the Great of Prussia (1712–86) in the years after 1745.

Aristocrats and successful merchants echoed royal patronage, by erecting and remodelling impressive country houses as well as mansions in town.

Throughout the period both new and remodelled palaces shared a layout that mirrored the formality and control that rigid codes of etiquette imposed on life at court. Sequences, or *enfilades*, of state rooms of ever-increasing luxuriousness and exclusivity led out from an impressive central staircase. These exemplified architectural theories such as those of Jacques-François Blondel (1705–74), who recommended in his important treatise, published in the mid-1750s, that 'one should be able to observe a gradation in richness and magnificence proportionate to the destination and function of each room'.[1] The biggest public rooms were near the staircase and were used for large receptions and public events, such as ambassadorial visits, royal marriages or balls. In contrast, the smaller rooms, further away from the staircase, were more intimate. It was a much greater honour to be received there. At the far end of the *enfilade* was the cabinet or closet, a small private chamber, comfortable for a company of four to six people at most, used for study, relaxation and select entertaining. Access to this inner sanctum was strictly controlled and proffered as a mark of special favour.

Perhaps as an antidote to such magnificence, smaller palaces – designed as quasi-informal retreats furnished in the latest taste – were also popular amongst royalty as an escape from formality. In Sweden, King Adolf Fredrik (1710–71) surprised his queen on her birthday in 1753 with a small Chinese pleasure palace in the Drottningholm Palace park, while Louis XVI's queen enjoyed exclusive use of the Petit Trianon in the grounds of Versailles, after his accession to the throne in 1774. Similarly, Catherine the Great's Kekerekeksinen (The Frog Palace) in Russia

was created to offer respite from the strict protocol
and lack of privacy of palace life in St Petersburg. The
more relaxed atmosphere of a private house presented
opportunities to experiment with new styles, which
might be thought too informal for an official residence.
Physical comfort was of paramount importance, and
innovations in heating, lighting, upholstery and dining
were enthusiastically embraced in this context.

The transmission of ideas, the trade in materials
and the migration of artisans, artists and patrons
during the period profoundly affected the design of the
wide range of objects created in different European
centres. Parisian cabinet-making, which set the fashion
for most of Europe, was dominated by immigrant
German craftsmen from the late seventeenth century,
and French Protestant goldsmiths like Paul Crespin
(1694–1770) cornered the London market for top-
quality silver (page 138). The travels of the Swedish
architect Nicodemus Tessin the Younger (1654–1728)
in Italy and France in the late seventeenth century
altered the course of Swedish design, while the
entrepreneurial German cabinet-maker David
Roentgen's visit to the court of Catherine the Great
in 1784 fed a growing appetite in Russia for western
European furnishings. International royal marriages
disseminated new fashions in everything from dresses
to dining. Such ideas swiftly filtered down to the
nobility and the increasingly wealthy middle classes.

Commercial and colonial expansion brought
new materials, such as tropical hardwood and
tortoiseshell, to the markets of Europe and increased
the popularity of imported products such as porcelain
and lacquer, as well as ornamental forms and motifs
from every part of the world. European inventors and
entrepreneurs were quick to set up new industries to
replicate them and serve ever-widening markets.

The free circulation of objects and people
did not, of course, create an entirely homogenized
Europe-wide taste. Distinct regional styles continued
to flourish, as design ideas were adapted to suit local

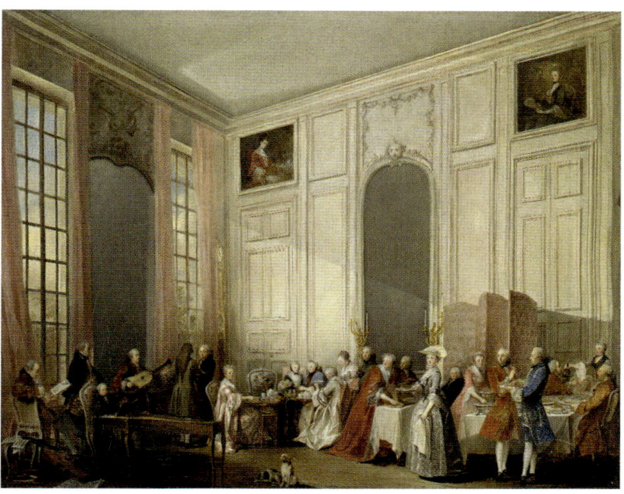

12 *Tea 'in the English style' served in the salon of the Four
Mirrors in the Temple, with the whole court of the Prince de
Conti*, by Olivier Michel Barthélemy. Oil on canvas. Paris, 1766
(Musée national des châteaux de Versailles et de Trianon)

aesthetic preferences, climate and way of life. Thus,
in southern Europe, ceramic tiles, long prized for their
coolness, decorated floors as well as internal and
external walls, while in more northerly countries tiles
were predominantly used around fireplaces or to cover
heating stoves. The succession of decorative styles that
appeared between 1600 and 1800 was interpreted
differently at different times across Europe. Baroque
drama, spatial complexity and opulent decoration
shaped both Bernini's St Peter's Basilica in Rome
(begun in 1626) and the palace of Mafra (begun in
1717) in Portugal. Rococo asymmetry and movement
can be seen in the Zwinger Palace in Dresden (built
1710–32) in Germany and in the textile designs of
Anna Maria Garthwaite (1688–1763) of London. The
light and colourful designs of Charles-Louis Clérisseau
(1721–1820) (page 142) brought neoclassical designs
to Paris in the 1770s. Jean-Demosthène Dugourc
(1749–1824) used the same repertoire of designs for
the Spanish market.

1 *Cours d'architecture*, 1752–6, quoted in Katie Scott, *The
Rococo Interior: Decoration and Social Spaces in Early
Eighteenth-Century Paris*, London and New Haven, 1995,
p.109

DESIGN FOR A CHINA CABINET

Daniel Marot (1661–1752)
The Netherlands; about 1700
Etching on paper
V&A: E.1672:20–1888; h. 24.1 cm, w. 19.4 cm

A CABINET WAS THE MOST PRIVATE AND intimate space within a palace or aristocratic house in the late seventeenth century. Houses in the fashionable baroque style were usually designed with separate suites of rooms (an apartment) for the owner and his wife, each set symmetrically on either side of the public rooms. Cabinets were richly decorated, but often in a less formal style than the other rooms of the apartment, possibly reflecting a more personal interest in the fashions of the day, particularly the taste for decorations in the Chinese style.

The designer Daniel Marot trained with Jean Le Pautre (1618–82) in Paris, working on designs for Louis XIV (1638–1715) at Versailles. As a Protestant, Marot was forced to leave France in 1686, after the Revocation of the Edict of Nantes the previous year, and went to the Netherlands where he became court designer for William of Orange (1650–1702) and his wife Mary, later King and Queen of Great Britain (from 1689 to the death of William in 1702). Marot made numerous designs for the palace of Het Loo near Apeldoorn, and it is probable that this etching shows a scheme developed to display Mary's collection of Chinese blue-and-white porcelain from the Ming and Qing Dynasties in her private apartments there. As part of a wider taste for all things 'in the Chinese manner', porcelain-collecting was highly fashionable across Europe from the 1670s well into the eighteenth century. Although some wares, such as teacups, were used for eating and drinking, the majority of porcelain was displayed in the home, arrayed on top of cabinets, over doors or on wall-brackets – even in special rooms. The density of display depicted here is an illustration of how much more widely available ceramics from China and Japan had become by the late seventeenth century. Prior to the establishment of reliable maritime trade routes from the Pacific Ocean in the sixteenth century very few examples of Asian porcelain were seen in Europe. Their rarity was reflected in the precious-metal mounts with which they were frequently embellished.

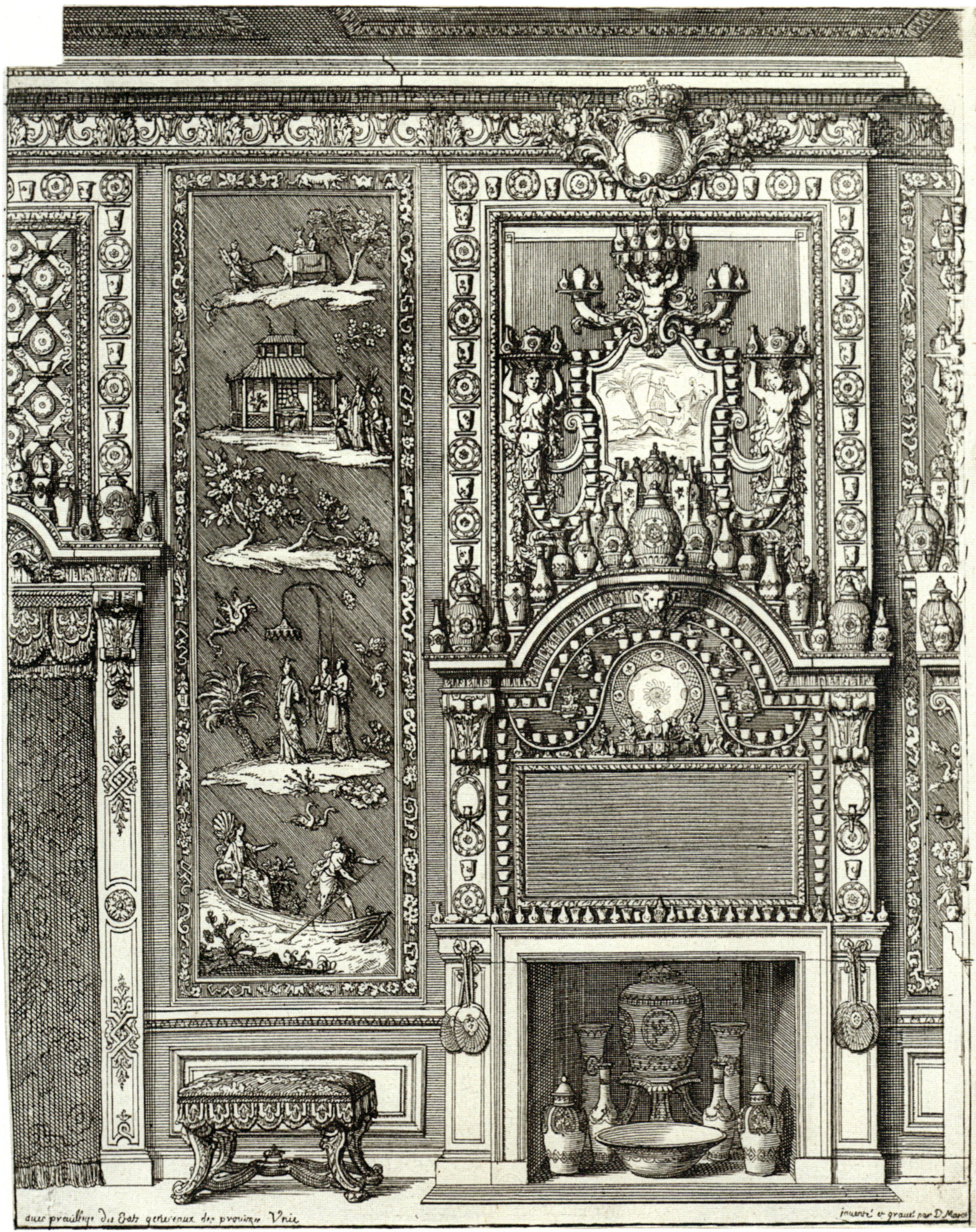

auec priuilege des Eats generaux des prouinces Vnie
inuenté et graué par D. Marot

VASE

Jingdezhen, China; about 1700
Porcelain, painted in underglaze blue
V&A: FE.3&A–1979; h. 36 cm, w. 9 cm, d. 9 cm

ULIPS, THE MOST SPECTACULAR OF WHICH are natives of Kazakhstan, were introduced to western Europe from the Ottoman Empire in the mid-sixteenth century and caused a sensation, especially in the Netherlands. Many new varieties of tulip were developed, and the most highly prized blooms were the flowers with delicate feathered patterning in two colours, now known to be the result of the mosaic virus.

Artists such as Jan Brueghel the Elder (1568–1625) depicted tulips in still-life paintings, celebrating their vivid colours and novel form. The enthusiasm for the new plants culminated in a brief period of intense speculation in the 1630s known as 'Tulip Mania', when bulbs were bought and sold for outrageous prices, and fortunes were made and lost in trading on them. The interest in tulips survived this hectic period, and special vases, intended to show tulip blooms to best advantage, were made in a wide range of sizes by manufacturers of tin-glazed earthenware in the Netherlands.

This form of vase, which used an obelisk to give height to the floral display and offered maximum support to the heavy blooms, was designed by Adriaen Kocks of the Grieksche A factory, active in Delft between 1686 and 1701, using underglaze-blue decoration, in imitation of the Chinese porcelain that was a fashionable import at the time. This particular vase, however, is made of porcelain rather than earthenware and was produced in one of the many ceramics manufactories at Jingdezhen in southern China. As the trade from China developed, European merchants initially bought wares made for the Chinese domestic market, but quickly realized that there would also be great European demand for further porcelain shapes that were until then unknown in China, such as chamber pots or this tulip vase. Samples of delftware were sent to Jingdezhen to be copied by the potters, who were quick to adapt their designs to the new markets. The results were novel designs that combined the fineness, durability and perfect whiteness of the ground to be found in Chinese porcelain with forms that were fashionable in the rich markets of the Netherlands.

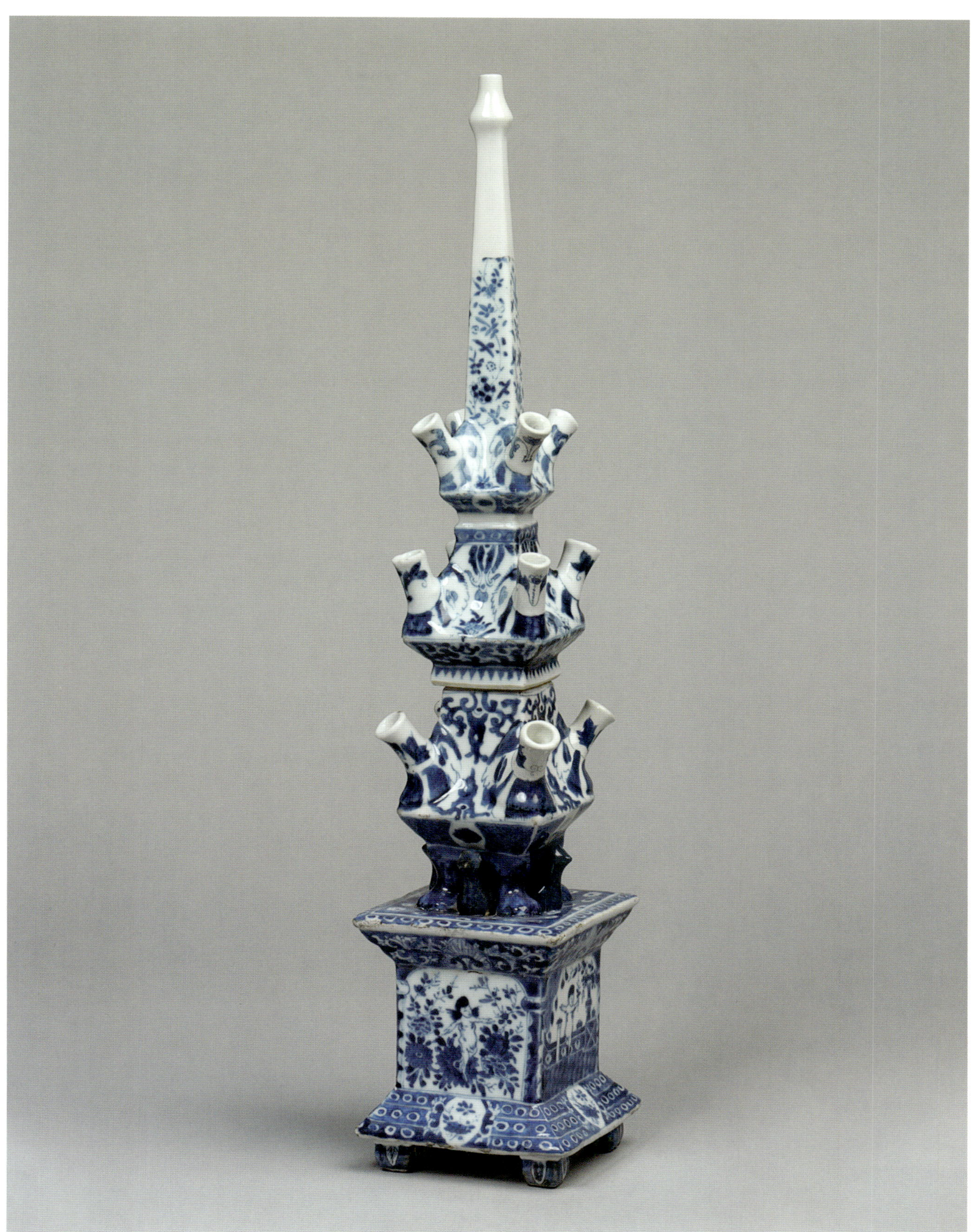

TILE PANEL

Lisbon; about 1720–30
Tin-glazed earthenware, painted
V&A: C.49–1973; h. 140 cm

THIS FINELY PAINTED PANEL EXEMPLIFIES A period of brilliance in the manufacture of pictures in Portugal in the early to mid-eighteenth century, a period in which the use of tiles simultaneously reached a peak of exuberance. The vendor to the Museum in 1973 believed that it was one of a series of six that had adorned the music room of the Quinta Formosa, to the east of Lisbon. A *quinta* was a country house, set in an estate, where the owners could take refuge in the summer from the heat of Lisbon. Tiles provided colour to the interiors of these houses and were well suited to the warm climate. They were deployed in a similar way to wood panelling, forming continuous dados around grand rooms, along corridors and up staircases.

Appropriately for a music room, these panels are decorated with scenes of dancing, music-making and relaxed entertainment. The combination of *trompe l'oeil* architectural framing and figurative scenes is characteristic of Portuguese baroque tiles and here gives an impression of figures on a terrace, with gardens beyond, an architectural conceit that would have echoed the more informal life of the *quinta*.

Tile-making in Portugal was established later than in Spain and developed a distinctive style. Technical innovations in the 1690s and the widespread participation of artists trained in their design and decoration created sophisticated wall-decorations with pictorial designs, sometimes on a large scale, imitating the effect of tapestries in a medium more suited to hot summers.

Success in the Portuguese Restoration War (1640–68) had freed Portugal from 64 years of rule by the Spanish Habsburg dynasty. This victory led to a surge in artistic confidence, which was also boosted in the first half of the eighteenth century by the wealth that came to the country from the gold and diamond mines of Brazil, its most important colonial territory. King João V (1689–1750) was particularly lavish in his patronage of architects and artists. Skilled designers and craftsmen came to Portugal from all over Europe, bringing new ideas to ornament buildings commissioned by the royal family and the nobility.

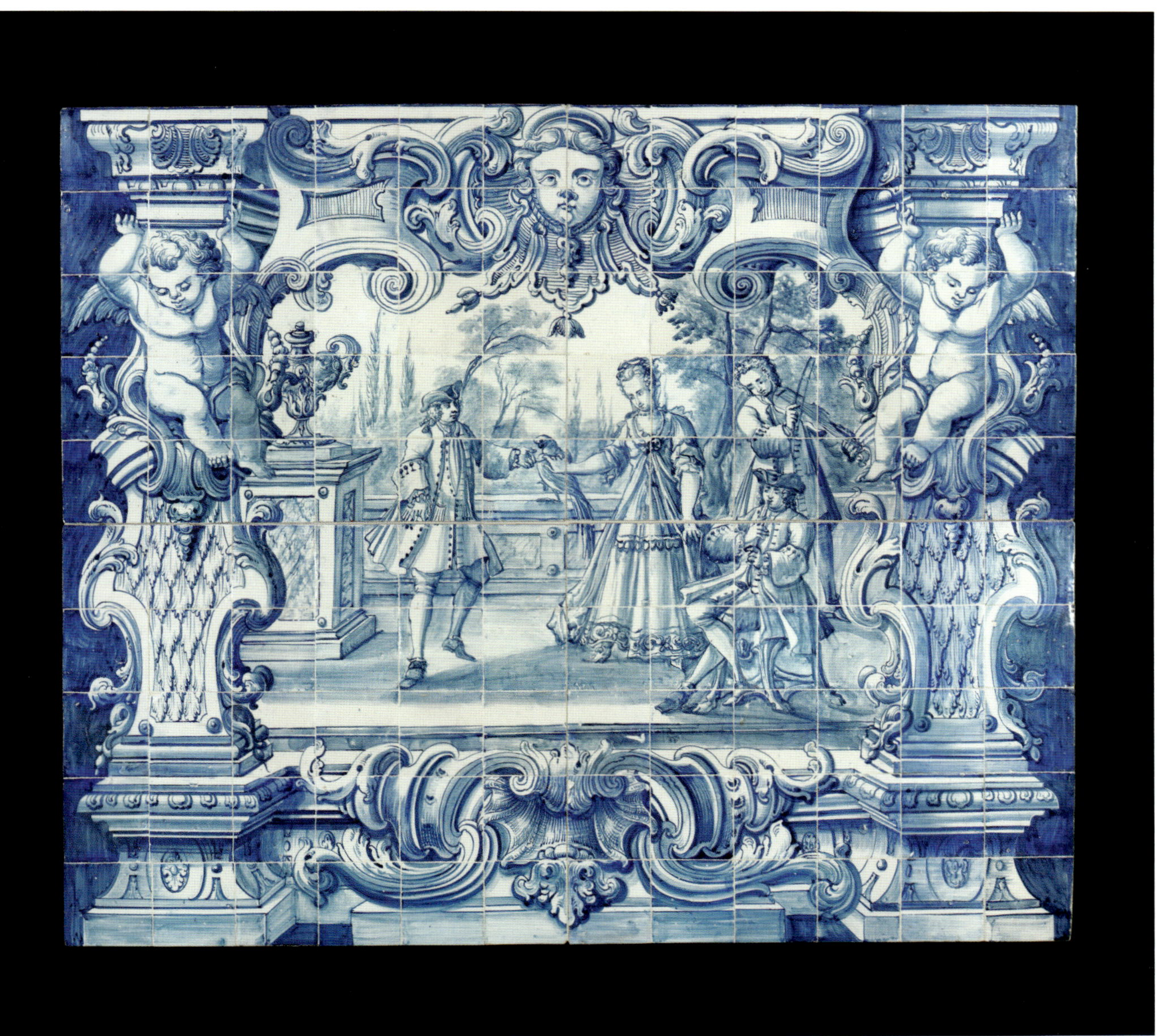

GUITAR

Joachim Tielke (1641–1719)
Hamburg; 1693
Ivory and turtle-shell veneer, with engraved
marquetry, gilt vellum rosette and carved ivory
openwork head
V&A: 676–1872; l. 102 cm, w. 30 cm, d. 13 cm

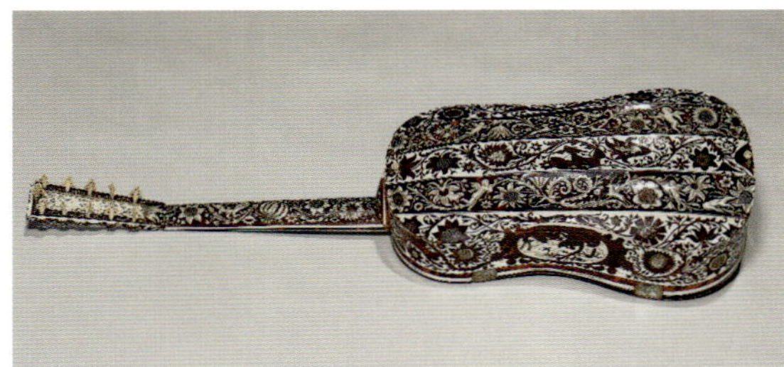

THIS SPLENDID INSTRUMENT IS AN EXAMPLE of the baroque guitar, which became highly fashionable across Europe in the late seventeenth century. Many professional guitarists made good livings at the courts of Europe, among them Francesco Corbetta (about 1615–81), guitarist to Charles II of England, and Robert de Visée (about 1650–1725), who served Louis XIV of France. Music also played a central role in domestic entertainment throughout the seventeenth and eighteenth centuries and, as a consequence, the ability to sing and play musical instruments was a vital social skill, to be cultivated by all who aspired to a polite education. Conduct manuals of the period stressed the importance of mastering these arts, which were central to the education of noblemen and women.

The guitars of the period were slightly smaller and of lighter construction than the modern classical guitar and had a more rounded back. They were easier to play than lutes, as the performer could simply strum the strings as an accompaniment while singing. The decoration of such instruments often meant that they were as much fashion accessories as musical instruments for virtuosic performances. In this example, the elaborate engraved marquetry of ivory and turtle-shell is a veneer that adorns the body of pine. The imported tropical materials from Asia, Africa and South America were highly expensive and suitable for decoration, while pine – the cheapest of woods – ensured a good sound.

Joachim Tielke, the maker of this guitar, built many beautiful stringed instruments for clients from the court of Cassel in central Germany; 15 guitars by him still survive, suggesting the esteem in which he was held, and the V&A alone has six stringed instruments by him.

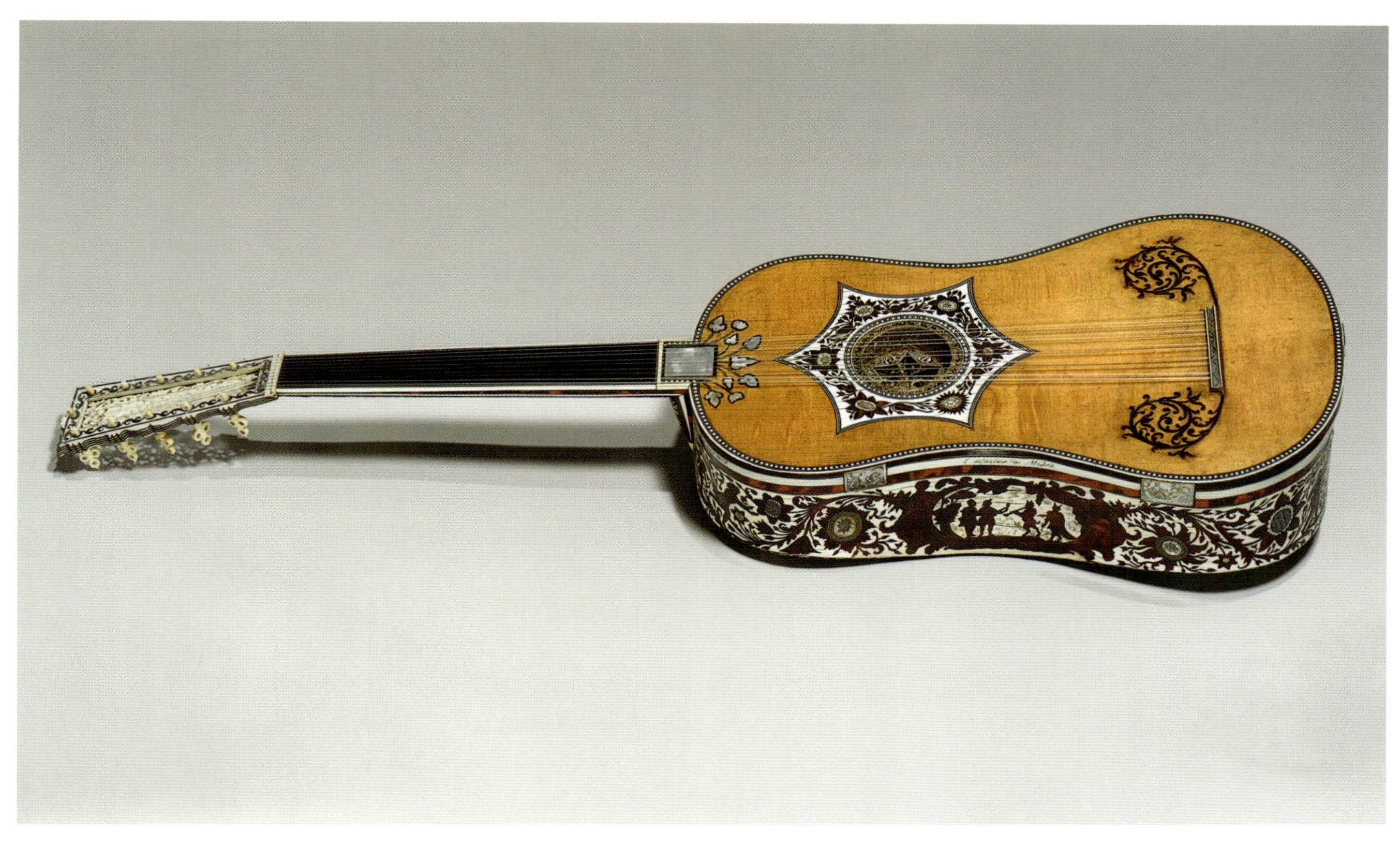

COMMODE

Charles Cressent (1685–1768)
Paris; 1745–50
Oak, veneered in *bois satiné* and purplewood,
gilt-bronze mounts, Brèche d'Alep marble slab
V&A: 1119–1882; bequeathed by John Jones;
h. 90.4 cm, w. 135.5 cm, d. 64.1 cm

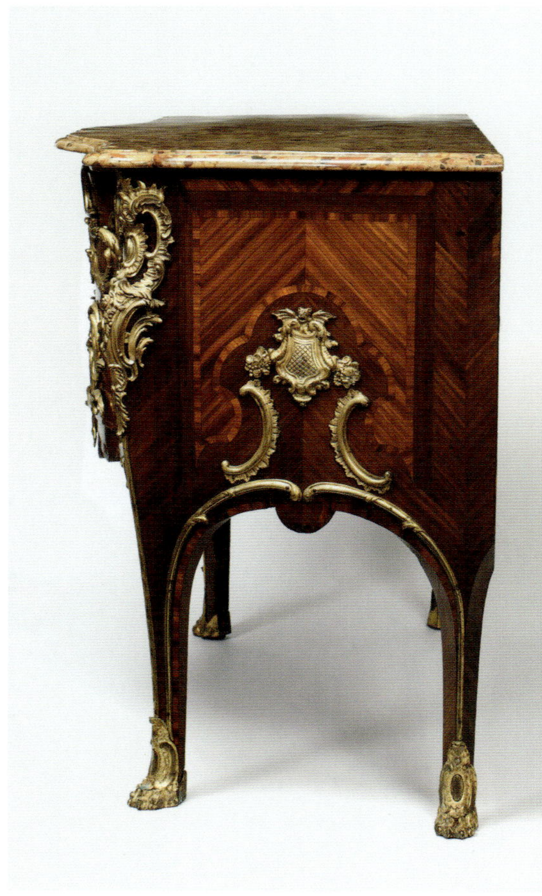

THE COMMODE (FROM THE FRENCH WORD for convenient), or chest of drawers, emerged as a new type of furniture in the second half of the seventeenth century. Combining features of the chest and the cabinet, it rapidly found favour in fashionable society throughout Europe, and by the end of the seventeenth century had taken the place of the cabinet-on-stand as the most prestigious form of furniture in the *enfilade* (the state rooms that were designed primarily to show the wealth and taste of the owner, rather than to provide comfortable accommodation). The commode was to retain this status throughout the eighteenth century, with cabinet-makers constantly redesigning the form and inventing new varieties of surface decoration to ensure its continued desirability.

Cressent specialized in creating carefully considered designs that relied for their effect on the contrast between the rich colouring of tropical hardwoods and the sculptural energy of his brilliant gilt-brass mounts. On this commode he used his favourite wood, *bois satiné* (a warm, red wood, not unlike mahogany, but with a more striped figure), giving the piece richness and grandeur. This was complemented by the colourful Brèche d'Alep marble slab that forms the top of the commode, a variegated marble from the Sarcolin quarry in the Pyrenees. They were often chosen to match or complement either the colour of the marble forming the chimneypiece in the room for which they were made or the marbles of the tables.

The mounts on this commode, one of Cressent's most celebrated designs, combine crossed palms with the C-scrolls and pierced scrolled mounts typical of the new rococo style. The design of the drawer handles, arising naturally from the scrolled mounts, which end in dragons' heads, is particularly skilful. Several of the mounts carry minute stamped mounts of a crowned C. This mark was struck on gilt-brass marks sold between 1745 and 1749, as evidence that tax had been paid on them.

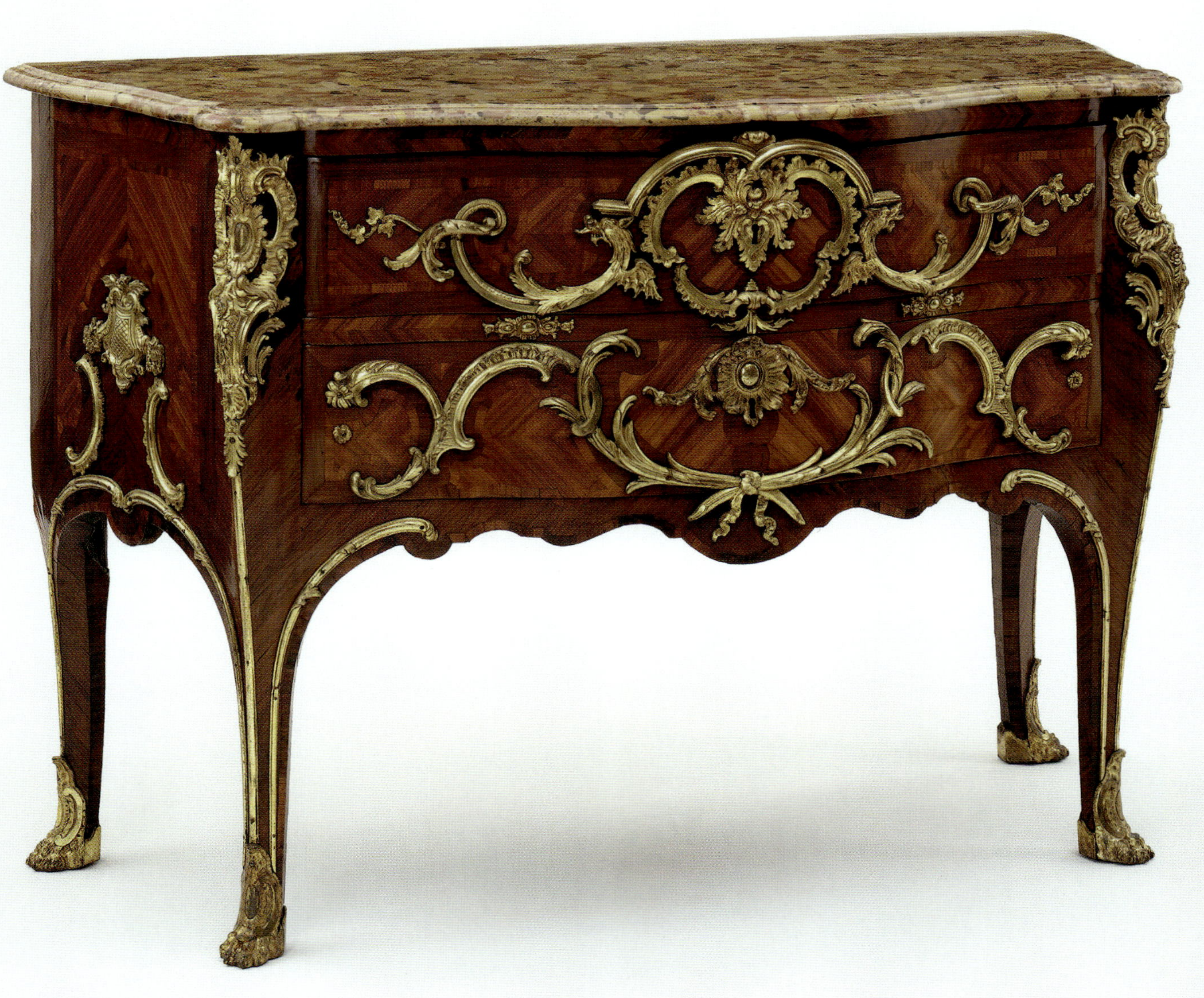

SILK-WINDER OR SPINNING WHEEL

Probably by Pietro Piffetti (1701–77)
Turin; about 1740–50
Turned ebony and ivory, the base veneered in
turtle-shell, mother-of-pearl and ivory, with
engraved decoration and walnut mouldings
V&A: W.159–1921; given by the Hon. Mrs
Carpenter; h. 56 cm, w. 53 cm, d. 25 cm

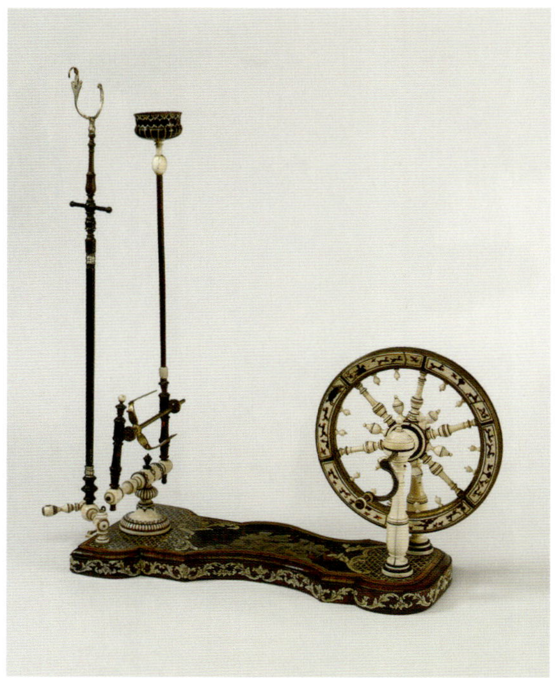

NEEDLEWORK WAS AN IMPORTANT activity for all women throughout the seventeenth and eighteenth centuries, as in earlier times, forming a vital part of every girl's education. For gentlewomen, who had no need to make basic linens for the household, embellishing garments and making decorative items using embroidery was still considered a suitable and virtuous occupation, and there is much evidence in diaries and letters of the long hours spent in sewing, often in a social situation. Even at court women would take their needlework with them to certain assemblies, and were frequently shown in portraits with their work in their hands.

A wheel like this would have been used for twisting filaments of silk into thread. Its elaborate marquetry decoration indicates that it was intended to be used and displayed in a drawing room. Pastimes such as sewing or spinning, in addition to being useful practical skills, also drew attention to elegant hands and could consequently become valuable assets in flirtation and courtship. Pietro Piffetti was cabinet-maker to the royal court of Turin from 1731 until his death in 1777. He made a wide range of furniture for the court, often collaborating with the royal architects Filippo Juvarro (1678–1736) and Benedetto Alfieri (1699–1767) to create integrated interior schemes. Piffetti specialized in furniture veneered with luxury materials – including, as here, ebony, ivory and mother-of-pearl. It is likely that the spindle and other turned elements of the wheel were made by a specialist turner under Piffetti's direction.

Piffetti's work both typified and influenced the northern Italian interpretation of the rococo style, with its weighty, curvilinear forms and intricate surface ornamentation. He embellished many of his materials with engraved decoration. On this winder the base is engraved with figures of Diana and Cupid. Diana is best known as the Roman goddess of hunting, but she was also the goddess of chastity and child-birth, both matters of concern to a good wife or to someone putting herself forward as a candidate for that role. There is further hunting imagery around the spinning wheel.

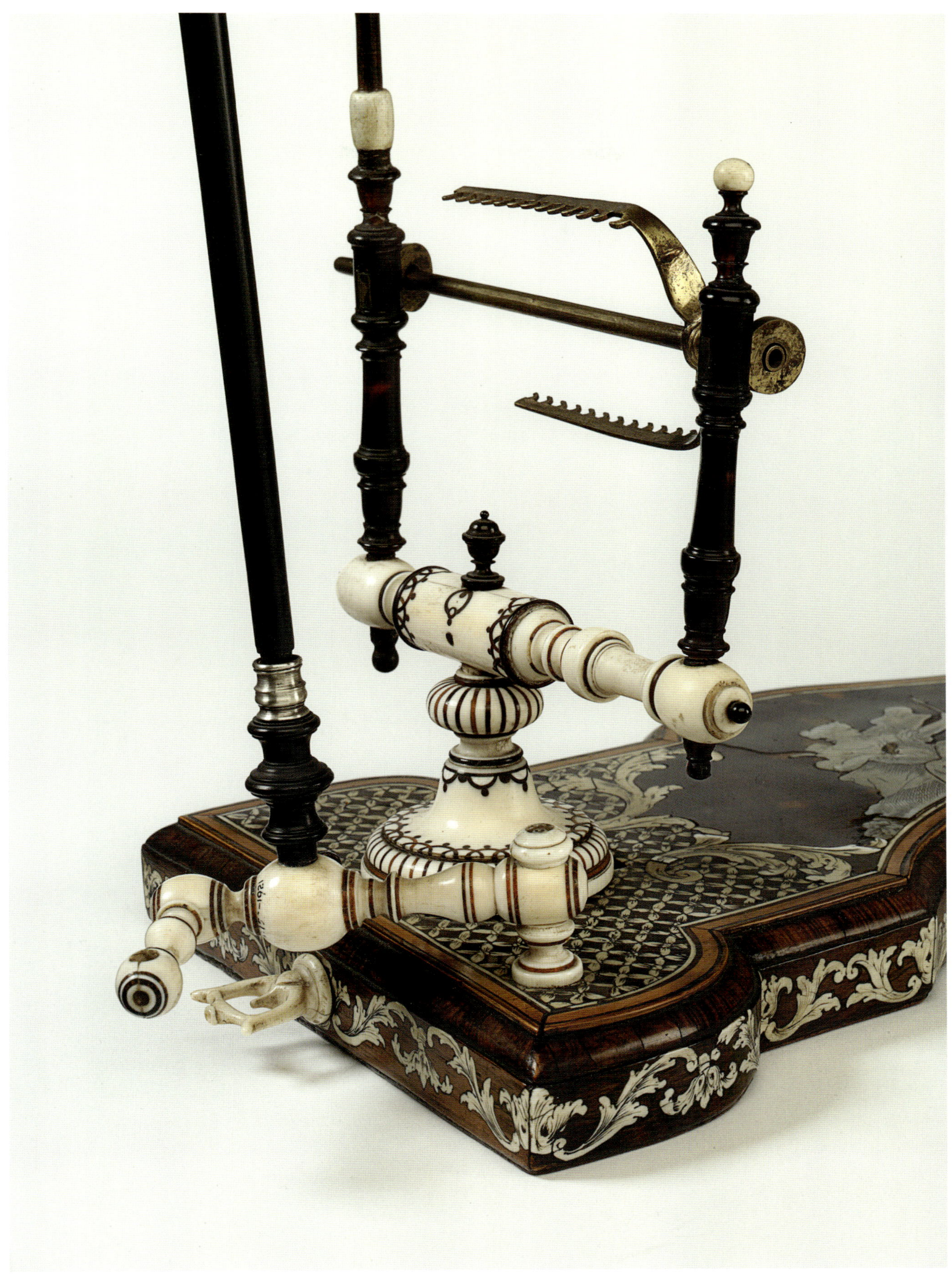

THE SWING (L'ESCARPOLETTE)

Nicolas Lancret (1690–1743)

Paris; about 1735

Oil on canvas

V&A: 515–1882; bequeathed by John Jones;

h. 70 cm, w. 89 cm without frame

THIS LIGHT-HEARTED GENRE PAINTING embodies the carefree love of pleasure that characterized Louis XV's court. It belongs to a type of painting known at the time as *fêtes galantes* (elegant entertainments) – imaginative depictions of fashionable people taking part in idealized country festivals or rural entertainments, usually with erotic undertones. The most famous exponent of this style was Antoine Watteau (1684–1721), best known for his depictions of scenes of aristocratic life. Although heavily influenced by Watteau, Lancret's interpretation of *fêtes galantes* is bright and playfully sensual, with none of the melancholy and world-weariness that permeate Watteau's work.

The subject of a young man pulling with a long rope a swing on which a girl sits was a popular subject for *fêtes galantes*, suggesting leisure and flirtation, but also control. This theme was interpreted by both Watteau and later by Jean-Honoré Fragonard (1732–1806). Lancret produced several versions of the subject for different clients. This painting is a typically rococo combination of naturalism and fantasy: the young man wears fashionable dress of the 1730s, but the girl is dressed in a whimsical shepherdess costume that draws on a long tradition of nobles playing at rural life.

Cleaning of the painting in the 1960s revealed a decorative framework around all four sides of the picture, suggesting that it was originally intended as a panel to go above a door, thus forming part of an interior scheme. Such subjects were popular for decorative painting in interiors, bringing a playful image of the garden or countryside into a town house and thereby creating a space for entertainment and forgetfulness of worldly cares. The same subjects might also appear on sets of tapestries and, on a smaller scale, decorating such items as ceramics, snuffboxes and fans.

The present frame, although a fine example of rococo carving, was probably added to the painting in the nineteenth century, before it came to the Museum as part of the bequest of John Jones.

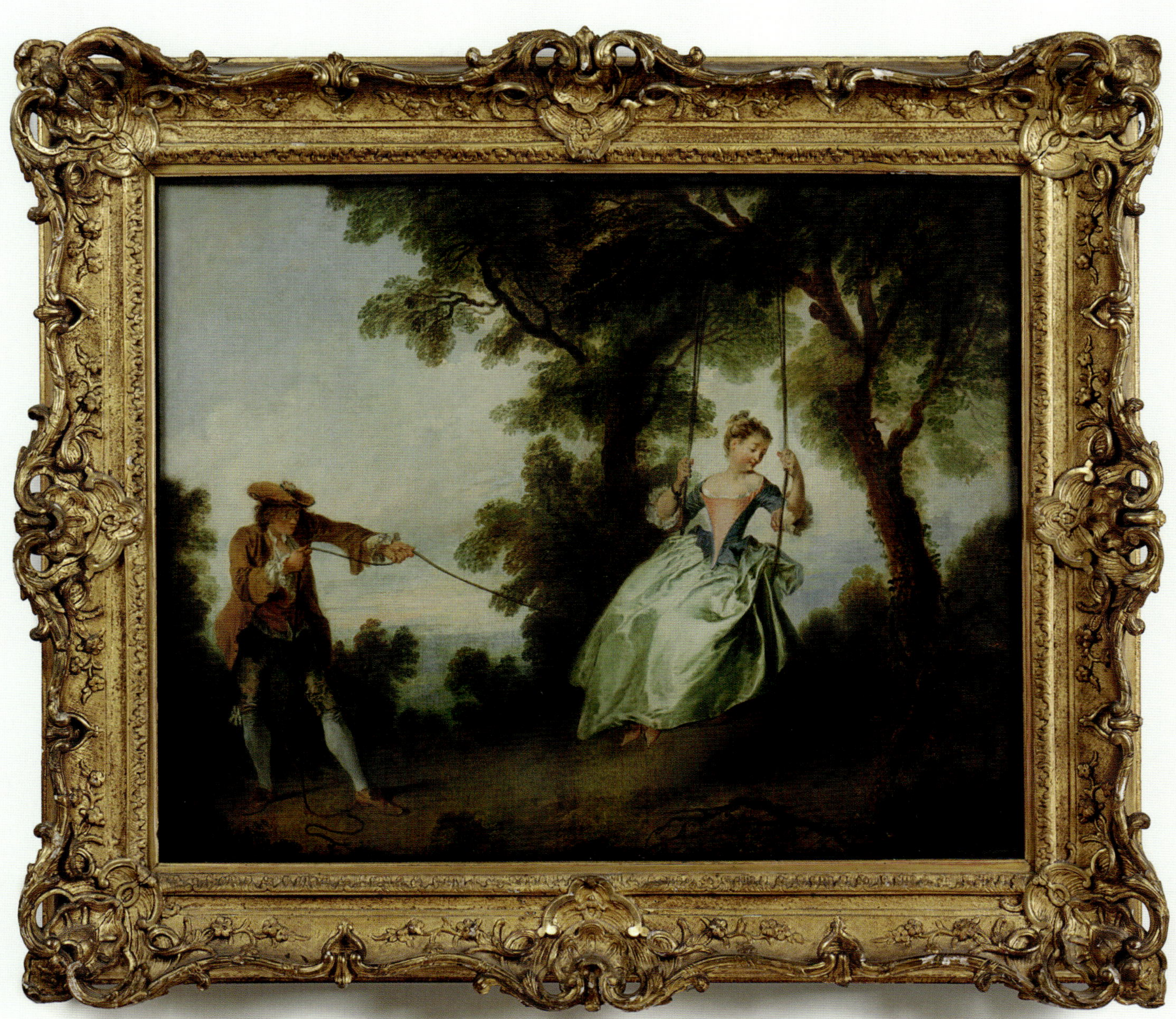

KNIFE AND FORK

Possibly northern Germany or the Netherlands;
1660–90
Forged and chiselled steel, gold
Knife: V&A: 2255–1855; l. 18.7 cm, w. 1.6 cm,
d. 1.1 cm
Fork: V&A: 2255A–1855; l. 15.7 cm, w. 1.2 cm,
d. 0.9 cm

BEFORE THE MID-EIGHTEENTH CENTURY cutlery was a portable, personal possession and did not necessarily come in large sets. Until that time, dining was an activity that might take place in one of several areas of a princely or aristocratic house, with tables and chairs being brought in as required. It was only in the eighteenth century that rooms dedicated to dining became a standard feature of such buildings, and along with them a whole repertoire of ceramics, silverware and glass, which became essential to polite dining. The etiquette of dining changed radically to take account of new implements that formed part of the new ceremonies of dining.

All but the very poorest in the seventeenth century carried a knife for eating and, whether at home, in a tavern or as a guest in someone's house, used their own utensils. Knives and spoons had been widely used in Europe from the earliest times, but forks, though known in the Roman world, took hundreds of years to gain widespread currency. Forks were still considered an Italian affectation by many in northern Europe well into the eighteenth century, although for anyone pretending to sophistication, such sets as this were essential luxuries.

Personal cutlery sets were often sold in a leather carrying case and offered similar opportunities to jewellery or writing equipment for displaying taste and wealth. The handles of this knife and fork, with their design of grape vines twining round the term figures of Bacchus, the god of wine (on the knife), and Cupid (on the fork), are based on designs for cutlery handles first carved in ivory and amber. These are, however, of chiselled steel, reflecting the skill in steelworking that developed in Germany in particular in the seventeenth century, much of it based on the skills required to forge swords, daggers or hunting knives. By creating these handles in steel, the maker has rendered a comparatively inexpensive material exceptional by means of superb craftsmanship.

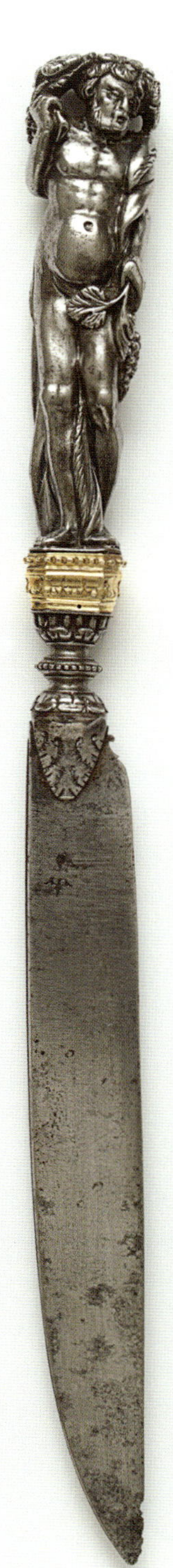
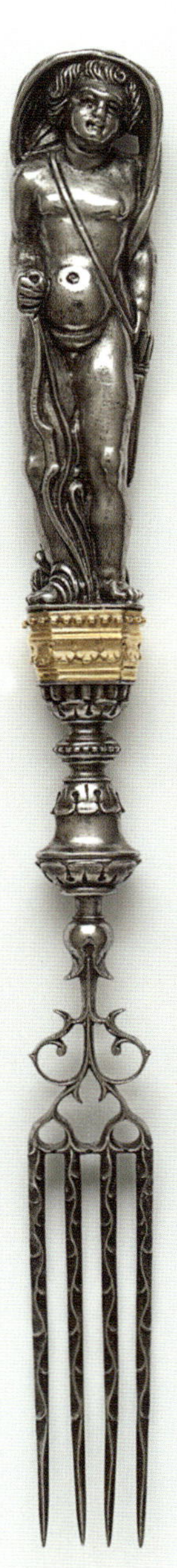

COVERED BEAKER

Hermann Schwinger (1640–83)
Nuremberg; glass about 1600,
engraving about 1680
Diamond and wheel-engraved glass, silver-gilt
mounts by Friedrich Hillebrandt (d. 1608)
V&A: 242–1872; h. 26.6 cm

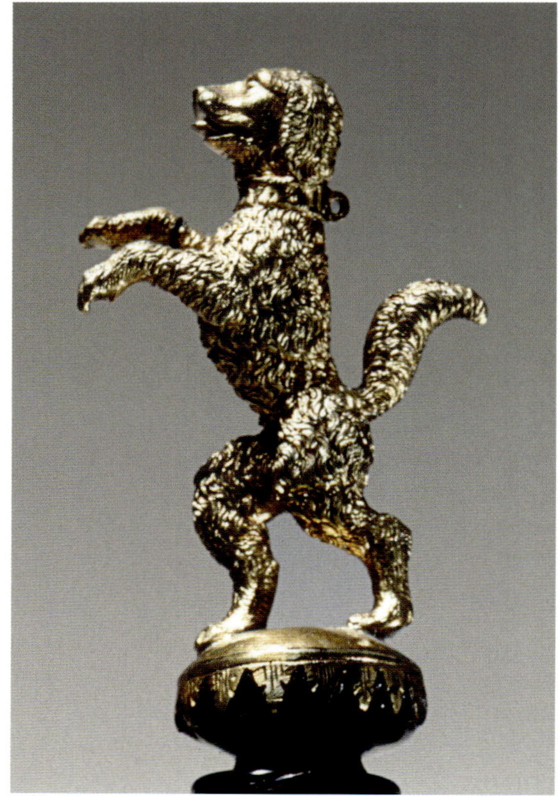

EREMONIAL TOASTING WAS AN IMPORTANT part of formal dining at the German royal courts, and elaborately decorated cups were often presented as gifts, reflecting their central role in rituals of patronage and duty, but also their importance as items for display. This beaker was probably made around 1600, but both beaker and cover were altered in the later seventeenth century to reflect more extravagant ideas of elegance. The dark-green colour of this high-quality glass was achieved by adding metallic oxides to the glass in its molten state. Reuse of luxury objects was common throughout the seventeenth and eighteenth centuries, reflecting the continuing reverence for items of rare or valuable materials or that revealed outstanding skill in their making.

Most of the silver-gilt mounts bear assay marks for Nuremberg and the mark of the maker FH, probably for Friedrich Hillebrandt, who died in 1608. The dog – probably a type of spaniel – that surmounts the cover is, however, by a different maker and was added later. It is inscribed 'I.A.V. 1656', a date that may be commemorative of a particular event for which the beaker was adapted and embellished. The figure of the dog most likely started its life as part of a pendant. Possibly the cup commemorates a particularly good hunting dog or expedition.

The wheel-engraving on the glass has been attributed to Hermann Schwinger, a glass engraver specializing in classical scenes. It can be dated by its style to around 1680, and includes the inscription *Vita quid est homnis* ('What is the life of man') and in the central roundel a naked child blowing bubbles. This sentiment reflects the popularity of *memento mori* (reminders of mortality) during the seventeenth century. At a time when religious belief was almost universal and dominated both political and personal life, it was expected that educated men and women would consider such questions very seriously. Both Protestants and Catholics were educated to undertake critical self-examination of their lives and their actions, and it was not unusual for items of high luxury to offer reminders to princes and nobles to remember their spiritual duties, even while enjoying the pleasures of life.

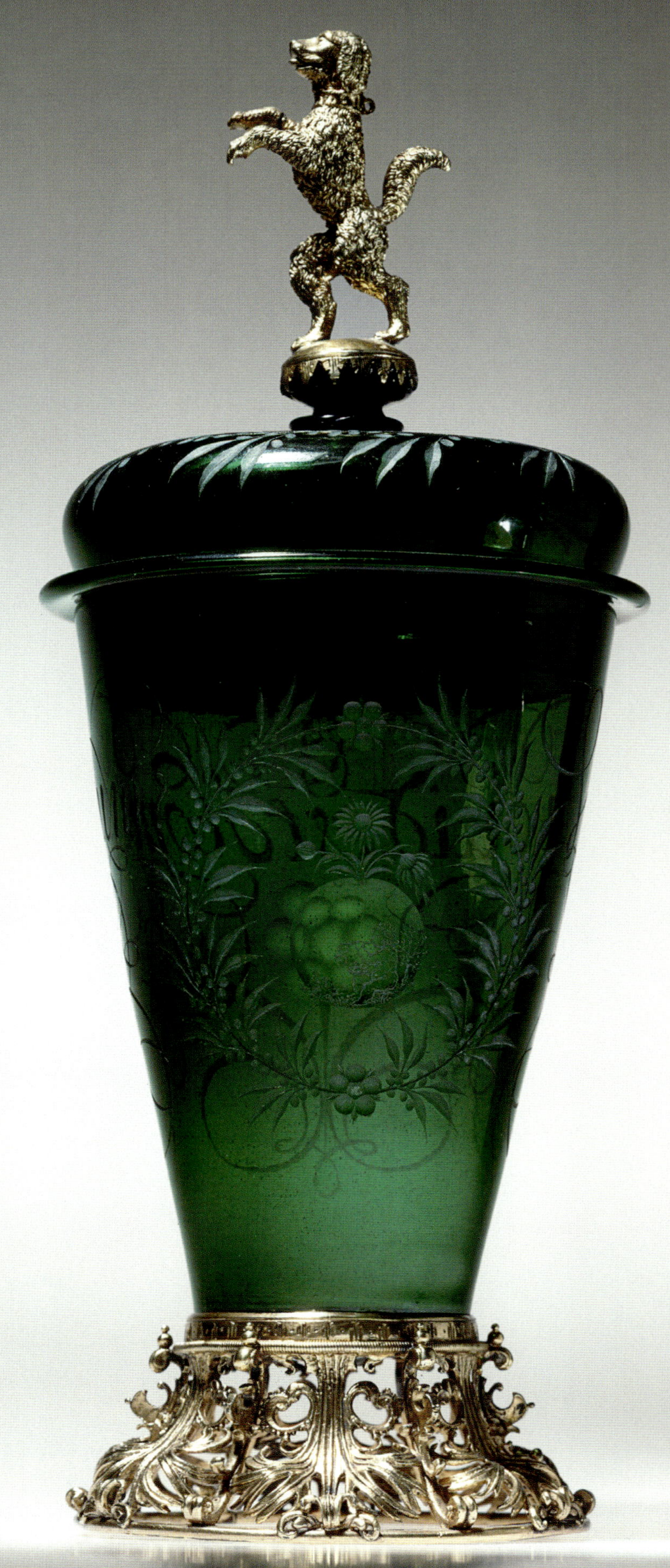

DISH

Meissen porcelain factory
Meissen; about 1735
Hard-paste porcelain painted in enamels and gilt
V&A: C.75–1957; given by Mrs C. Staal in memory
of the late Charles Staal; diam. 57.2 cm

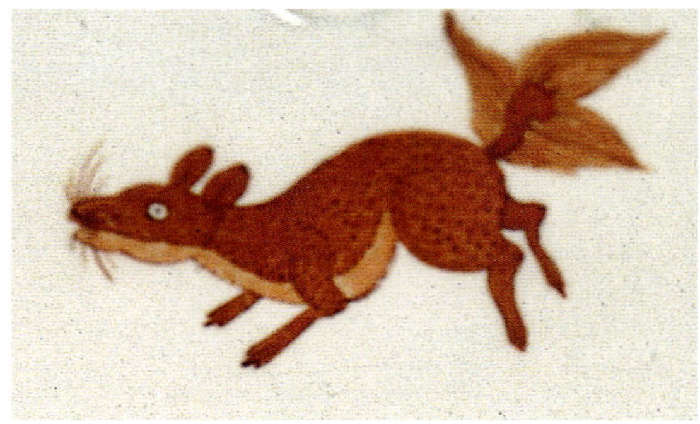

EUROPEAN COLLECTORS WERE FASCINATED BY the fine quality of Japanese porcelain and by its glassy, translucent body, which offered a pure-white surface in contrast to the colourful decoration. Such whiteness had eluded European potters, and it was not surprising that many attempts were made to imitate it in various European centres. The first to succeed was the Meissen factory in Germany, founded by Augustus the Strong (1670–1733), Elector of Saxony and King of Poland, who was an enthusiastic collector of Asian ceramics. For some years his employees struggled to replicate the imports from China and Japan. In 1710 Meissen became the first European factory to make true hard-paste porcelain. Key to this early success was the combination of kaolin, quartz and alabaster, fired at very high temperatures.

Early Meissen production imitated the forms and decoration of the Chinese and Japanese porcelain so admired by Augustus. Although these wares remained popular, especially those inspired by Japanese Kakiemon porcelain, the factory expanded its repertoire with a range of carefully modelled figures, the most impressive of which were the almost life-size animals and birds made for the Elector to complement his menagerie of live animals (pl.5).

This dish, while ostensibly copying Japanese porcelain, combines two patterns that would never appear together on wares made in Japan. The dense patchwork effect and rich polychrome enamel colours on the lower half of the dish imitate Imari porcelain, while the flowers and sparrow on the upper half are inspired by Kakiemon wares. Both styles were produced for export at Arita on the island of Kyushu between 1680 and 1725.

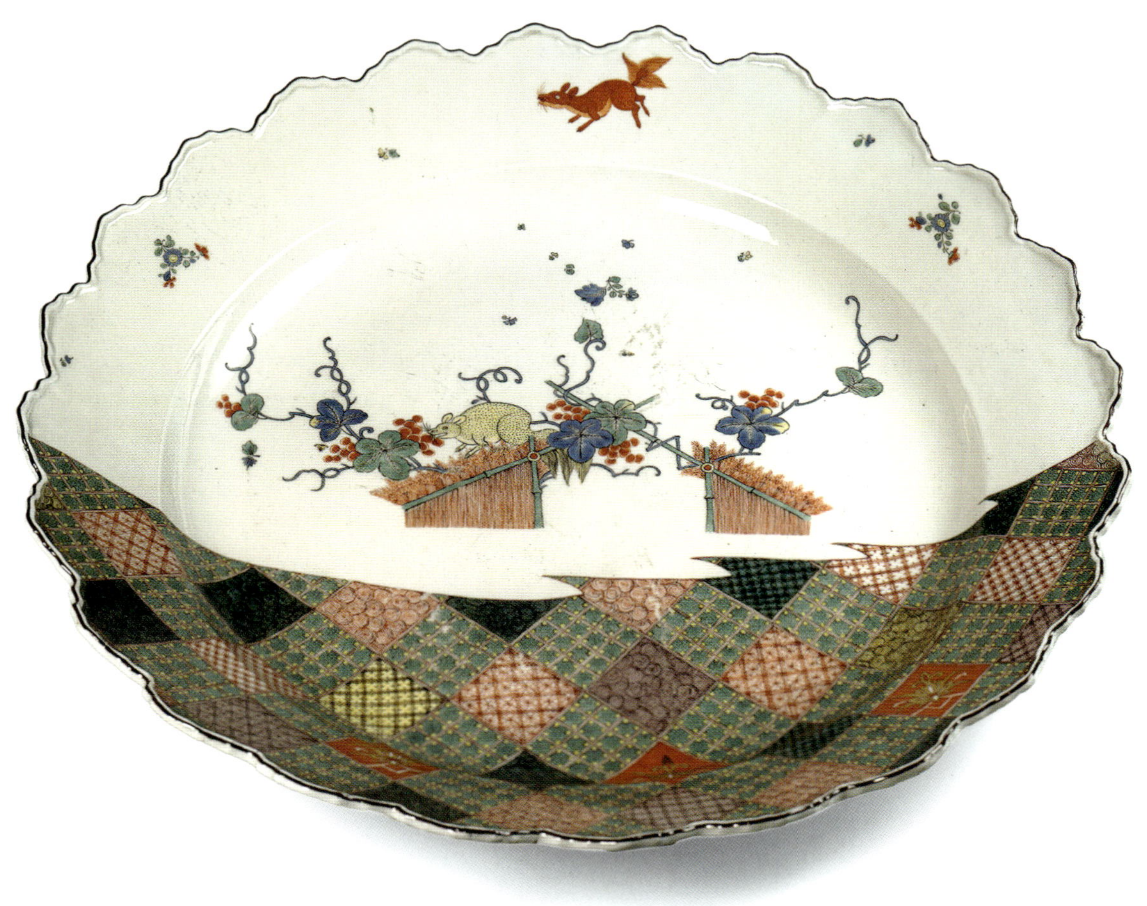

PLATE FROM THE 'FROG SERVICE'

Josiah Wedgwood & Sons
Chelsea; 1773
Creamware, painted in enamels
V&A: C.74-1931; Alfred Williams Hearn Bequest;
l. 39.37 cm, w. 29.84 cm

BY THE SECOND HALF OF THE EIGHTEENTH century the oppressive weight of absolute rule in much of Europe was being challenged by intellectuals such as Voltaire (1694–1778), Montesquieu (1689–1755) and Rousseau (1712–78). The ideas of these great thinkers of the era of the Enlightenment were discussed throughout Europe, not just in their own countries, and many owed their origin to English philosophers. Such thinking fuelled a Europe-wide enthusiasm for all things English, which came to be known as 'Anglomania'. Catherine the Great of Russia (1729–96), who might be seen as the epitome of an authoritarian ruler, engaged deeply with the modern ideas circulating in western Europe.

In 1773, moved by her enthusiasm for such ideas, the Empress commissioned a 50-setting dinner and dessert service from the English pottery manufacturer Josiah Wedgwood (1730–95). Like her predecessor Peter the Great, Catherine looked to western Europe for artistic inspiration and was a great patron of German and French, as well as English, craftsmen. The service was intended for a new royal retreat designed by Yury Velten (1730–1801) in the fashionable Gothic style, halfway between St Petersburg and the palace of Tsarskoe Selo. The site of the new palace was known as Kekerekeksinen, which means 'frog marsh' in the local Finnish dialect. This explains the frog motif in the border, and the popular name that has remained with this service.

Catherine left the design of the service to Wedgwood, stipulating only that she wished it to be decorated with views of England and that no two items should be the same. Wedgwood's partner, Thomas Bentley, selected the views from engravings and paintings. This dish shows the gardens of West Wycombe in Buckinghamshire, copied from a print by William Woollett (1735–85). It was never sent to Russia, however, because of a discrepancy in the design. Although it is a dinner dish and should have a domed cover, it is decorated with the border design intended for the dessert wares. Before the service was dispatched to Russia, Wedgwood displayed it in his London showrooms on Greek Street in Soho.

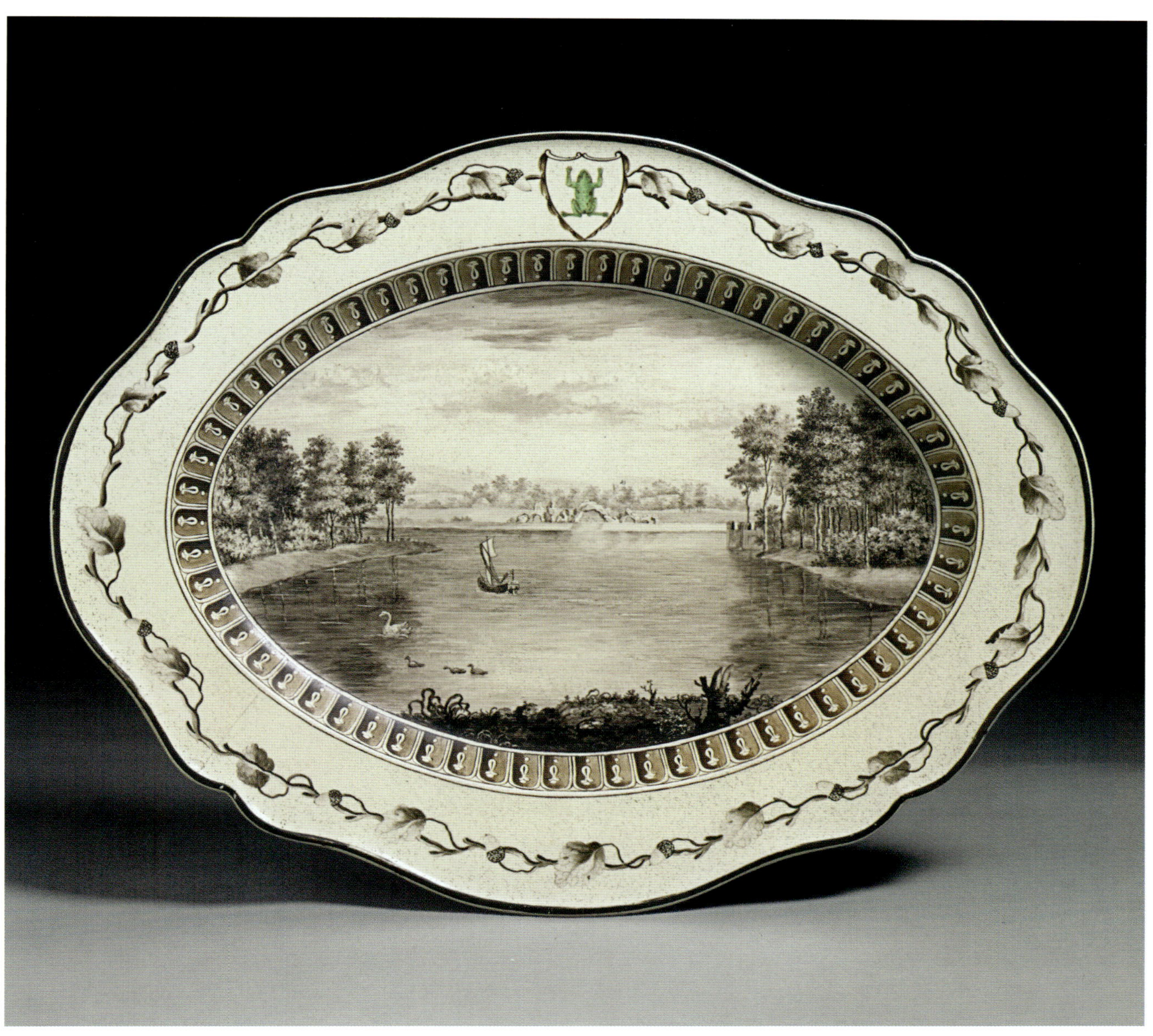

CABARET SET: TRAY, CUP AND SAUCER, COVERED SUGAR BOWL AND CREAM JUG

Sèvres porcelain factory

France; about 1757–8

Soft-paste porcelain, painted with enamels and gilded

V&A: 2020:A-E–1855

Cup: V&A: 2020–1855; h. 6.1 cm, w. 9.4 cm, d. 7.5 cm

Saucer: V&A: 2020A–1855; diam. 13.3 cm

Tray: V&A: 2020B–1855; w. 24.5 cm, d. 17.3 cm

Sugar basin and cover: V&A: 2020C&D–1855;

h. 5.7 cm, diam. 7.3 cm

Cream jug: V&A: 2020E–1855; h. 9.2 cm, w. 9.9 cm,

d. 7.3 cm

THIS DELICATE SET OF PORCELAIN, DESIGNED for a single person to take tea in the comfort of the bedroom or cabinet, epitomizes the level of luxury available to princely patrons in the middle of the eighteenth century. The care with which such pieces were designed and made far outstrips that of many of the celebrated luxury products of today. Princes competed with one another in fostering the luxury trades in their own territories, following the example of France, which had poured money into such royal patronage since the reign of Louis XIV (1643–1715).

Tea, coffee and chocolate had all become highly fashionable in the late seventeenth century, bringing with them designs for necessary new equipment, such as teapots and bowls. The latter soon developed into the handled cups still in use today. By the middle of the eighteenth century, serving these drinks – initially enjoyed outside the home as a novelty – had become an ingrained habit and was central to home-based entertaining. The drinking of tea in particular could form the centrepiece to an occasion of domestic sociability or, as with this set, private indulgence.

Porcelain production began in Europe in 1710 at Meissen in Germany, under the patronage of Augustus the Strong (1670–1733). The Royal Porcelain Manufactory at Sèvres, south-west of Paris, developed from a factory established by businessmen at Vincennes in 1745. Early production copied Asian porcelain and Meissen wares, but, with the support of Louis XV (1710–74) and his influential mistress, Madame de Pompadour (page 34), quickly evolved to create stylish and distinctive ceramics. Famous for its beautiful white paste and translucent glaze, Sèvres was also celebrated for its innovative shapes and unique decoration. This cabaret set is an early example of the best-known house style, which combined rich ground colours with delicately painted flowers and finely tooled gilding.

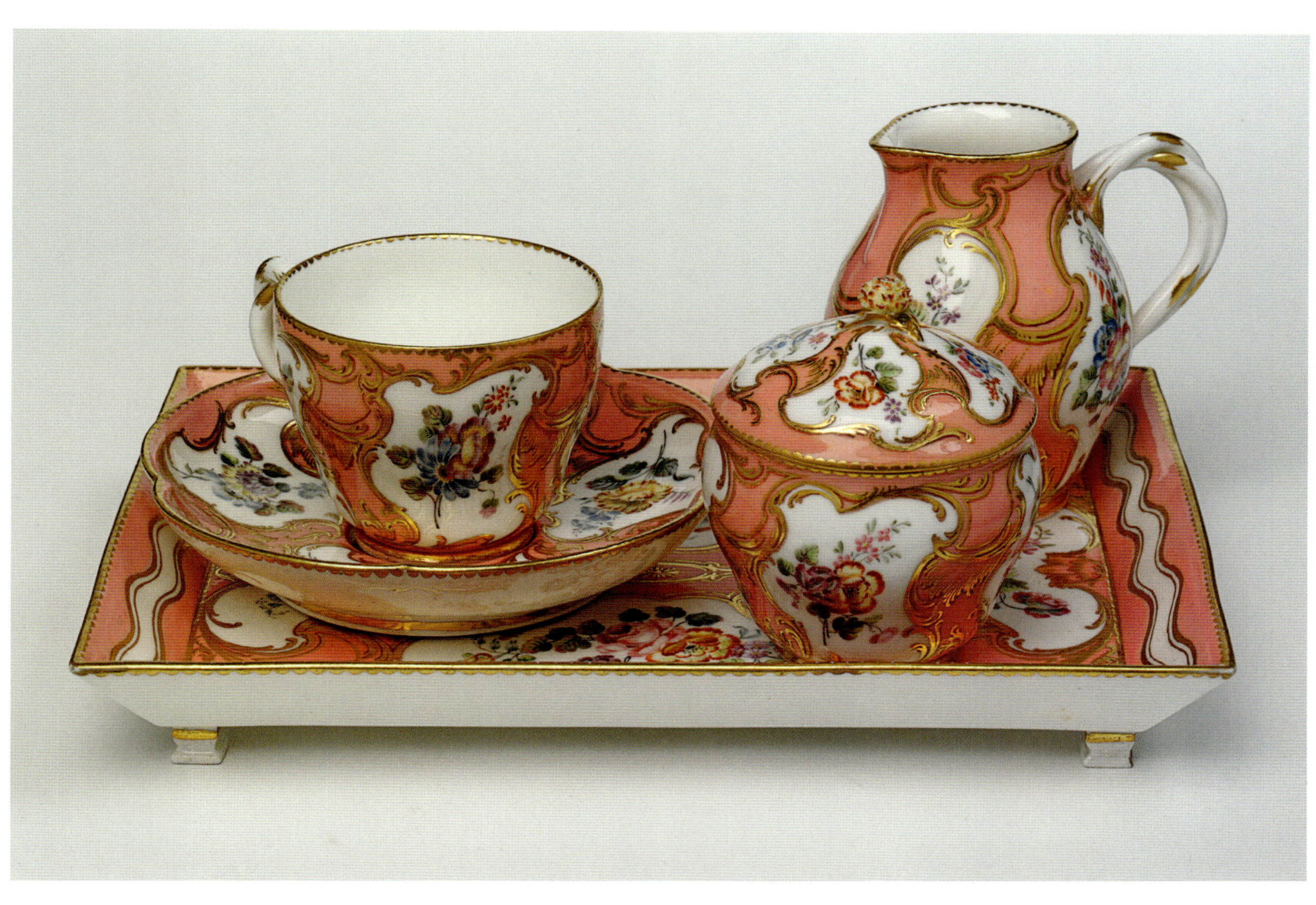

CABINET-ON-STAND

Probably by Pierre Gole (about 1620–84)
Paris; 1661–5
Pine, oak, walnut and pearwood, veneered in ivory
with marquetry of various woods, turtle-shell,
bone and horn
V&A: W.38–1983; h. 126 cm, w. 84 cm, d. 40 cm

BY THE MIDDLE OF THE SEVENTEENTH CENTURY the cabinet-on-stand was the single most important type of furniture for fashionable interiors. It was used to contain a variety of small, precious objects, from turned ivory or carved amber to jewellery, miniatures or shells and samples of minerals. The decoration was suitably sumptuous, with veneers of tropical hardwoods such as ebony, from newly acquired colonies, or imported materials that were richer still, such as turtle-shell or ivory, the former imported from Africa since the fifteenth century, the latter from India since the sixteenth century.

This unusually small cabinet was almost certainly made for the household of the Duc d'Orléans (1640–1701), brother of Louis XIV, and his wife Henriette Anne, daughter of Charles I of England. The inventory, made after her death in 1670, of their apartments at the Palais Royal in Paris, describes a cabinet that closely matches this one, in the *Cabinet Blanc*. Little is known about the decoration of this room, but it seems reasonable to assume that it was predominantly white. Thus the extraordinary ivory veneer that provides a ground for the floral marquetry on the cabinet would have been particularly appropriate. The inventory was certified by Pierre Gole, cabinet-maker to Louis XIV (1638–1715), and this, in addition to the cabinet's similarity to known pieces by Gole, makes it very likely that this cabinet is his work.

Pierre Gole was born in the Netherlands and must have trained as a cabinet-maker there before coming to Paris around 1643. By 1656 he was making furniture for Louis XIV, and five years later supplied some of the first pieces commissioned for the extended and refurbished palace of Versailles, including three tables decorated with floral marquetry. The floral marquetry on this cabinet shows the influence of Italian *pietre dure* (hard stone), but probably also reflects the popularity of pictorial marquetry in Dutch cabinet-making. Originally, the colours of the marquetry would have been much more vivid, imitating the colours of real flowers.

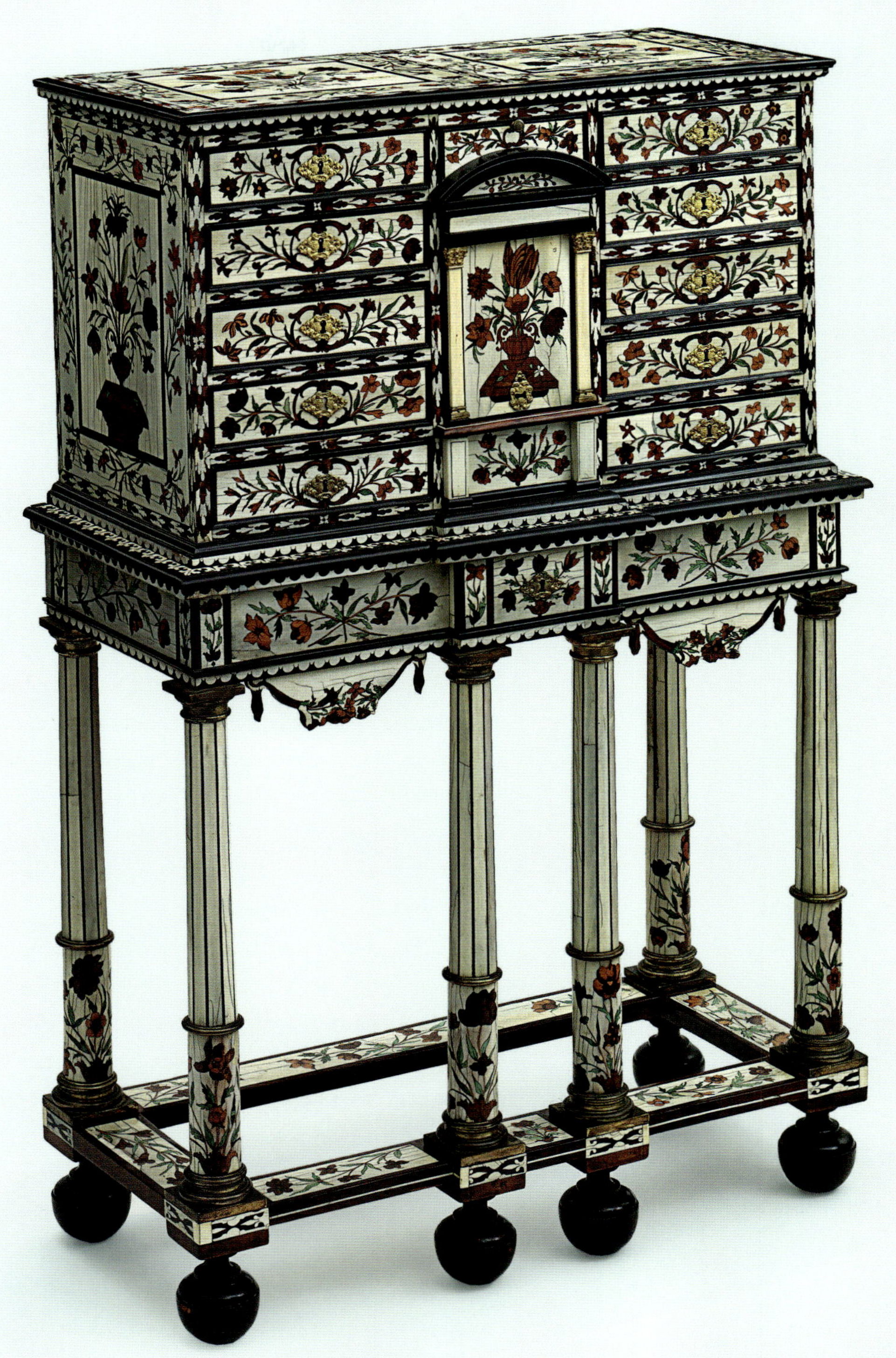

EWER AND BASIN

Possibly designed by Lavazzo Tavarone
(1556–1641), probably made by Giovanni
Aelbosca Belga (active *c*.1620)
Genoa; 1621–2
Silver, cast, chased and embossed
V&A: M.11&A–1974; purchased with the assistance
of The Art Fund
Ewer: M.11–1974: h. 53.5 cm, w. 17.5 cm
Basin: M.11A–1974: diam. 64 cm

THIS EWER AND BASIN FORM PART OF A spectacular garniture of silver for display on a buffet or set of tiered shelves, a universal method of displaying princely wealth in the seventeenth century. The set also comprises two further ewers and basins, all decorated with the arms of the Lomellini family. They are now in the Ashmolean and Birmingham museums. In total, the complete set weighs almost 10 kg. Large and impressive silver of this kind was primarily for display. Ewers and basins could, however, be used for washing hands before meals, playing an important part in setting the scene for formal dining, and the scenes on them might form a didactic display for guests.

The Lomellinis were influential merchants in the Italian city of Genoa, whose wealth came from successful trading in, among other things, coral, cork and slaves. The family's opulent palace in the city was built at about the time that the basin and ewer were made, and still survives. Three Lomellinis were elected Consuls, or high officials, of Genoa, and Anthony Van Dyck (1599–1641) painted portraits of several members of the family. They were linked by marriage to all the other important families in the city, including the Dorias and the Grimaldis.

The meaning of the embossed decoration on the ewer and basin is uncertain. It is thought to depict scenes from the Battle of the Po in 1431, when the Grimaldi family of Monaco joined the Visconti family of Genoa in their struggle against the Venetians. The standards of Grimaldi of Monaco and of the imperial family of Habsburg can clearly be seen. The relevance of these events to the Lomellinis is, however, unclear. The most likely explanation is that the pieces were originally commissioned from Giovanni Aelbosca Belga, a Flemish goldsmith working in Genoa, by a member of the Grimaldi family and were only later passed by marriage to the Lomellinis.

In the late eighteenth century an English aristocrat, the 5th Earl of Shaftesbury (1761–1811), bought the complete garniture in Naples for £300.

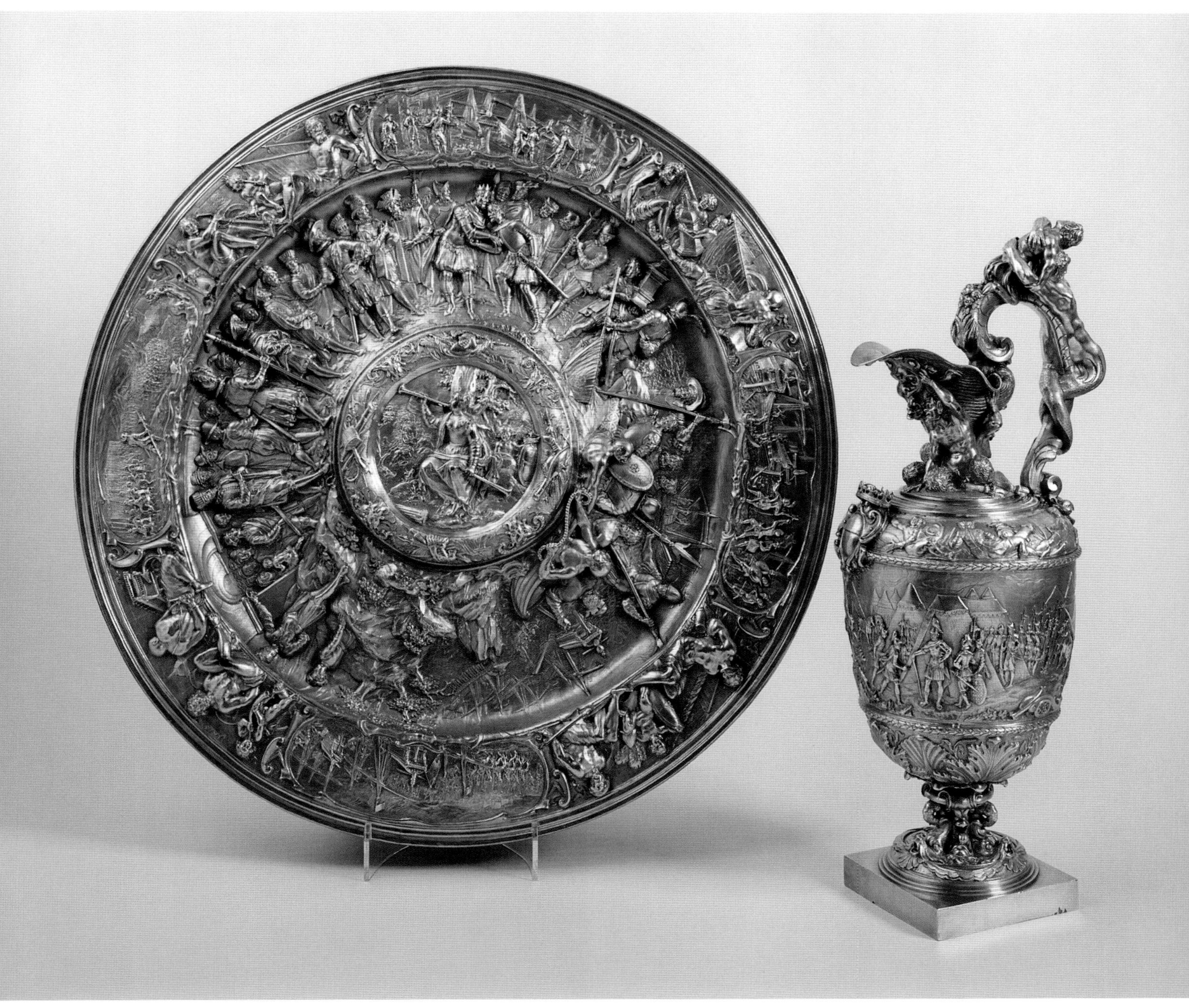

PERFUME BURNER

Spain; about 1630
Silver, embossed and chased
V&A: M.21–1966; acquired with the aid of the
Hildburgh Fund; h. 59 cm

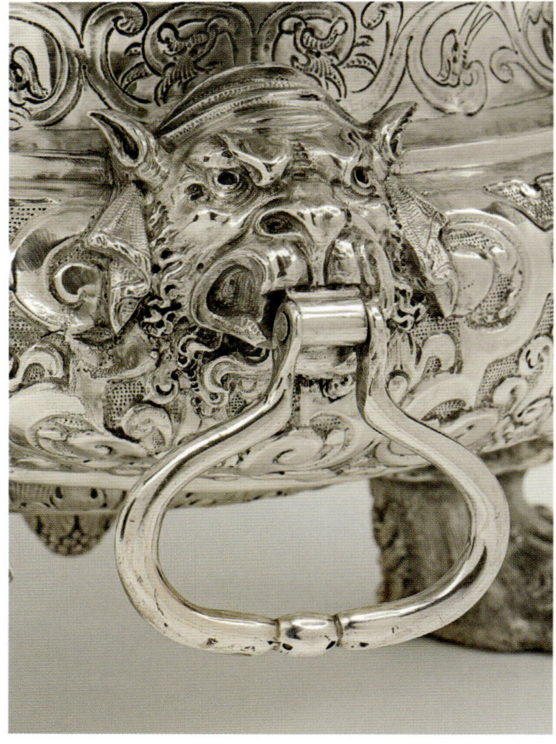

THE HOMES OF THE WEALTHY NEEDED TO delight all the senses and be not only beautiful to look at, but also comfortable and full of pleasing sounds, tastes and smells. The existence of only basic sanitation and limited personal hygiene, however, meant that few interiors smelt pleasant. Burners like this one were used to heat incense or perfumed oil, releasing a strong scent that would help to disguise any lingering bad odours. Burners were made in sections. The lower chamber was for burning charcoal, while the pierced upper section would have contained perfumed materials such as juniper leaves, turpentine or frankincense, which would have released their aroma as the charcoal heated them. Spanish inventories have many references to perfume burners, while in England 'chafing dishes' were charcoal burners that heated either food or perfume.

This burner, made in three pieces, is unusually large, weighing some 5.5 kg. A rather crudely engraved inscription around the central section indicates that it belonged to Don Gerolamo Cao, Professor of Law at Cagliari University in Sardinia and also Canon of the cathedral there. The slightly later coat of arms emblazoned on the shield of the warrior surmounting the cover is that of Don Francesco Cao, who was granted these arms in 1646. Given its ownership, it is possible that the burner was made for use in a church setting. However, as many priests kept house lavishly, it is equally likely that both Don Gerolamo and Don Francesco in turn used it to fragrance their private rooms. In churches, pleasing smells were provided by the incense in the thurible (a perfume burner that was carried on a chain), which was used in Catholic church services.

Between 1323 and 1713 Sardinia was ruled by the Kings of Aragon, resulting in strong trading links between that island and Spain. Although there were significant silver deposits in Sardinia, and some silversmiths there also, clients looking for high-quality pieces in the latest fashion had to commission them from elsewhere. The well-established connection between the Spanish mainland and Sardinia made Spain the obvious source.

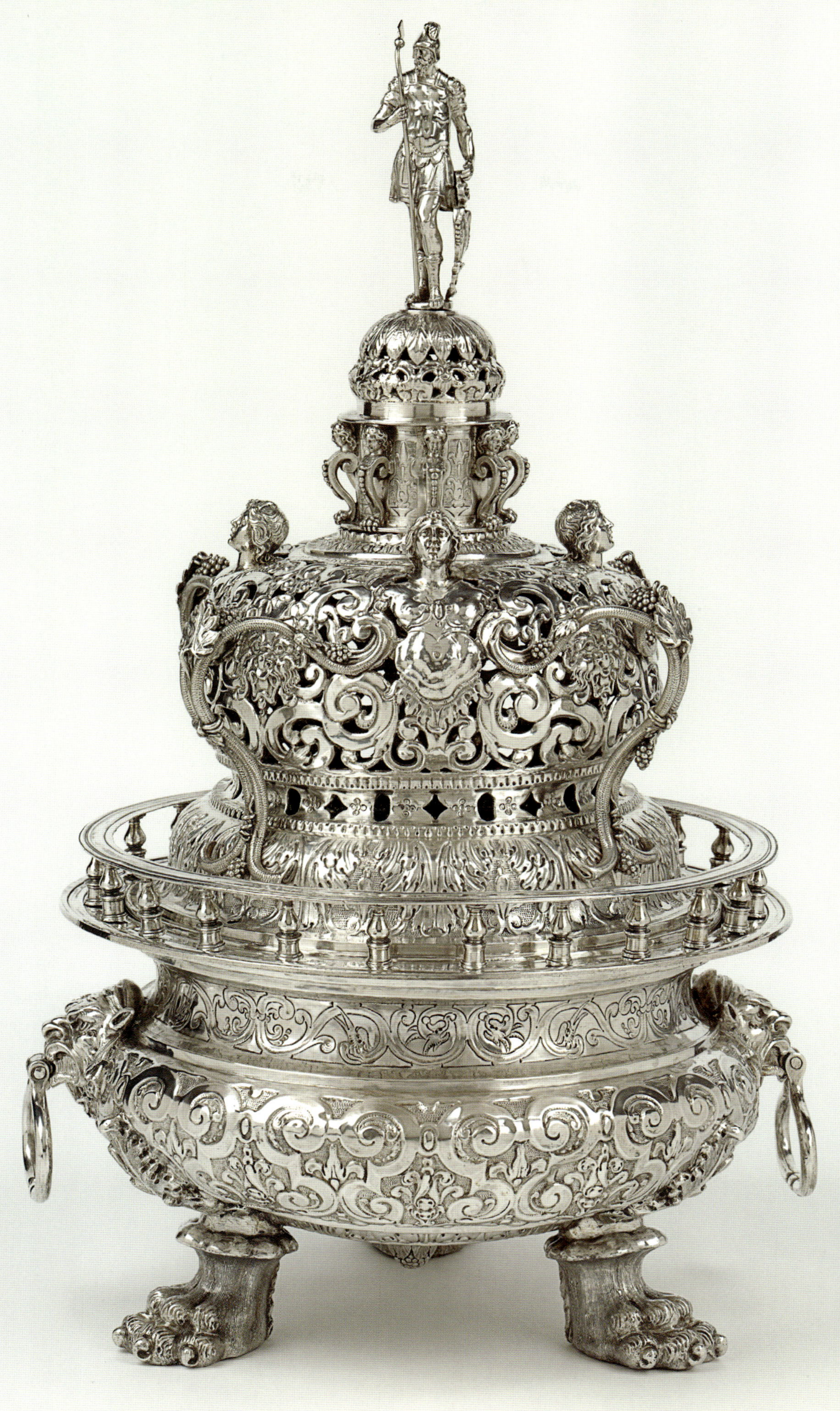

CHAMBER CANDLESTICK

Paul Crespin (1694–1770)
London; 1744–5
Silver, embossed, cast, chased and engraved;
originally gilded
V&A: M.2–1980; h. 11 cm, w. 19.5 cm, d. 14.3 cm

IN THE CENTURIES BEFORE GAS OR ELECTRICITY, lavish (or even just efficient) lighting was a mark of luxury. Servants prepared and lit candles in wall-sconces or candelabra, in anterooms or salons, but the simpler chamber candlestick was an important piece of personal equipment.

A chamber candlestick, with its handle and large drip-pan, was designed to be carried easily without covering the user's hand with hot wax. It also needed to hold a candle firmly to prevent it wobbling, and for this reason it had a short stem below the candle nozzle. Despite its very practical design, this candlestick is a fine example of the rococo, displaying the asymmetric arrangement of motifs, the S-scrolls and the engaging naturalism typical of the style. The winged cupid holding a bow, that supports the candle-holder is another characteristic rococo motif that combines charm with wit.

Elements of what was to become the rococo style first appeared in France in the 1720s and spread across Europe in the 1730s and 1740s. The English interpretation of the style was less flamboyant than its Italian or German manifestations and lacked the internal tension that gave the best French rococo its dynamism. It was, however, fluid, imaginative and made with the refined sculptural detail seen here.

Although Paul Crespin was born in London, he was the son of French Protestant (Huguenot) refugees and had considerable contact with French fashions in silverware, which heavily influenced his work. The impact of the designs of Juste-Aurèle Meissonnier (1695–1750) (page 68) and the rococo silver of Thomas Germain (1673–1748) can be seen in this chamber candlestick.

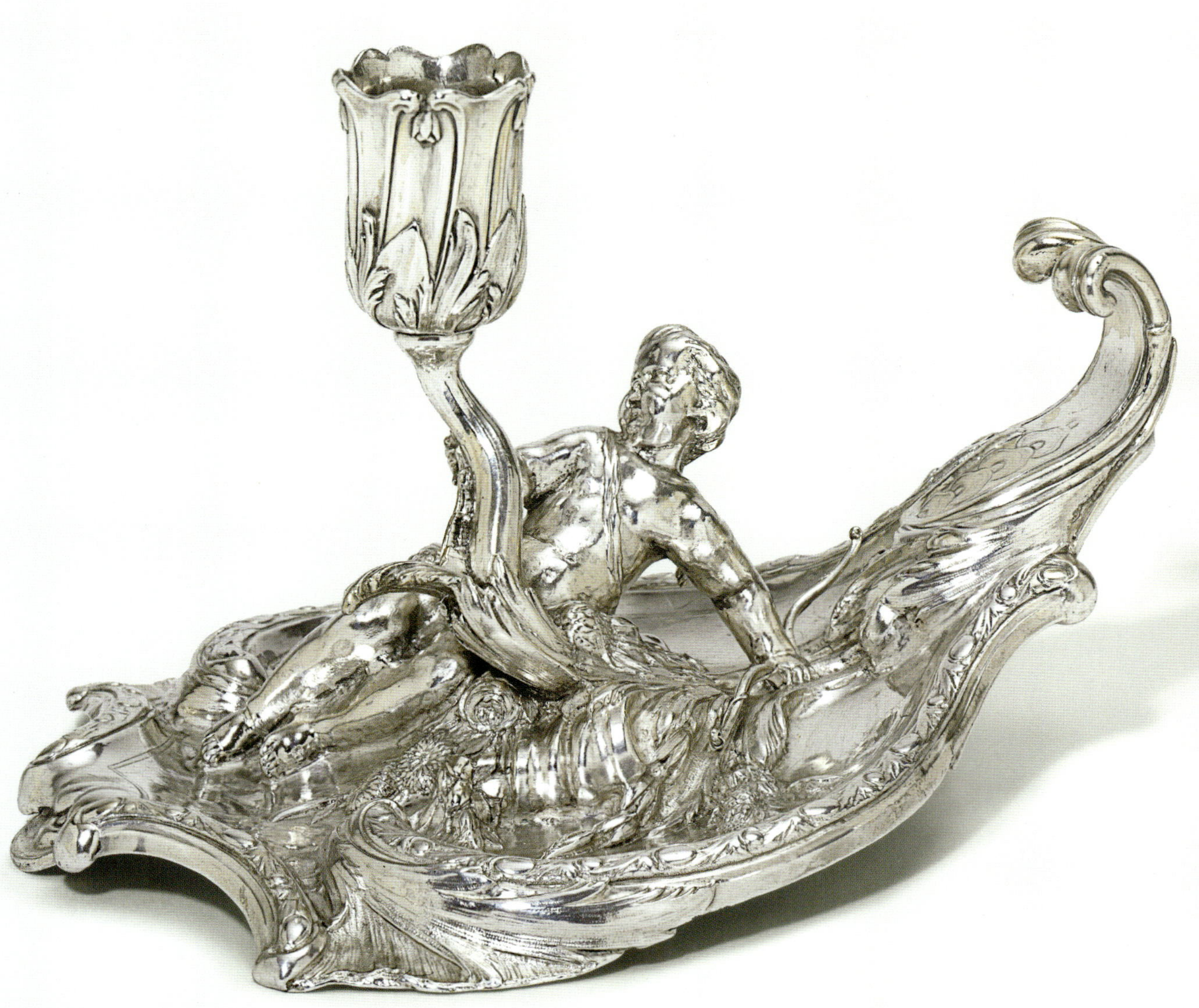

READING, WRITING AND MUSIC STAND

Martin Carlin (d. 1785),
Jean-Jacques Pafrat (d. 1793)
Paris; 1777–85
Oak with marquetry of tulipwood, sycamore
and other woods, gilt-bronze mounts, Sèvres
porcelain plaque
V&A: 1057–1882; bequeathed by John Jones;
h. 78 cm, w. 41 cm, d. 34 cm

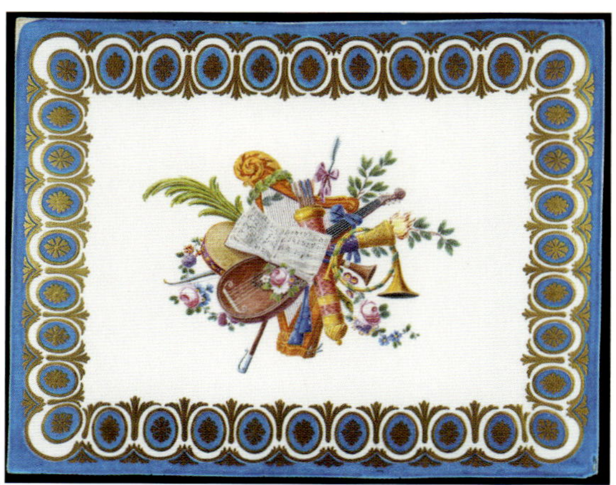

S MALL ITEMS OF MULTI-FUNCTIONAL FURNITURE became popular in the middle years of the eighteenth century, as princes and courtiers sought spaces that were more intimate and more comfortable, as an escape from the strict etiquette of court life. Such pieces provided a showcase for new materials and mechanisms. The top of this reading, writing and music stand is hinged and can be angled to provide a slope, and the drawer hides a writing surface. Novel and modish pieces like this also presented an opportunity for their owners to show their sophistication, by using the object to display the elegance with which they adjusted the mechanism and their mastery of the different activities for which it was intended.

The Sèvres porcelain plaque that forms the top of the stand is finely painted with a trophy comprising musical instruments and emblems of love. Unusually, the plaque still bears its original price label, showing it to have cost 216 *livres*, equivalent to the annual wages of an unskilled labourer. Several other stands of this design are known, incorporating different porcelain plaques or panels of oriental lacquer. Items of this kind were usually commissioned by *marchands-merciers* – dealers in luxury goods – to provide a fitting setting for the plaques of high-quality Sèvres porcelain on which they held a monopoly and the imported lacquer of which they held large reserves. The completed objects were innovative, extravagant and very fashionable, highly appropriate merchandise for the grand retailers of the rue Saint-Honoré in Paris.

By tradition, this stand is one of several objects given by Queen Marie Antoinette (1755–93) to Eleanor Eden (1758–1818), wife of the diplomat William Eden (1745–1814). The Edens visited Paris in 1786 in order to negotiate a trade agreement between Britain and France. William Eden's correspondence during the visit noted that Marie Antoinette was very attentive to Eleanor, making all the more convincing the handwritten label recording the gift, that was added to the table by Eleanor's daughter Emily (1797–1869) in 1852.

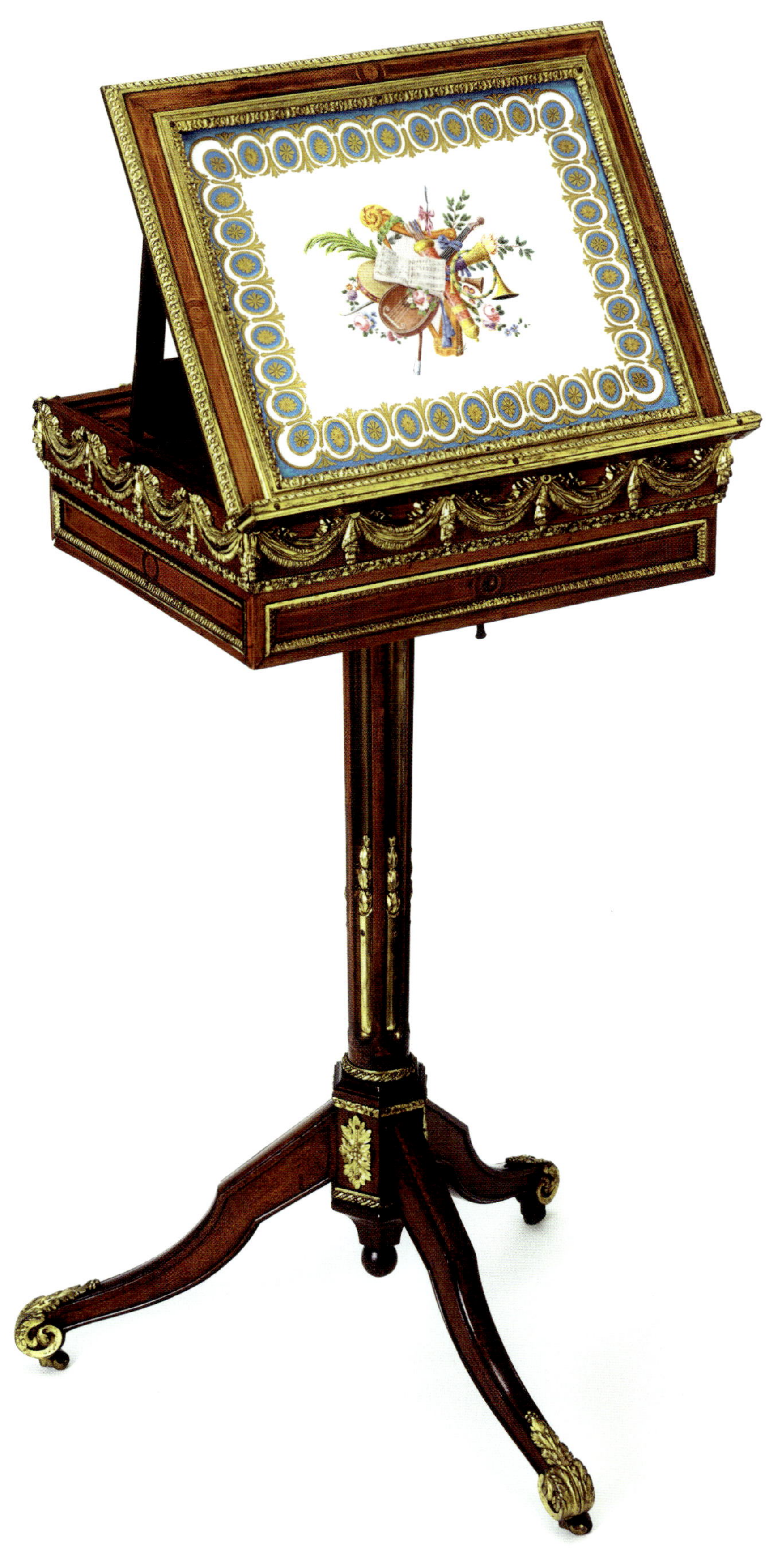

THREE FROM A SET OF WALL-PANELS, PAINTED WITH SCENES FROM THE STORY OF ACHILLES

Charles-Louis Clérisseau (1721–1820)
and Étienne de Lavallée-Poussin (1735–1802)
Paris; *c.*1777
Oil on canvas
V&A: W.2A–1957; h. 350.5 cm, w. 126.5 cm, d. 3 cm
V&A: W.2R–1957; h. 350.5 cm, w. 35 cm, d. 3 cm
V&A: W.2G–1957; h. 350.3 cm, w. 127 cm, d. 3 cm
Presented by The Art Fund

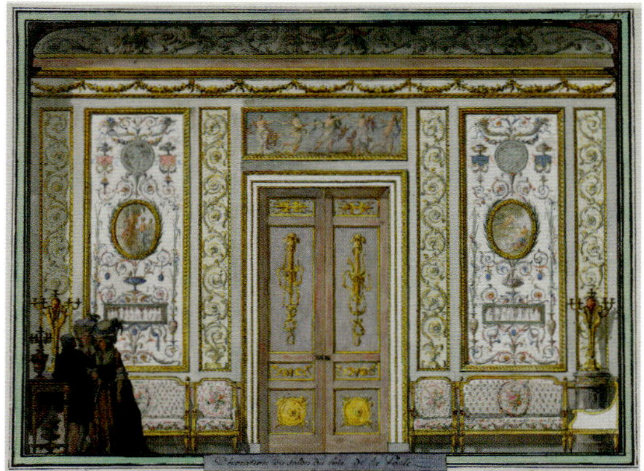

Design for a salon, Jan Chrystian Kamsetzer after
Charles-Louis Clérisseau. Pen and brown ink,
watercolour and graphite traces, gouache and wash.
Paris, 1782. Print Room, Warsaw University Library
(INW 2B.D.8137, IV)

THESE PANELS ARE FROM A SET ORIGINALLY created for the Hôtel Grimod de la Reynière, the Parisian townhouse of Laurent Grimod de la Reynière (1733–93), an extremely wealthy and successful financier. The *hôtel* was built on the site of a former royal sculpture store, given to Grimod de la Reynière by Louis XV (1710–74). Floor-to-ceiling wood panelling had generally been used to decorate smart rooms throughout the seventeenth and eighteenth centuries in Paris. Painted panels such as these were an innovation well suited to the lightness and elegance of the neoclassical style of the 1770s and '80s, which retained some of the playfulness and romance of the rococo, while incorporating accurately rendered motifs from the buildings of ancient Greece and Rome. Here, scenes from the story of the ancient Greek Achilles combine with architectural ornament and grotesque figures to create a refined and highly fashionable interior scheme.

Clérisseau spent four years studying at the French Academy in Rome and visited many important Roman sites during his stay in Italy. The decoration of these panels blends elements derived from wall-paintings in the Golden House of Nero and the buried cities of Pompeii and Herculaneum. Clérisseau, who was renowned in Rome as a draughtsman, collaborated with the Scottish architect Robert Adam (1728–92) on his volume of illustrations of the Roman Emperor Diocletian's Palace at Spalatro (Split, in Croatia). He also presented a collection of designs to Catherine the Great of Russia (1710–96).

In the nineteenth century the panels were purchased by the Earl of Ashburnham, a noted collector of books, manuscripts and *objets d'art*, and installed at his country house, Ashburnham Place in Sussex. The last of the family inherited the house in the early 1950s and, unable at that time to afford its maintenance, sold off the contents and demolished large portions of the house, before donating it to a charitable foundation as a religious retreat.

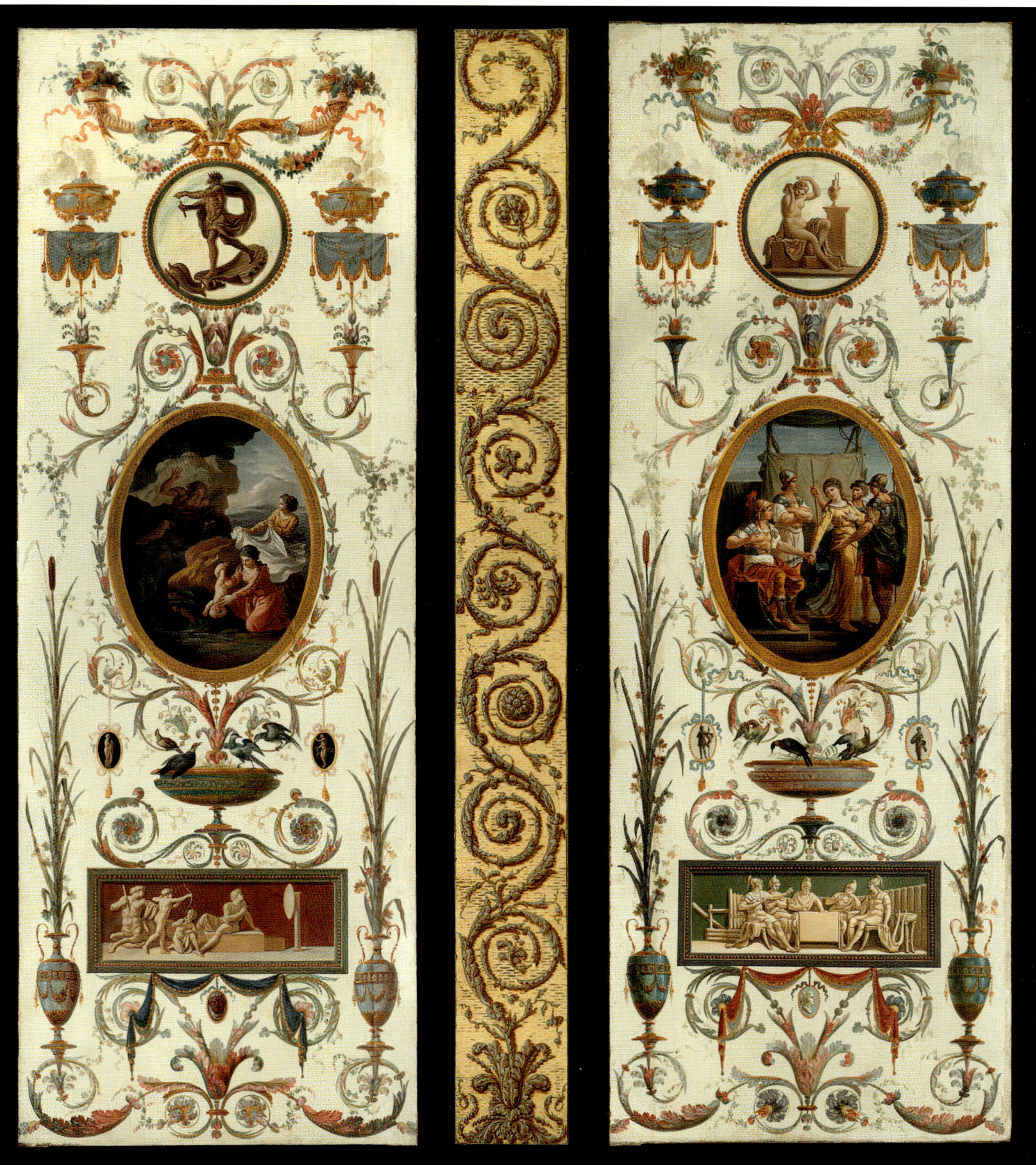

ARMCHAIR

Paris; about 1760–70

Carved and gilded walnut, modern silk damask
upholstery

V&A: W.10–1973; h. 102 cm, w. 77.5 cm, d. 80 cm

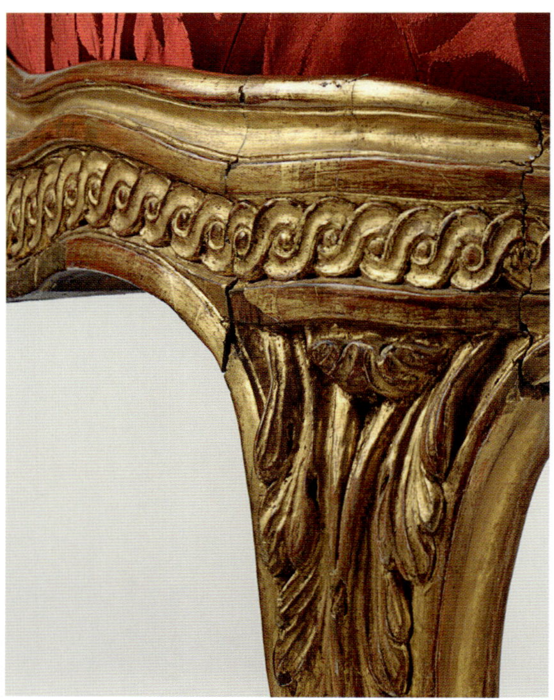

TEXTILES, IN THE FORM OF WALL-COVERINGS, tapestries, curtains and the coverings of beds or chairs, were always a dominant, often matching element in interiors, but are now frequently lost, changed or so faded that it is impossible to imagine their initial effect of richness and glamour. This chair, which had lost its original upholstery, has been re-covered in red silk damask, the most popular colour for upholstery in grand interiors in France in the eighteenth century.

The underside of the chair is branded with the inventory mark of the Château de Chanteloup, used between 1786 and 1793, when it was home to the Duc de Penthièvre (1725–93). The chair, made in the 1760s, is in the style known as 'Transitional', because it displays elements of both the rococo and neoclassical styles, with classical guilloche motifs or interlaced bands forming a series of circles, decorating a frame that still retains the curving outline of a rococo chair. It may well have been purchased for Chanteloup by the chateau's first owner, the Duc de Choiseul (1719–85), but is not recorded in any inventories. A chisel-struck V on the chair's underside indicates that it was originally one of a set, probably of at least six armchairs.

From the late seventeenth century onwards upholstery became increasingly sophisticated, reflecting a growing awareness of physical comfort as an important consideration in the domestic interior. Significant advances followed in the making of seat furniture. The frames of both the upholstered back and seat are screwed into the chair frame, a style of construction known as *à chassis*, which came into fashion in the 1730s. They could be taken out and replaced by other frames as appropriate, being stored or re-covered for future use. The style was never universally used, but is to be found on some of the grandest seat furniture, on which it enabled the entire textile furnishings of a room to be changed seasonally, with dark, sumptuous and heavy hangings and upholstery for the winter and lighter-weight fabric for the warmer months. This chair is a rare piece of physical evidence of this housekeeping practice.

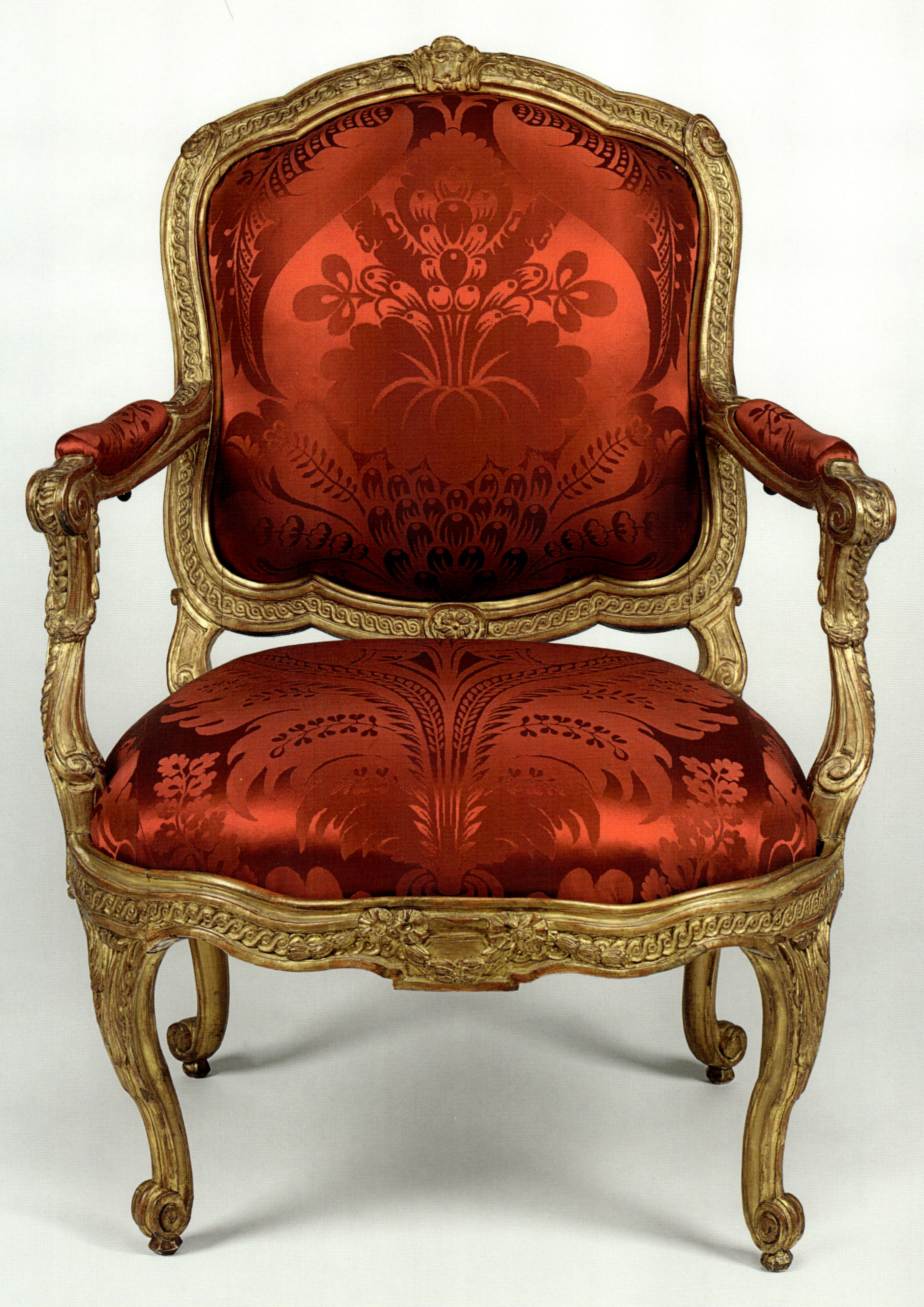

GARNITURE

Sèvres porcelain factory
France; 1780–90
Porcelain, painted with enamels and gilded,
with gilt-bronze mounts and later replacements
Clock: V&A: 171–1879; h. 44.5 cm
Vases: V&A: 172&A–1879; h. 29.8 cm, w. 26 cm

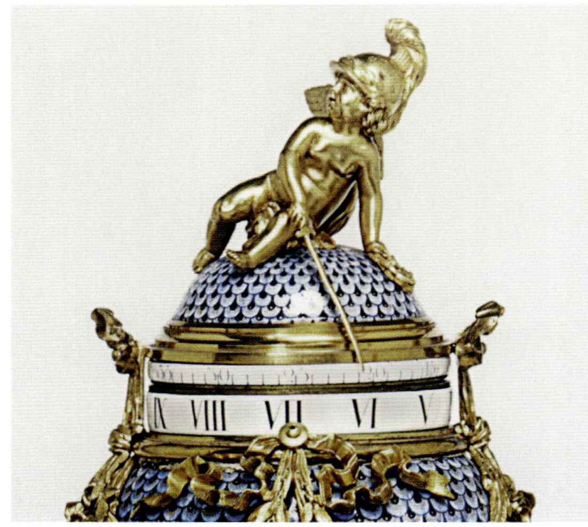

VASES WERE AMONG THE MOST EXPENSIVE items produced at the Sèvres porcelain factory. Between 1745 and 1800 Sèvres produced more than 250 models for vases, the newest of which were launched at yearly sales in the King's apartments at Versailles. Vases were sold individually, in pairs or in groups known as garnitures, and were often assembled by *marchands-merciers*, or dealers in luxury goods. These merchants were also frequently responsible for commissioning the gilt-bronze mounts that formed such an important element in the final effect.

Garnitures – usually comprising three, five or seven components – were used to create formal symmetrical arrangements on chimneypieces, tables and commodes. Purpose-made garnitures like this one replaced the garnitures of Asian porcelain that had been avidly collected and displayed in the same way since the late seventeenth century. Those who bought these newly created garnitures could choose the shape, colour and ornament to complement other elements of furnishing in a room.

This example is composed of two potpourri vases and an unusual oviform (egg-shaped) clock. Potpourri – a dried mixture of fragrant leaves and flowers – was widely used in fashionable interiors to scent rooms and thus mask the unpleasant odours widespread in eighteenth-century life. A gilt-bronze grille between the vase and the lid enabled the perfume to circulate, without displaying the drab-brown potpourri. At first glance the clock appears to be another vase, but closer inspection shows the two dial bands that turn to indicate the time, against a pointer held by the helmeted cupid. The base and lid of the vase on the left must have been damaged and replaced, as is evident from the slightly different colouring on the replacement pieces. This repair indicates the value of such pieces to collectors in the nineteenth century.

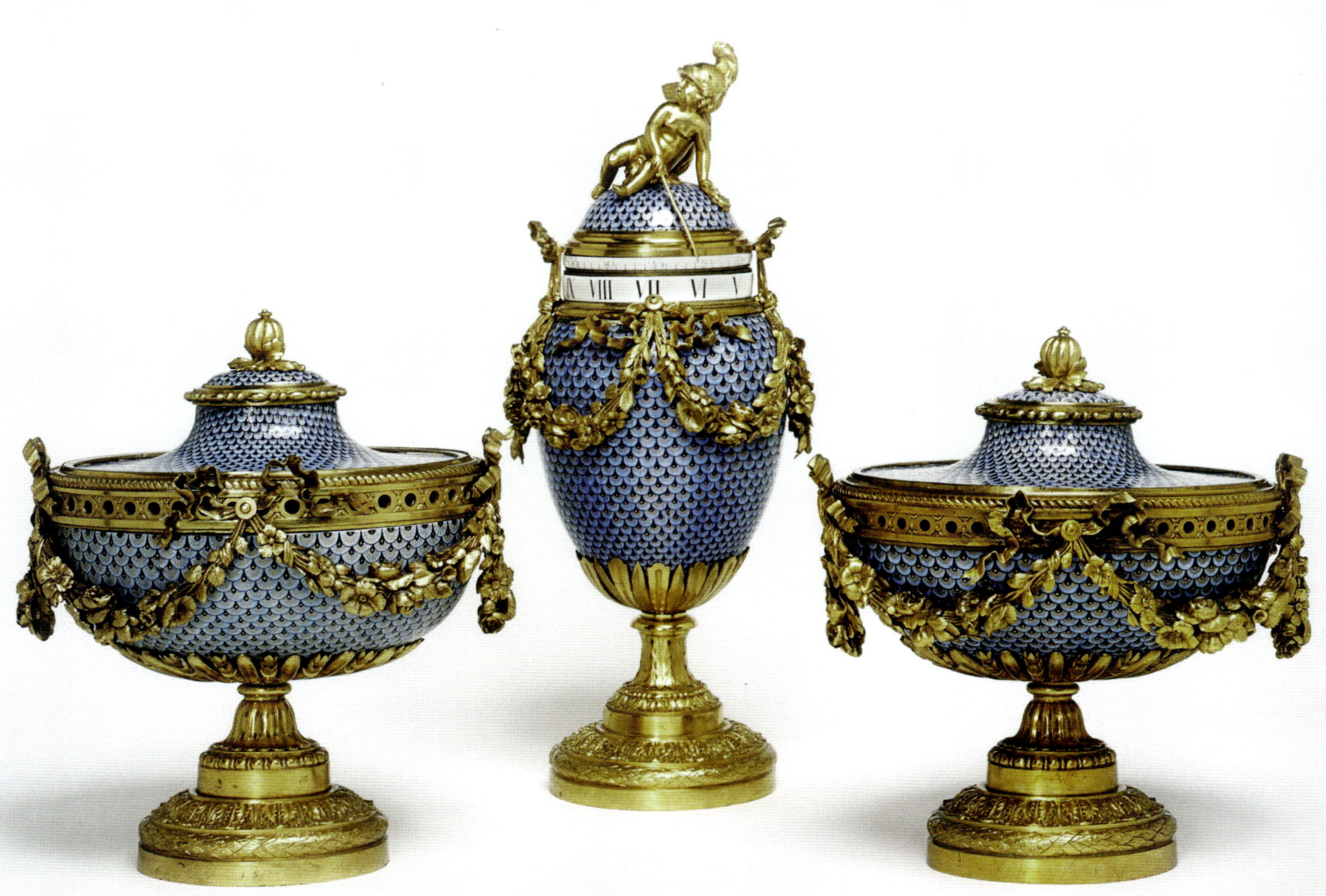

FIRE-GRATE

Pierre-Philippe Thomire (1751–1843)
Paris; 1788
Cast-iron and gilt-brass, patinated
Fire-grate: V&A: M.19–1987; h. 84.5 cm,
w. 109.5 cm, d. 48.5 cm
Columns: V&A: M.19A–1987; h. 105 cm

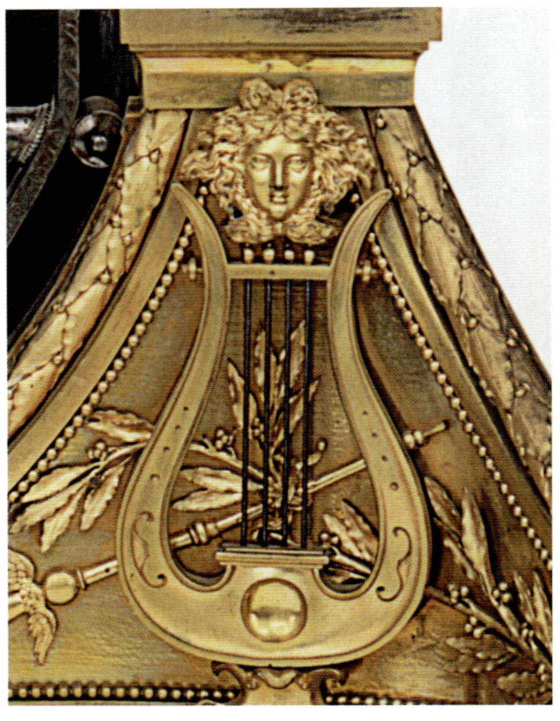

THIS FIRE-GATE AND ITS FLANKING COLUMNS are an unusual fusion of French style and English form. Although made in France, by one of its most celebrated makers of gilt-brass, they were clearly intended for a British client. Grates of this kind were only used for burning coal, and were consequently unknown in France where wood was the predominant domestic fuel, burned on the open hearth, with the logs raised on fire-irons, decorated at their front ends with small, decorative sculptural groups in gilt-brass. The grate was clearly designed in the British fashion, to burn coal, but lacks a working fire-basket and has obviously never been used, suggesting that it may have been commissioned primarily for its decorative splendour, and perhaps that the maker in France misunderstood the way in which it was intended to be used.

The grate was probably commissioned by the top London cabinet-maker and dealer John Linnell (1729–96). Among his drawings are two designs that relate to the grate, one of which is annotated in what may be Thomire's hand. In 1785 Linnell had been given the contract to furnish Uxbridge House in Burlington Gardens, London, for the newly created Earl of Uxbridge (1744–1812). Linnell is known to have had links with the Parisian *marchand- mercier* (dealer in luxury goods) Dominique Daguerre (active 1722–93), who was working in London on the design and decoration of Carlton House for the Prince of Wales at this time. It is likely that the order was placed through him.

Unusually for a gilt-bronze, the grate and one of the columns are signed and dated. They were made in the workshops of Pierre-Philippe Thomire, the foremost modeller and caster of the day, and show exceptional craftsmanship in the refined detail of the modelling and the contrasting matt and burnished gilding. The figures that surmount the columns are of Apollo, the god of the sun, light and truth, and Euterpe, the muse of music, and the fire-basket is decorated with engraved lyres and masks, suggesting that the ensemble was intended for a music room. In the early nineteenth century, however, the grate was recorded in the library at Powderham Castle in Devon, home of the Courtenay family.

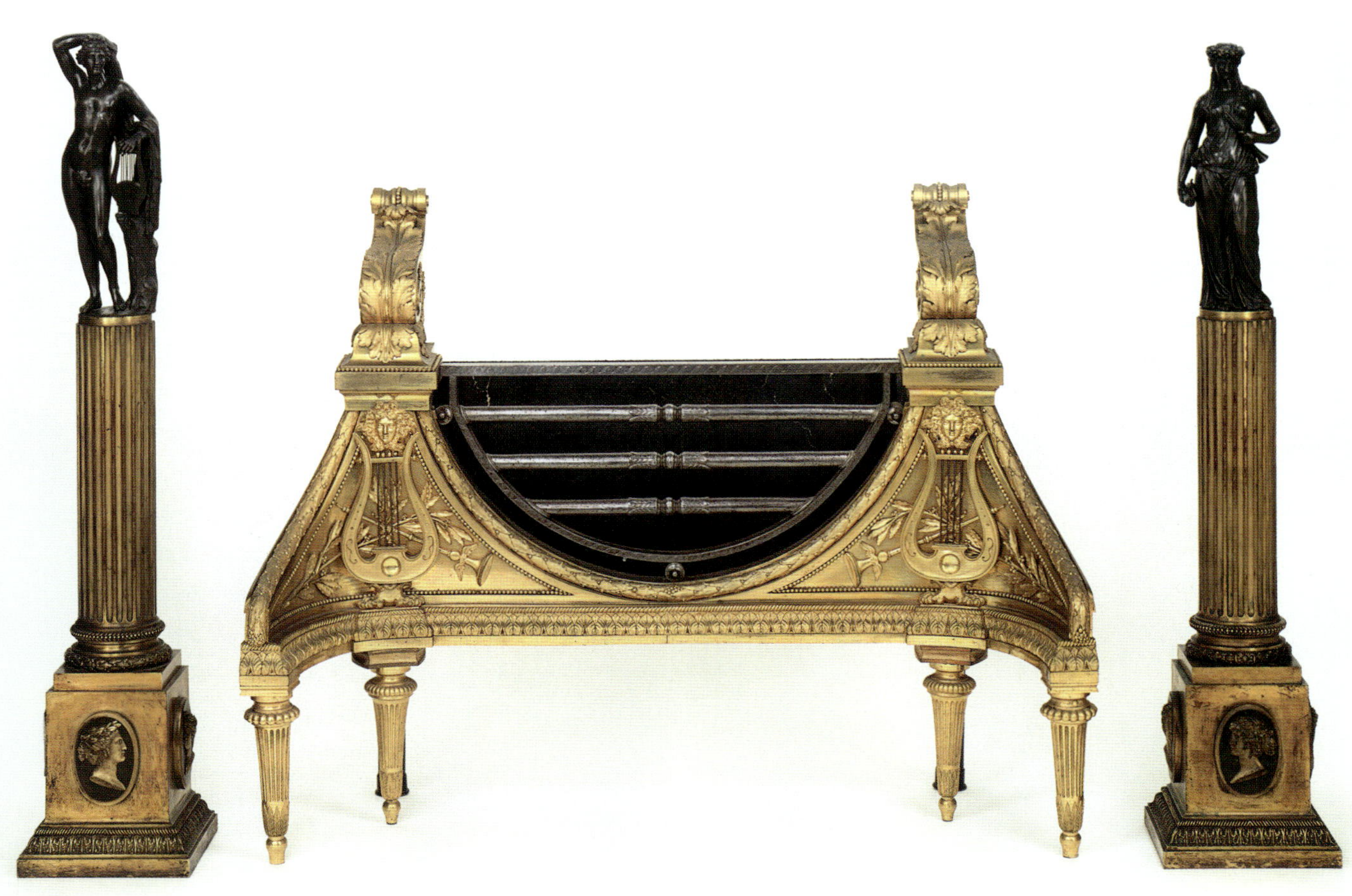

TABLE CABINET

Probably Vienna; 1715, altered about 1735
Oak, with marquetry of turtle-shell,
mother-of-pearl, brass, copper and silver,
gilt-copper mounts, printed paper lining to drawers
V&A: W.17–1958; h. 73.5 cm, w. 120 cm, d. 47 cm

THE BOLD USE OF ARCHITECTURAL FORM AND ornament on this table cabinet gives an impression of substance and size to a relatively small piece of furniture. In particular, the scrolling, gilt-copper mounts on the feet add drama to the composition. The magnificent marquetry of turtle-shell, mother-of-pearl, brass and copper uses the same technique as that made famous by André-Charles Boulle (1642–1732) – from whom the technique takes its modern name of boulle marquetry – cabinet-maker to Louis XIV of France (1638–1715). The skill of working in such materials was, however, also practised to a high level in several cities, including Augsburg, Munich and Vienna.

Like all small cabinets, this one functioned both as a work of art in its own right and as storage for small items of interest and value, the treasures of its original owner. In addition to the lockable drawers and central cupboard, the cabinet has a number of small concealed compartments, which could be used for hiding private correspondence, paper money in the form of bankers' drafts or promissory notes, or jewels. In an era when private life could involve the constant presence of servants, secrecy was valued.

The coat of arms in the centre of the pediment is that of Count Johann Franze von Khevenhüller (1707–62). The arms may have been altered or added, probably when Count Johann became Bishop of Wiener Neustadt in 1734, but the cabinet may have been owned by his family before that date. The proud display of his arms on such a richly ornamented piece reminds us of the status of the higher clergy, whose interest in luxury goods could be quite as strong as, if not stronger than, that of their secular contemporaries.

The central door of the cabinet is decorated with a city scene in perspective, to the left of which is a palace whose façade carries a coat of arms with a crowned eagle and the date 1715 in Roman numerals. The marquetry of this panel is different in style and materials from the rest of the cabinet. It has been suggested that it may be a later addition, although such differences are not uncommon in late seventeenth and early eighteenth-century cabinets.

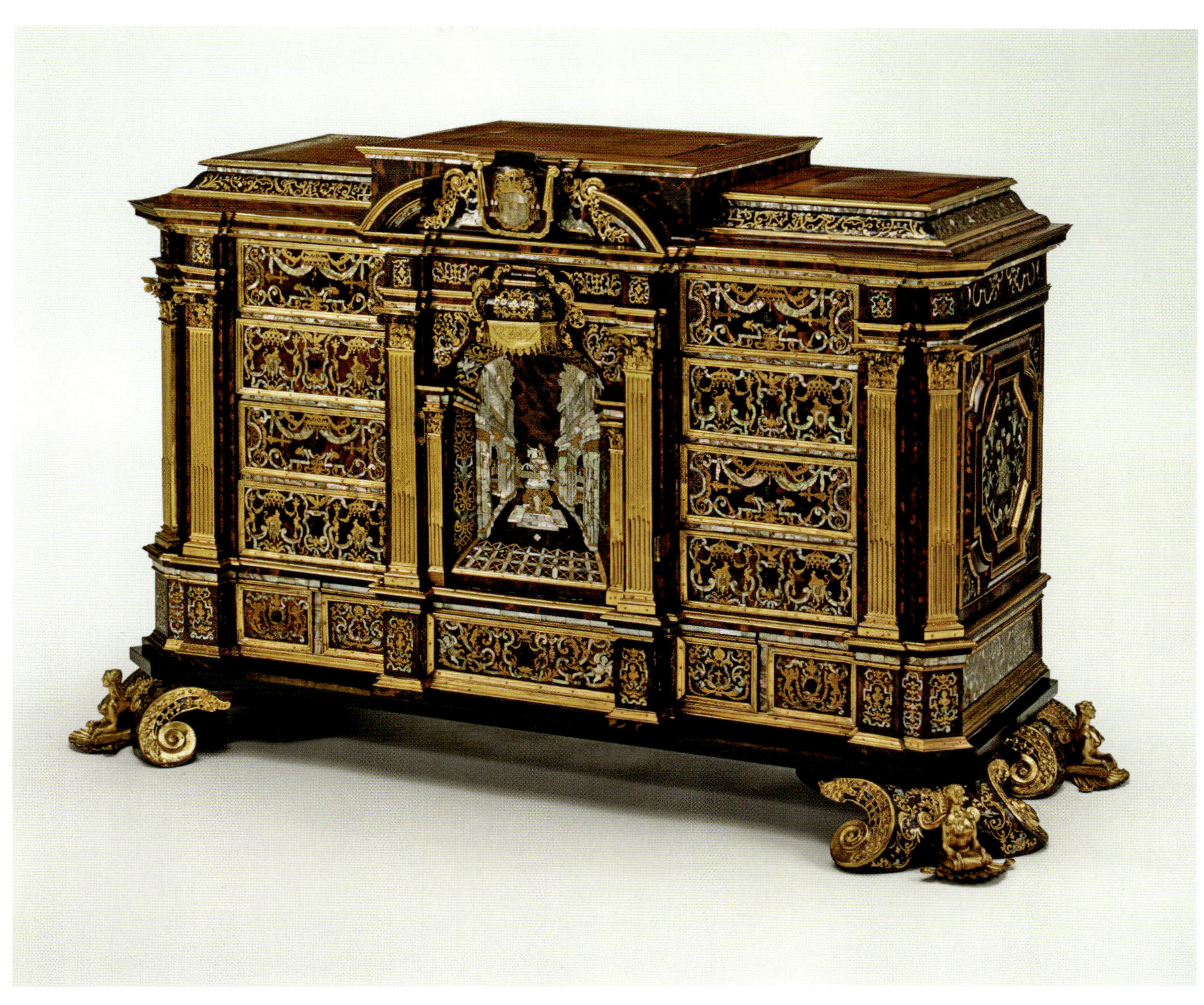

BED-COVER

Coromandel Coast; 1725–50
Resist- and mordant-dyed cotton, quilted
V&A: IS.17–1976; h.335 cm, w.217 cm

LTHOUGH COTTON WAS GROWN IN southern Europe from the ninth century, it only became widely available in Europe during the early seventeenth century when both the English East India Company and the Dutch East India Company began importing it in quantity from the Indian subcontinent. The most successful of these imports was Indian resist- and mordant-dyed cotton. Known as chintz, the anglicized version of an Indian word meaning 'spotted', it was admired for its strong fast colours, light weight and exotic designs. The density and fine gradation of the colours in this piece illustrate the sophisticated effects that could be achieved by skilful Indian dyers and fabric-painters.

The arrival of chintz in Europe coincided with the first large-scale importation of other luxury goods from East Asia, such as porcelain and lacquer. All three contributed to the new fashion for interiors in the 'chinoiserie' style – a combination of elements of Asian design, imported objects and fanciful European interpretations of such pieces. This new style was taken up in particular by women, and was favoured for bedrooms and dressing rooms and occasionally for the small, private rooms known as cabinets (page 108). Chintzes became fashionable for both dress and furnishings.

Quilted bed-covers of chintz were popular with both British and Dutch consumers, though they were later superseded by thinner cottons. Other quilts with bold medallion motifs like this one survive in Dutch collections, making it likely that this example was intended for the Dutch market. The transfer of design ideas back and forth between Asia and Europe is very clear in this bed-cover, which uses large, symmetrically placed motifs in the European baroque manner, but drawn in a decidedly Indian style. In each corner a shield-shaped space has been outlined, ready for the coat of arms of the customer to be added in embroidery, once it was sold. It is likely that the Indian textile-painters were carefully targeting their designs for the Dutch market. Correspondence between merchants and their agents in India indicates that smaller patterns on a white ground were preferred in Britain.

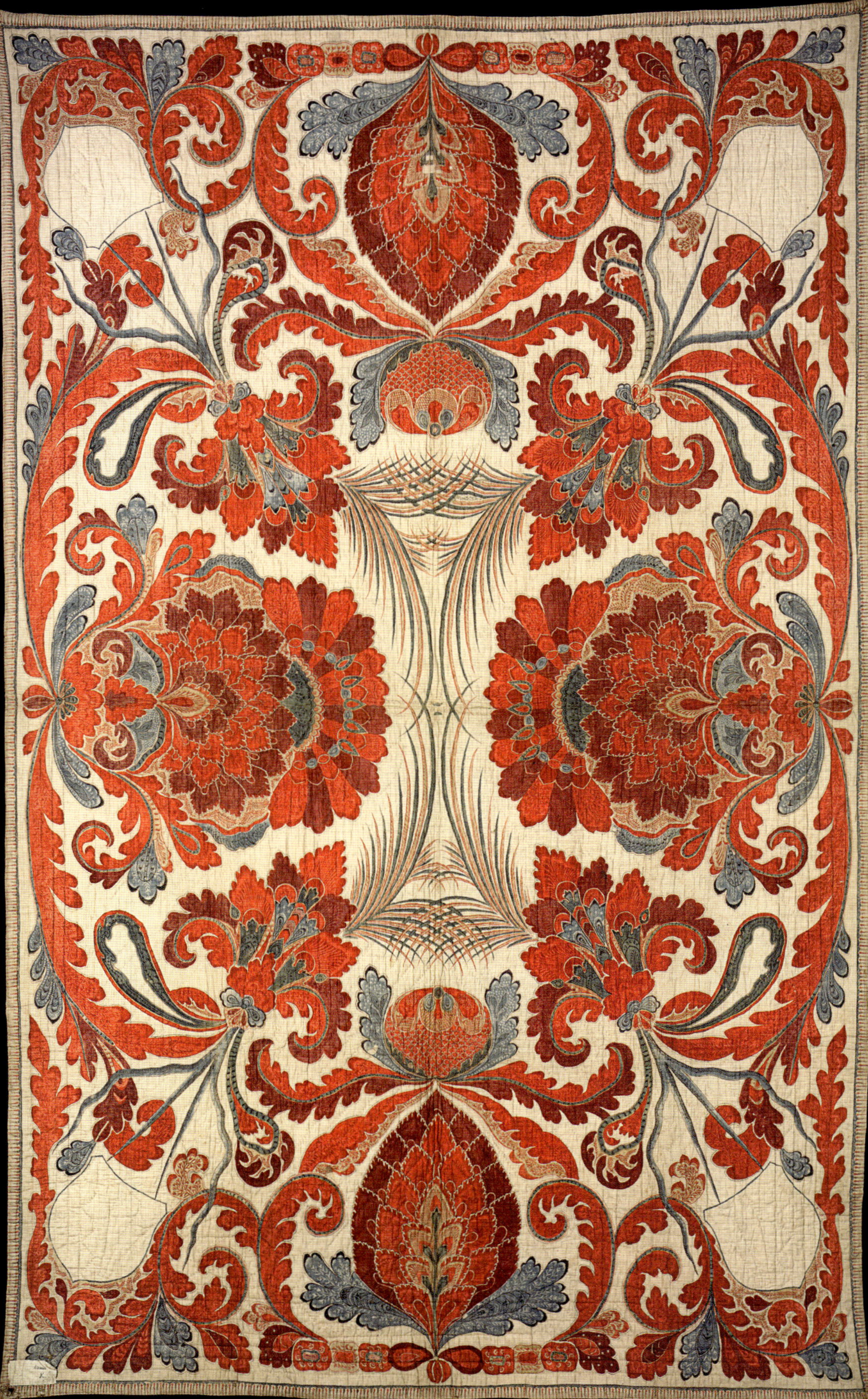

FASHION AND PERSONAL ADORNMENT

LESLEY ELLIS MILLER

PRINCES AND ARISTOCRATS CONSCIOUSLY proclaimed their social status and cultural aspirations most immediately through their personal appearance – how they dressed head and body, and what accoutrements they selected for specific occasions, ceremonial, formal, semi-formal and informal. Even a monarch might tutor his son in matters sartorial, as James I of England (VI of Scotland) (1566–1625) did in 1606 in the following terms: 'In your clothes, keep a proportion, as well with the seasons of the year as of your age: ... and fail never in time of wars to be galliardest [brightest] and bravest, both in clothes and countenance ... '[1] At the end of the eighteenth century the Empress of Austria counselled her daughter, the ill-fated Queen of France Marie Antoinette (1755–93), in not dissimilar terms: 'You know that I always have thought that fashions should be followed moderately ... the simplicity of your adornment will show you off better and is more suitable to the rank of a Queen ... '[2] Both royal parents echoed widely held views on courtly manners. They did not reject magnificence entirely, but rather advised that display should be used discreetly and when appropriate.

Many objects from the V&A collections offer insights into the paraphernalia of 'being fashionable', even into supremely ephemeral aspects such as the *toilette*, the process of dressing. Sculpture, paintings and engravings captured hairstyles for posterity (pages 156, 160, 162), while luxurious shaving, hairdressing or make-up tools reveal the importance attached to these procedures (page 158). Personal adornment was clearly an expensive and skilful affair, as was the adornment of glamorous objects contributing to its success. In both cases, the raw materials were often rare and invariably costly, and a range of skilled craftsmen invested time and labour in creating and

maintaining them. Often the raw materials cost much more than the work that transformed them into luxurious, but functional objects.

In an age when most personal adornment was bespoke (made to measure), hand-made, but not yet signed or labelled, a prince employed full time – often for his own or his household's exclusive use – a number of employees who made fabrics into garments, cared for garments while in use and recycled them appropriately afterwards: a tailor, a lace-man or -woman, an embroiderer, seamstresses, a shoe-maker, a hat-maker, a supplier of gloves and boots, a jeweller. A barber and hairdresser/wig-maker cultivated the currently fashionable head – trimming beards in the early seventeenth century, keeping the face clean-shaven thereafter. Good fit and cleanliness were emphasized as marks of distinction, the British aristocrat Lord Chesterfield advising his son, who was on his Grand Tour in Italy in 1751, 'Dress is ... an article not to be neglected ... By dress, I mean your clothes being well made, fitting you, in the fashion and not above it; your hair well done, and a general cleanliness and spruceness in your person.'[3] The significance of the process of dressing was underlined by princes who developed a ceremonial that focused attention on their daily routine, including rising (*lever*) and dressing and undressing before retiring to bed (*coucher*). These two events were semi-public and enabled a prince to show his favour by selecting which aristocrats might serve him in the inner sanctum of his bedroom or closet (*cabinet*).

Dress distinguished between the upper and lower echelons of society in different ways over these two centuries. Attempts to control who could wear certain luxuries via sumptuary laws continued in some states, although the policing of such laws was a rather arbitrary affair. Britain abandoned any attempt after

1604, while Philip IV of Spain (1605–65), desperate to
protect dwindling supplies of gold and silver from
South America, successfully implemented his *Chapters
of Reformation* in 1623. He set an example by wearing
the stiff white linen collar (*golilla*) and plain black suit
that were to characterize the Spanish court for 80
years. Emperor Peter I of Russia (1672–1725), in
contrast, imposed modernization on the urban
population of Russia between 1701 and 1724 through
insistence on the use of western European dress. This
differentiated his court from country dwellers, who
continued to wear traditional Russian gowns. The
fashions that he introduced were subject to seasonal
change, since, by the end of the seventeenth century,
across Europe mercantilist views of luxury as a positive
boost to the economy successfully promoted an
increasingly rapid cycle of built-in obsolescence in
design (colours, materials, pattern). By the second half
of the eighteenth century keeping up with change set
those in the know apart from the masses, as did their
ability to accumulate well-stocked wardrobes.

France dominated fashion for most of this
period, reaping the rewards of Louis XIV's strategy of
sponsoring high-end fashion trades from the 1660s
onwards. As early as 1730 the merchants and
manufacturers of Lyons, the European centre for
avant-garde silk textile production, worked on the
basis that fashions initiated at the French court were
copied at other European courts and in the city of
Paris, before spreading to the provinces. At the end of
the eighteenth century, however, the plain country
fashions and tailoring favoured in Britain were
assimilated into the urban wardrobes of continental
neighbours, who associated such styles with that
nation's liberal climate and democratic government.

The European elite's diplomatic and cultural
travels facilitated the dissemination of fashions around
European courts and cities, as did royal marriages and
alliances. Nobles described their foreign purchases in
their letters, and brought them home with pride. By the

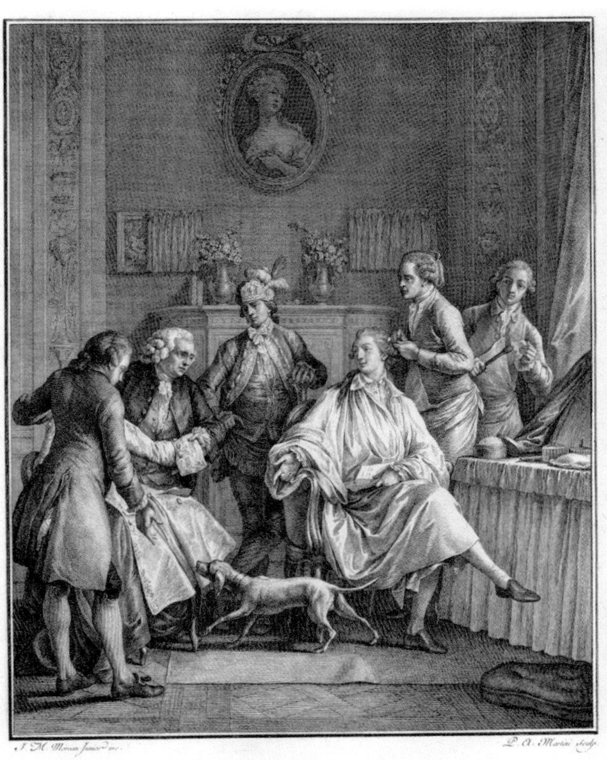

13 'La Petite toilette', from *Monument du Costume Physique et
Moral à la fin du dix-huitième siècle*, after J.M. Moreau. Engraving.
Paris, 1789. The British Museum, London (P&D 1925,0114.28)

end of the eighteenth century dressing fashionably was
not restricted to the court, fashion intelligence being
widely relayed by a variety of means, including an
ever-increasing range of periodicals, such as *Le
Mercure Galant* (from 1678) and the *Cabinet des
Modes* (from 1785) in Paris, *The Lady's Magazine*
(from 1756) and Heideloff's *Gallery of Fashion* (from
1794) in London, and the *Journal des Luxus und der
Moden* (from 1786) in Berlin.

1 James I, 'Basilikon Doron. Or, His Majesties Instructions to his
  Dearest Sonne, Henry the Prince (1606)', cited in David
  Kutcha, *The Three-Piece Suite and Modern Masculinity
  England, 1550–1850*, California, 2002, p.45

2 Letter dated Vienna, 5 March 1775, transcribed in Olivier
  Bernier (ed.), *Imperial Mother, Royal Daughter: The
  Correspondence of Marie Antoinette and Maria Theresa*,
  London, 1986, p.159

3 Charles Strachey (ed.), *The Letters of the Earl of Chesterfield to
  His Son*, London, 1932, p.150

PORTRAIT BUST OF THOMAS BAKER
(1606–58)

Gianlorenzo Bernini (1598–1680)

Rome; about 1638

Marble

V&A: A.63–1921; h. 82.5 cm, w. 70 cm (approx.),
d. 36 cm (approx.)

THIS BUST OF THE ENGLISHMAN THOMAS Baker reveals the sculptor's attention to the detail of young men's fashions from the court of Charles I of England, Scotland and Wales (1600–49) in the 1630s and '40s. Baker's flowing locks, tied with a ribbon on the left shoulder, in careful disarray, contrast sharply with his neatly trimmed moustache and beard, both equally difficult to achieve and maintain without the daily attentions of a hairdresser and barber. Over his doublet and the cloak held in place by his gloved hand, Baker displays what was probably the most expensive element of his attire: a lace-edged linen collar. Technically, his collar looks as if it was made of Flemish bobbin lace, but the design corresponds closely to engravings in an Italian pattern book by Bartolomeo Danieli, *Vari disegni di merletti*, published in 1639, just a year after Baker's visit to Rome and conserved in the collection of the V&A. While the most expensive laces came from Italy, designs were available across Europe, and it may well be that this lace was made in Flanders to an Italian design.

Gianlorenzo Bernini was the leading sculptor in Rome, where he worked primarily for the papal court and other heads of state, attaining an outstanding reputation and high status. This bust is unusual because it was a private commission from a comparatively modest member of society. Baker was the Englishman thought to have delivered Anthony Van Dyck's famous triple portrait of Charles I to Bernini in Rome so that the sculptor could carve his bust. The King's bust was an important diplomatic gift from the Pope, who ordered Bernini to stop work on Baker's commission because it would deflect him from his more prestigious task. Baker's bust was completed by an assistant of Bernini. Bernini's working method was to make numerous drawings of his sitters in action so as to get to know their movements and expressions. Working from memory, he then carved the Carrara marble block using chisels and drills. He prided himself on being able to give marble the appearance of flesh.

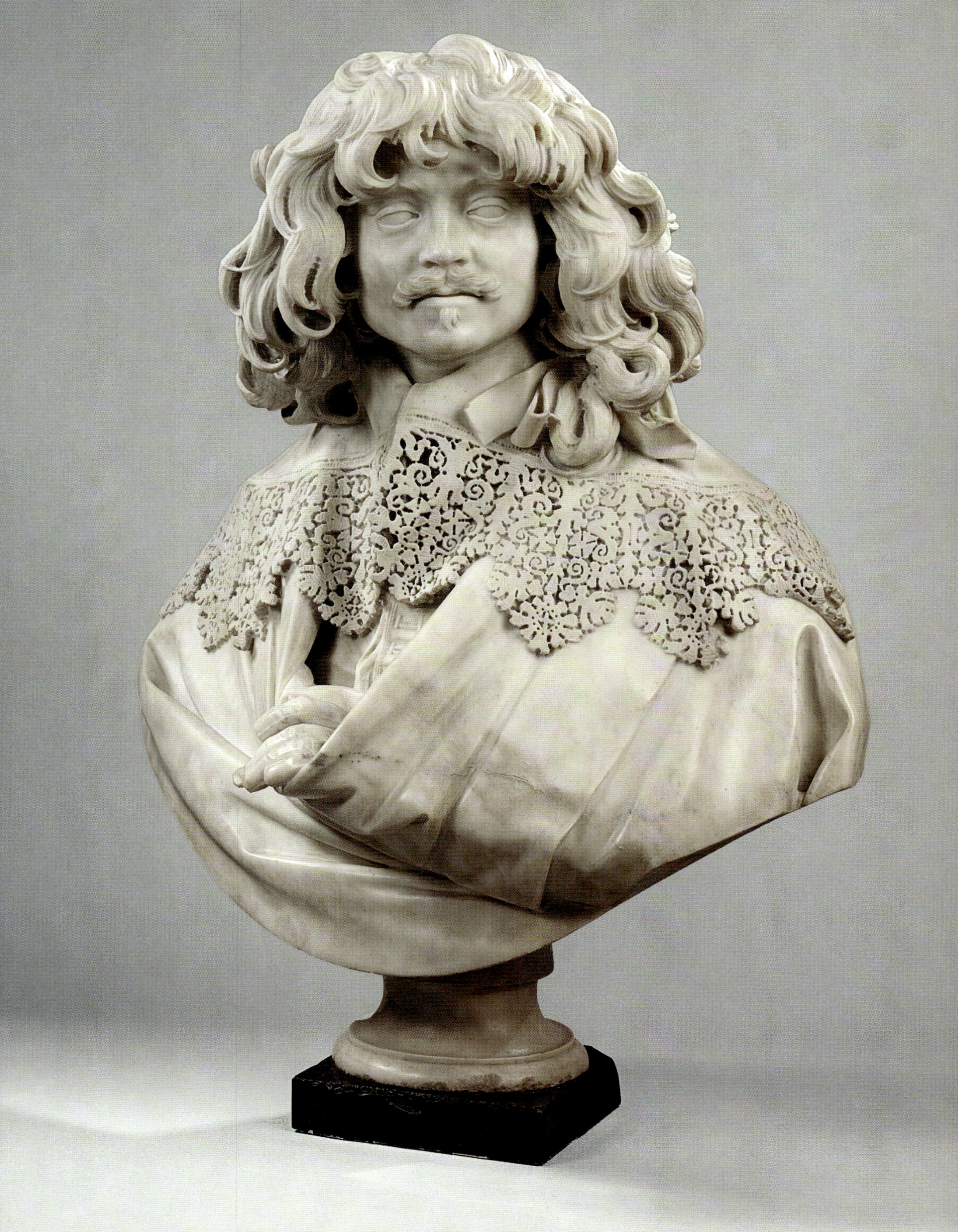

TRAVELLING RAZOR SET

Possibly Dutch; probably 1700–30
Silver, tortoiseshell; the steel blades are a later
nineteenth-century replacement by the Sheffield
firm of Wade and Butcher
V&A: 192–1881
Case: h. 28.6 cm, w. 13 cm, d. 9 cm
Mirror: h. 16.6 cm, w. 9.5 cm, d. 0.8 cm
Comb: h. 16.5 cm, w. 3 cm
Razors: h. 16 cm, w. 2.5 cm, d. 0.7 cm
Shaving-set sharpener: h. 17.5 cm, w. 2.9 cm,
d. 1.2 cm
Scissors: h. 18.5 cm, w. 5.5 cm

THE LAVISH DECORATION AND FINE MATERIALS of this travelling razor set suggest that it was as much for display as for use. It contains all the necessary tools for shaving – a mirror, scissors, a two-sided comb, a file for sharpening razors as well as six razors (to save sharpening a new razor every morning), but its prime use may have been to demonstrate the ownership of luxurious goods at the *toilette*, which might be attended by friends. At the time it was made, the fashion was for a clean-shaven face. The head was often shaved, too, so that the wig would sit comfortably.

Princes and aristocrats owned shaving sets, which might be kept at home or accompany them on their travels, so that a valet or barber could attend to their needs daily in their apartments. Wardrobe accounts reveal just how much was spent on the pomades and ointments required as part of the process. The privilege of having such private, personal service is thrown into relief by the commentary in *Pogonotomie ou l'Art d'Apprendre à se raser soi-même (The Art of Learning to Shave Oneself)*, a treatise written by J.J. Perret, published in Paris in 1769 and clearly intended for men who could not afford this dedicated personal service, yet who sought to stay clean-shaven. Patronizing the local barber was fraught with danger because he used the same razor for all clients, which meant that diseases might be caught from strangers because steel has pores that absorb pus and dirt.

The set is decorated with a style of ornament fashionable in the years following the death of Louis XIV in 1715, when his brother was Regent of France. Elements of the ornament – the tassels, the cockleshell shapes, the straight-edged strapwork and C-curves – recall designs for clock and watch cases by Daniel Marot (1661–1752), the French Huguenot designer who worked in France, then Holland and England in the late seventeenth and early eighteenth centuries.

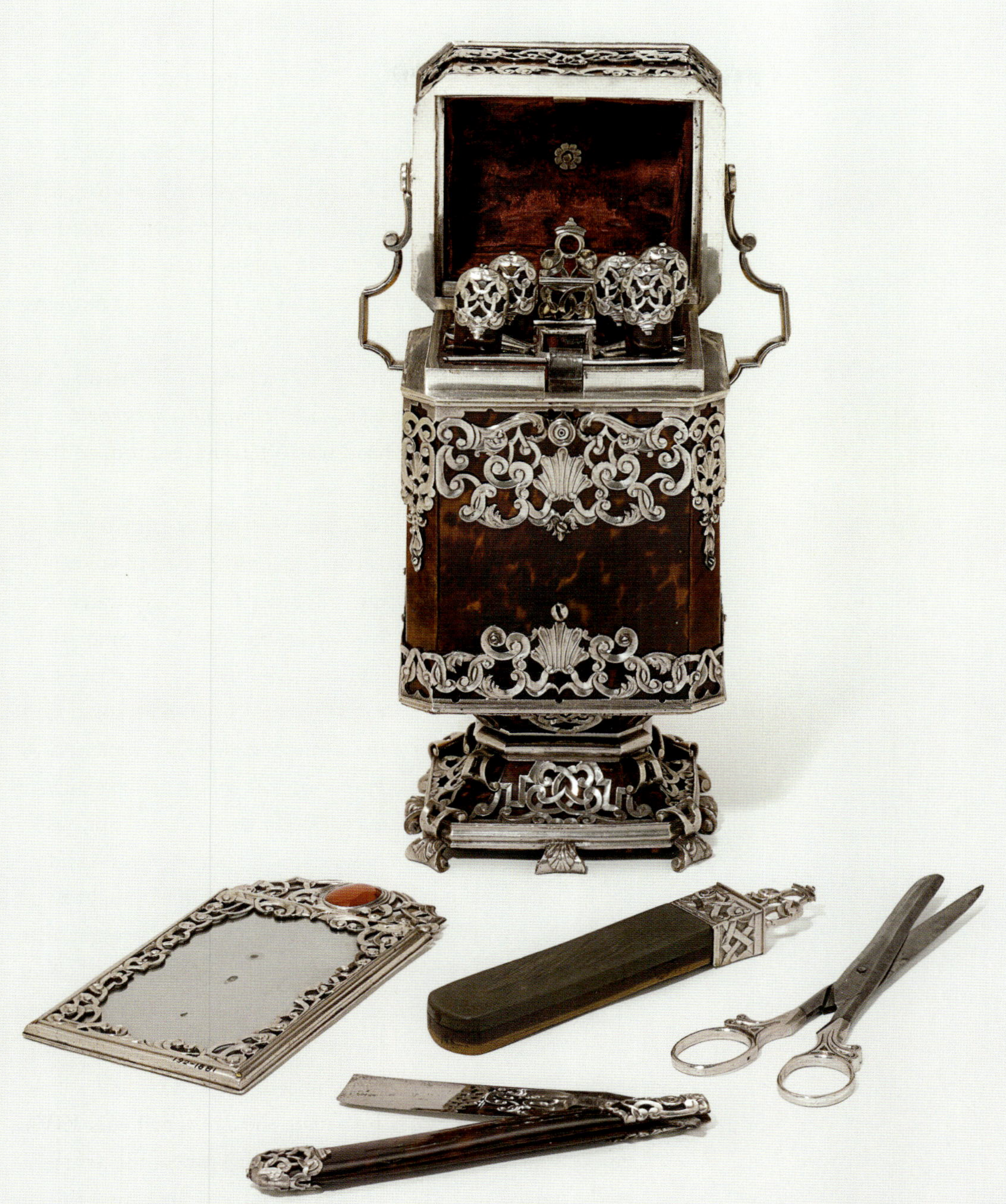

A MASKED LADY

Luca Carlevarijs (1663–1730)
Venice; about 1700–10
Oil on canvas
V&A: P.72–1938; h. 17.2 cm, w. 9.3 cm

THREE STUDIES OF MEN

Luca Carlevarijs (1663–1730)
Venice; about 1700–10
Oil on canvas
V&A: P.43–1938; h. 17.8 cm, w. 15.5 cm

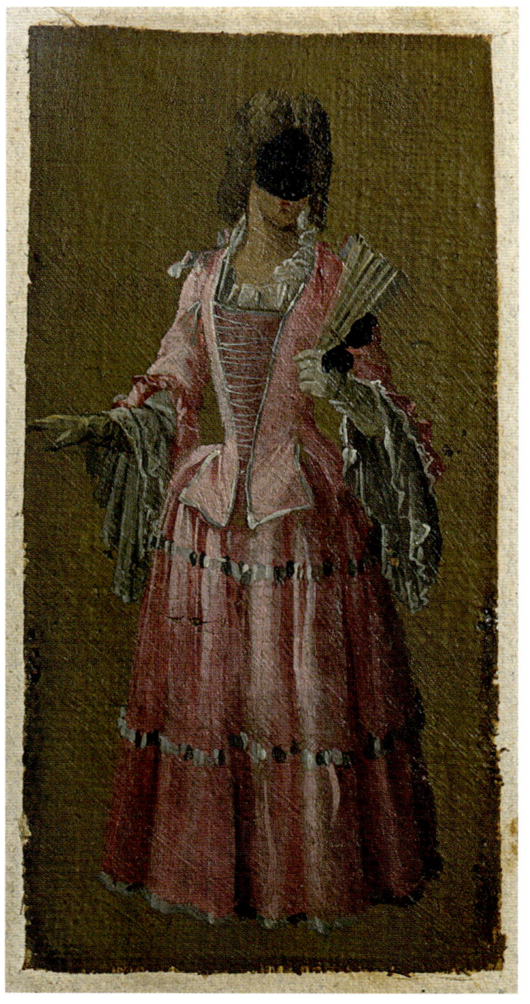

ARLEVARIJS'S SKETCHES REVEAL A PARTICULAR attention to costume. They are part of an album of 53 sketches, which includes figures that he appears to have painted in the open air in preparation for insertion into formal compositions. The figures and objects are closely related to his 104 etchings, *Le fabriche et veduti di Venetia (The Buildings and Views of Venice)* (1703), in which he intended 'to render more clearly the magnificence of Venice to foreign countries'. These original sketches served the painter for nearly two decades between 1707 and 1726, partly because the cut and silhouette of dress altered very slowly, and partly because he showed a range of different social and occupational groups, not all of whom were fashionable. The unpatterned textiles that most figures wear were not easily datable, unlike the distinctively new patterns that were manufactured every six months.

Most elements of dress in these two studies would have been familiar to contemporary Europeans, and were not specifically Venetian fashions: the woman's tight-fitting bodice with long sleeves is worn over a full skirt or petticoat, the only noteworthy local accessory being her mask (*volto* or *larva*). This accessory was used in Europe either as a protection for the skin in extreme weather conditions or for carnival and masquerade. In Carlevarijs's paintings this woman always appears surrounded by male figures wearing carnival masks. The three men wear variations on the coat, waistcoat and breeches, although the man on the right in his wig and coat with large turn-back cuffs in contrasting figured silk is much more fashionably dressed than the other two men. The latter do not wear wigs, and probably wear dark livery coats, whose seams are outlined with contrasting braid and whose sleeves end in practical slits rather than cuffs. The strange hat is not familiar from western European dress, and may be an example of a local style adapted from hats that were brought to Venice by merchants coming from further east.

The maritime republic of Venice had been a great commercial power and was still one of the major centres visited on the Grand Tour. By this period, however, that power was dwindling and the government was corrupt.

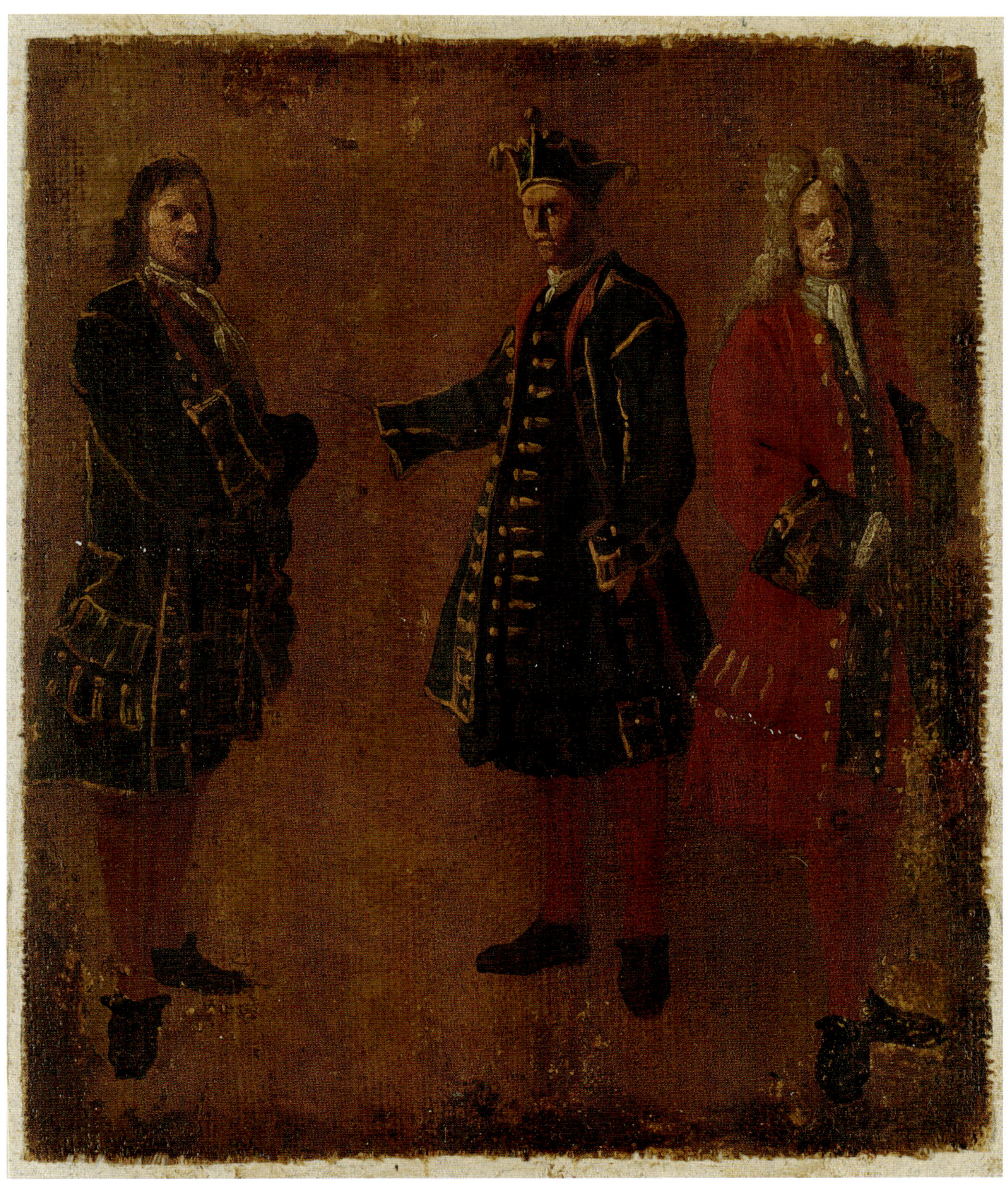

DRAWINGS FROM *THE EXACT DRESS OF THE HEAD, DRAWN FROM THE LIFE AT COURT, OPERA, THEATRE & PARK ETC.*

Bernard Lens III (1682–1740)

London; 1725–6

Pen and ink and watercolour on paper pasted into a sketchbook

V&A: E.1652–1926, E.1674–1926 and E.1678–1926; h. 9.5 cm, w. 15.3 cm (each drawing)

THIS SKETCHBOOK CONTAINS THE ORIGINAL preparatory drawings for engraved plates, 87 of which were published in the mid-1720s. Drawn from life at court, the opera, theatre and park in London, they reveal the formal dressing of the head for occasions when the 'Quality and Gentry of ye British Nation' were on public display. They are the work of Bernard Lens, an English artist known primarily for his portrait miniatures. He was miniature painter at the courts of George I (1660–1727) and George II (1683–1760). He also taught miniature painting and acted as a fine-arts consultant to upper-class families, and was therefore well placed to observe and record the ways in which both gentlemen and gentlewomen covered their heads.

For women, Lens illustrated 60 or so variations on the theme of a pair of hanging lappets (long, narrow bands of lace attached to the cap and hanging loose down the back or pinned up), a cap-back and a frill to make a headdress. The variations depended on the position of the cap on the head, the exact position in which the lappets were attached and their length. The moment of putting up or letting down the lappets was a subtle point of eighteenth-century etiquette. This style of lappet was fashionable from the early 1710s through to the late 1720s. In this latter decade women's hair was dressed close to the head, their tresses swept up into a knot at the back or curled elaborately in rows. The smooth style was most common in England. The rows of curls, or *tête de mouton* (sheep's head), was imported from France. Only unmarried women went bareheaded in this period.

Gentlemen's wigs also varied in style, the hair being combed flat on the crown and curled at the sides, with a 'pig-tail' or 'queue' hanging down the back. The best-quality wigs were made to measure from human hair. They were worn over a shaven head, powdered white or grey, and needed redressing regularly. The 'bag' wig was more formal than the 'pig-tail', its black silk bag protecting the coat from the markings of the powder. The three-cornered hat was an outdoor accessory, worn over the wig. Lens matched the formality and functions of the head covering with different types of coat.

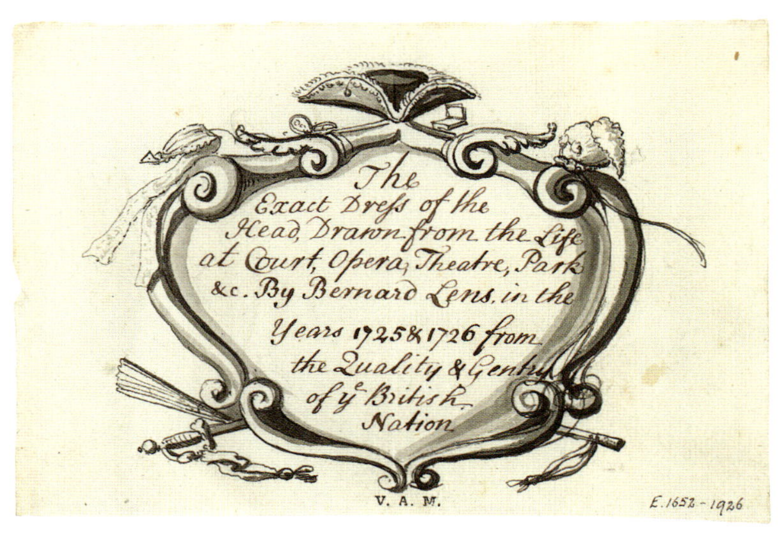

The
Exact Dress of the
Head, Drawn from the Life
at Court, Opera, Theatre, Park
&c. By Bernard Lens. in the
Years 1725 & 1726 from
the Quality & Gentry
of ye British
Nation
V. A. M.
E.1652-1926

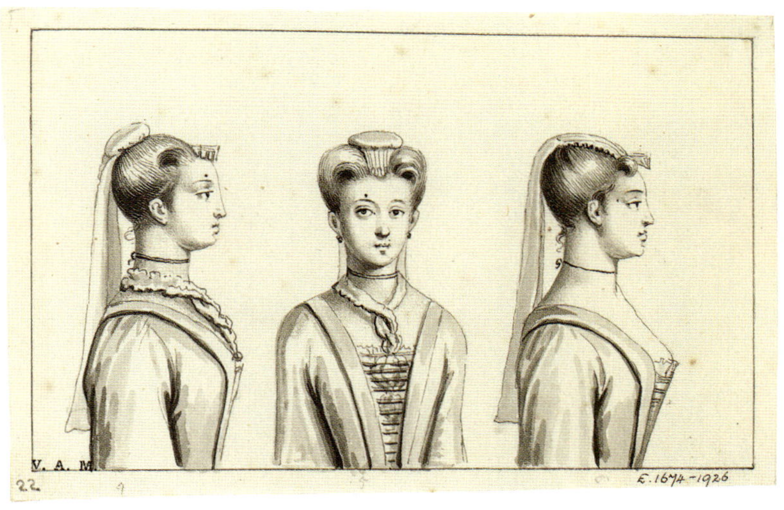

V. A. M.
22
E.1674-1926

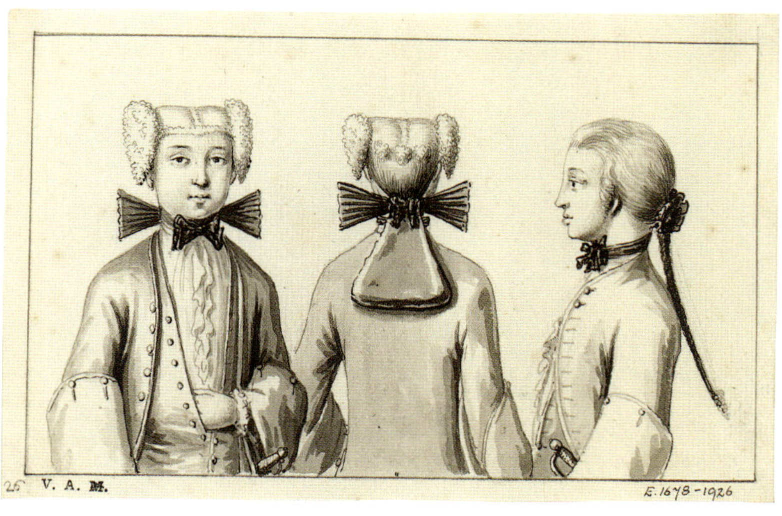

25 V. A. M.
E.1678-1926

HAT

Probably Italy; 1775–1800
Straw and silk appliqué
V&A: 157–1865; h. 5.5 cm, diam. 38.5 cm

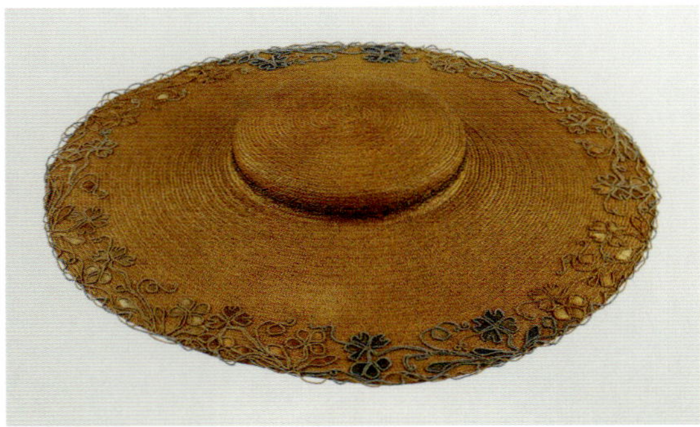

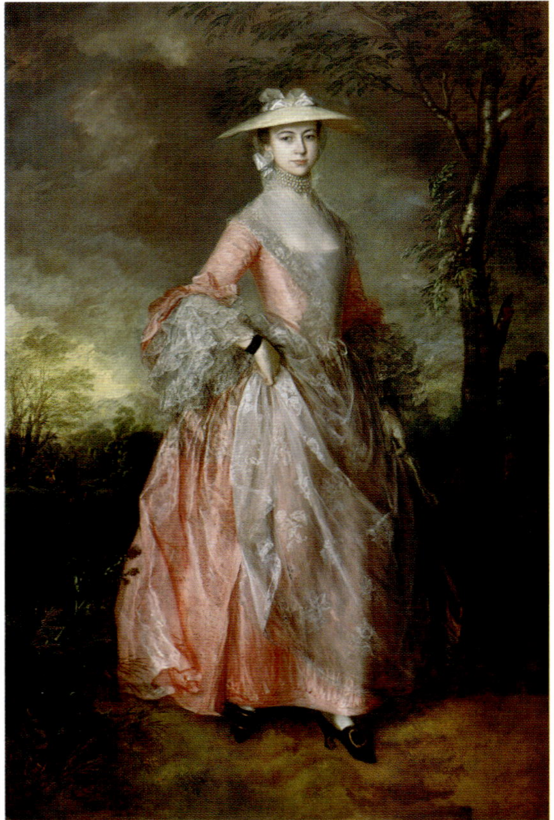

Mary, Countess Howe (detail), by Thomas
Gainsborough. Oil on canvas. London, *c.*1760 (English
Heritage, Kenwood House, The Iveagh Bequest)

BY THE 1740s WIDE-BRIMMED STRAW HATS
with shallow crowns had become a
fashionable accessory for women. They
continued in fashion, worn at various angles
and with varied decorations, until the late
1780s. Originally inspired by the hats
traditionally worn by working women in rural areas in order
to protect themselves from the sun, in higher-class contexts
they were worn in the garden or out walking in clement
weather. In the second half of the century they gained a new
standing because they were in tune with an idealized
appreciation of country life. In France the rural association
was explicit in the name given to such hats: *bergère* (or
shepherdess). Numerous paintings attest to their popularity
among wealthy women in France and Britain, from the
rococo fantasies of the French artist François Boucher
(1703–70) to the neoclassical portraits by Elisabeth Louise
Vigée Lebrun (1755–1842), who famously depicted Marie
Antoinette in a simple white shift and straw hat in 1783
(National Gallery of Art, Washington).

This particular hat is almost certainly of Italian
manufacture. The straw plaits are sewn edge to edge, and the
decoration consists of flowers cut from sheets of flattened
straw, dyed in a range of colours and stuck side by side. The
fineness of the plait made the hats lightweight and flexible, as
did the method of construction, which could not be imitated
in England until much later. The straw-plait industry had
begun in Tuscany, a trade guild having been established by
Florentine straw-hat merchants by the sixteenth century. In
Britain these hats were called Leghorn(s) – the English version
of Livorno, the important Mediterranean port through which
they were exported. After 1675, and until 1860, Livorno was
a prosperous and cosmopolitan city where goods could be
traded duty-free. Many merchants and craftsmen from other
countries, including a significant number of Englishmen,
chose to live there. The Napoleonic Wars (1803–15) resulted
in an end to most European imports to Britain and
encouraged the development of the British straw-plait
industry.

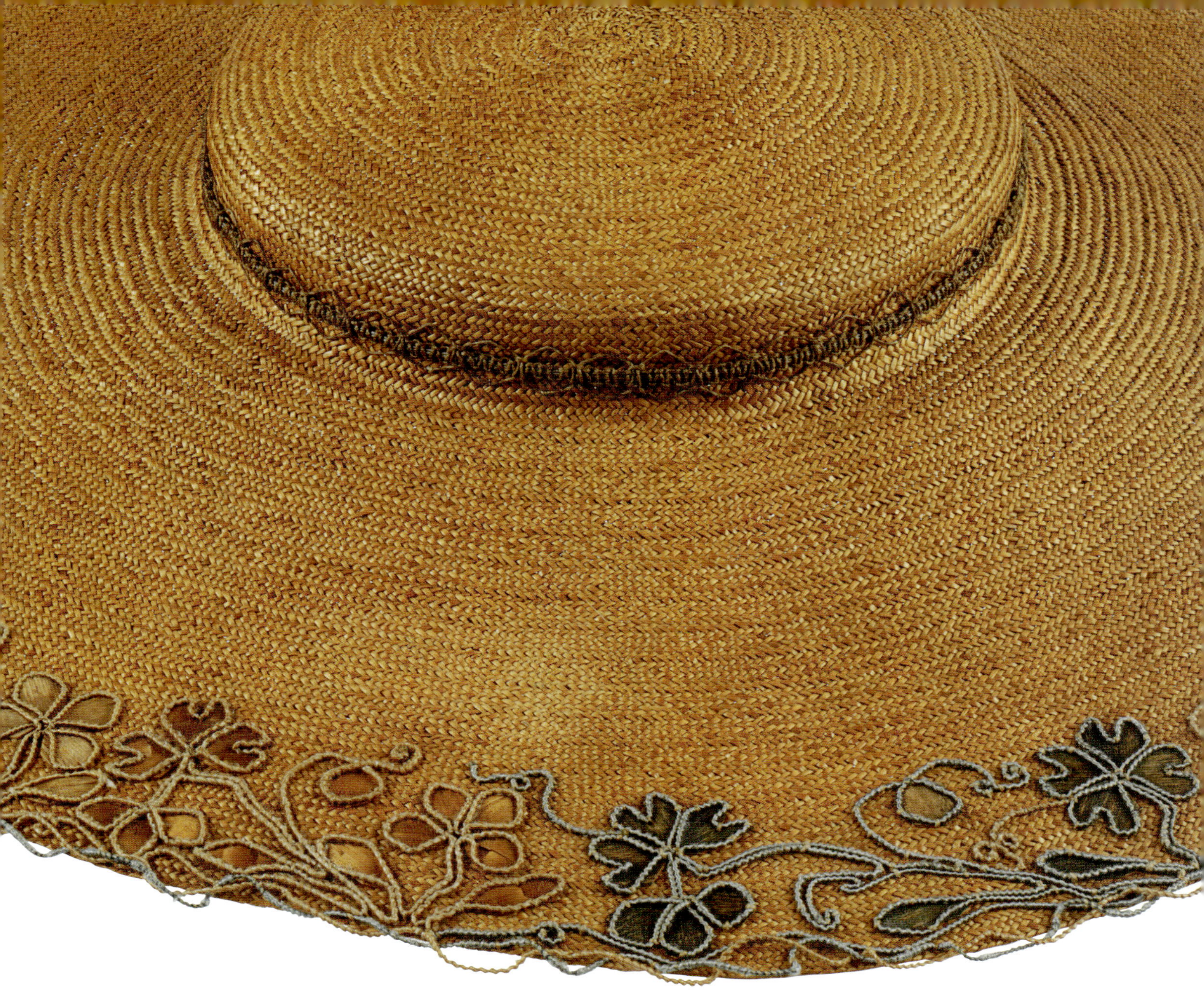

PAIR OF GLOVES

Probably Spain; about 1800
Kid, printed
V&A: T.169&A–1922; given by Mrs C. J. Wallace
V&A: T.169–1922: l. 22.5 cm, w. 9 cm
V&A: T.169A–1922; l. 22.5 cm, w. 8.5 cm

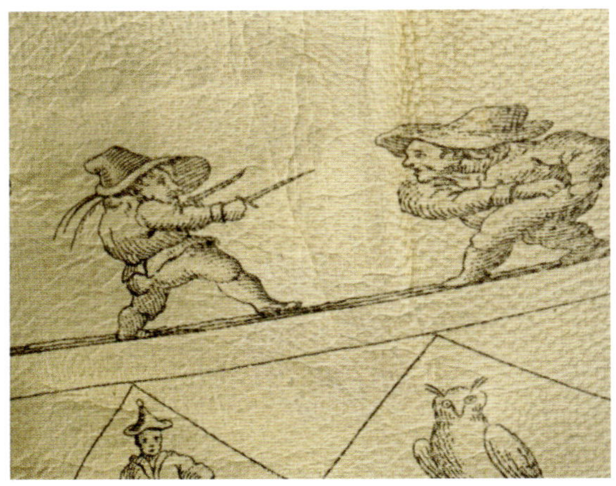

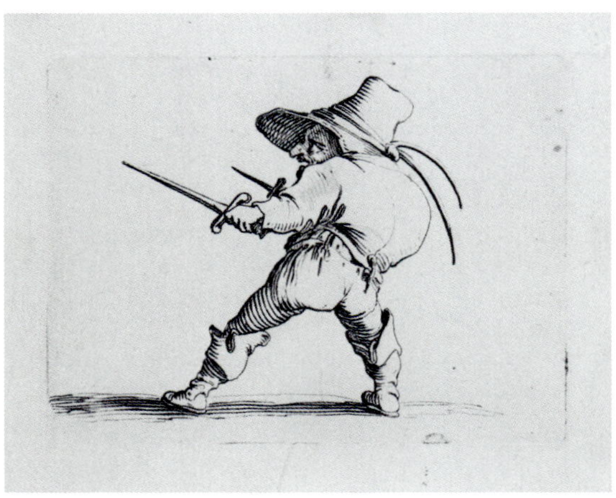

'The duellist with a rapier and dagger', from *Varie Figure Gobbi*, by Jacques Callot. Etching. Published in Paris, *c.*1621–5 (V&A: 24586.5)

PRINTED KIDSKIN GLOVES OF THIS TYPE WERE fashionable from the 1790s until the 1820s. They were suitable for wearing with the long-sleeved day-dresses that women adopted in the last decade of the century. Long gloves continued to be required for court dress, which retained its short sleeves. By this date many European countries were manufacturing gloves, both in leather and in woven or knitted textiles made of silk, cotton, linen or wool. Stylistically these particular gloves fit with others known to have been made in Barcelona in Spain – a country with a long tradition in working leather.

The motifs in the diamond shapes contain flowers, birds and human figures, possibly from the *commedia dell'arte*, professional itinerant troupes of actors who travelled across Europe from the sixteenth century onwards making improvised performances. Here, some dance, while others carry musical instruments. The unusual figures on the band at the wrist are similar to the *Gobbi* – or hunchbacks – engraved by Jacques Callot (1592–1635) (below left). His work was well known and had a lasting impact in Spanish artistic circles, including on the work of the prominent court painter Francisco de Goya (1746–1828). The *Gobbi* were well known in early seventeenth-century Italy, where they were a popular entertainment at festivals.

The design was transferred onto the leather by intaglio engraving. The pattern was incised into a copper plate, which was then covered in ink and wiped clean, leaving ink only in the engraved areas, to be transferred to the leather under the pressure of a screw-press. Several different pairs of gloves could be printed on one piece of leather at a time. The pattern gradually wore off the leather, but the owner might have the gloves reprinted. Denis Diderot's *Encyclopaedia*, published in the late eighteenth century, reveals just how skilled and specialist the craft of leather glove-making was. In contrast, fabric gloves were the province of dress-makers or milliners who dealt in soft goods and haberdashery, a completely different trade.

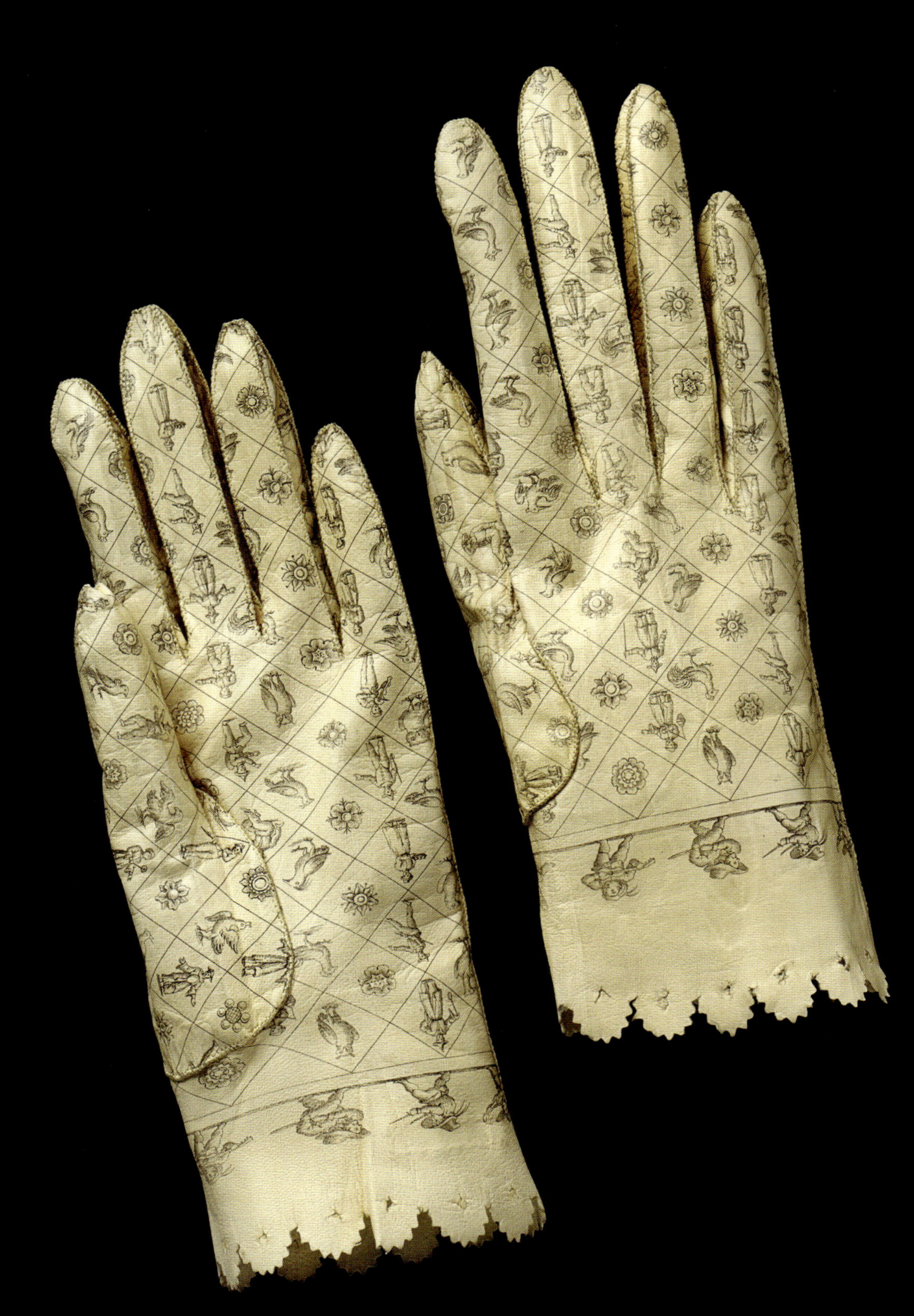

PAIR OF SHOES

Probably Britain; about 1720–40
Leather, silk satin, silver-gilt braid
V&A: 230&A–1908; given by Miss C.E. Keddle;
h. 14 cm, w. 8 cm, l. 25.6 cm

PAIR OF SHOES

Britain; about 1800
Leather, with stencilled decoration
V&A: T.115&A–1933; h. 7.5 cm, w. 7 cm, l. 26 cm

THESE TWO PAIRS OF LADIES' SHOES demonstrate how fashion changed between the early and late eighteenth century. Both pairs were made for genteel indoor rather than heavy outdoor use. They would not have survived the wear and tear of walking regularly in mud on unpaved roads. Both were made by hand, and in both cases the left and right foot were made in exactly the same shape. In shoe-making this practice had been constant since the introduction of heels in about 1600.

In some respects the two pairs differ radically, notably in materials, height of heel and method of fastening. The earlier pair is representative of the decorative and impractical styles of court society. Adorned with silk and silver-gilt braid, high-heeled and pointed-toed, the shoes originally fastened at the front with a decorative buckle. For court wear, such buckles would have been made of precious metal and might even have been set with gemstones. Such shoes contrasted sharply with the heavy leather or wooden shoes worn by ordinary working women in the same decades.

The spotted kid shoes represent the simplification of styles favoured at the end of the century. A very similar pair is illustrated in 1801 in *The Lady's Magazine*, whose commercial and artistic engraved fashion plates had shown the latest metropolitan fashions to provincial readers since 1759. Characteristic were the low heels, pointed toes and pastel-coloured kid leather with painted, stencilled or engraved patterns. The material and form of decoration echo to some extent those of gloves (page 166). These shoes slip on, requiring no elaborate fastening. Their very simplicity – the fact that they did not need an aristocratic buckle to fasten them – has often been associated with ideas about a more natural form of dress and life, as advocated most forcefully by the French philosopher Jean-Jacques Rousseau (1712–78).

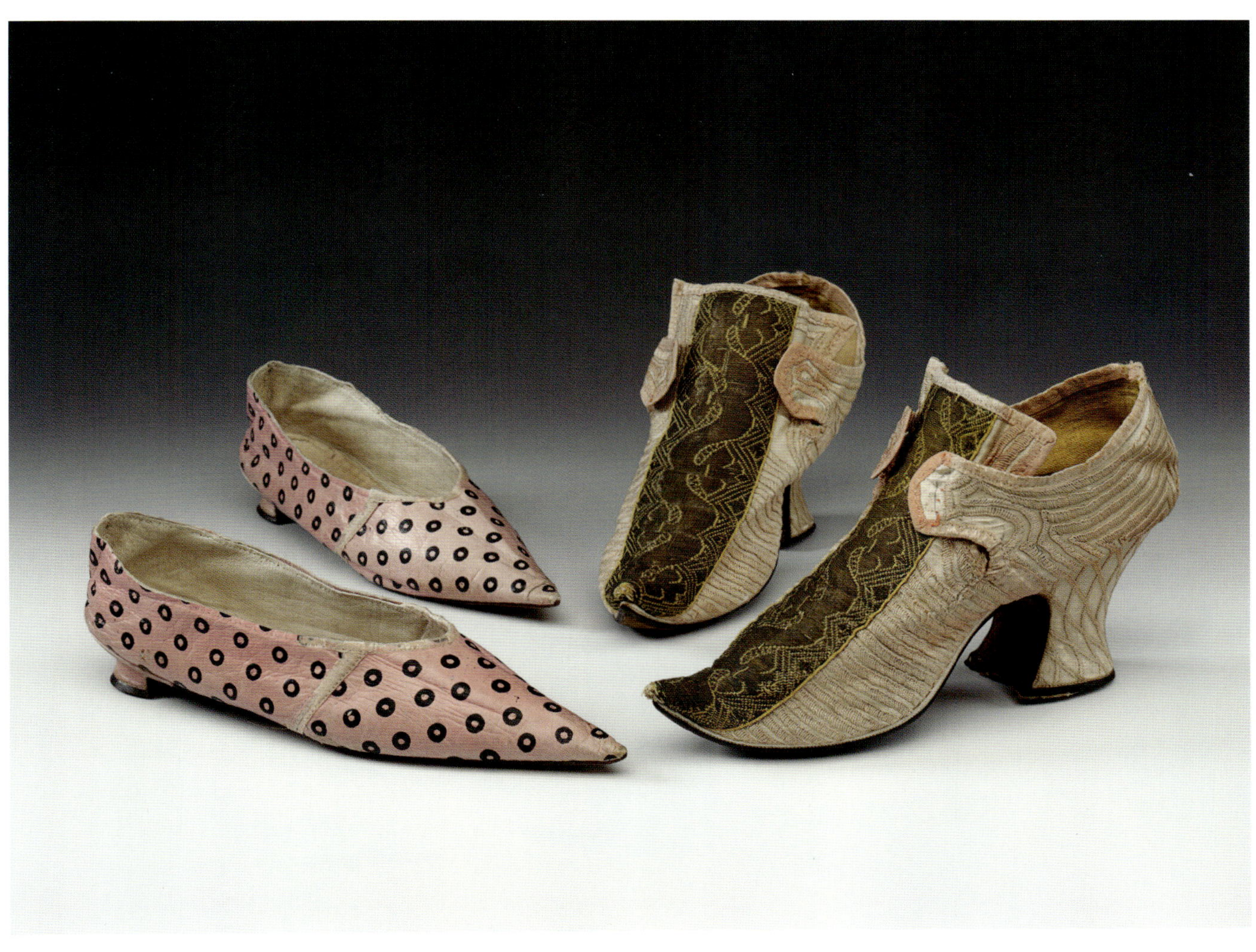

SACK-BACK GOWN

England; 1760–65
Silk, with linen lining
V&A: T.426&A–1990; h. 178 cm (neck to hem),
circ. 87 cm (waist, approx.), w. 19.75 cm (silk,
selvage to selvage)

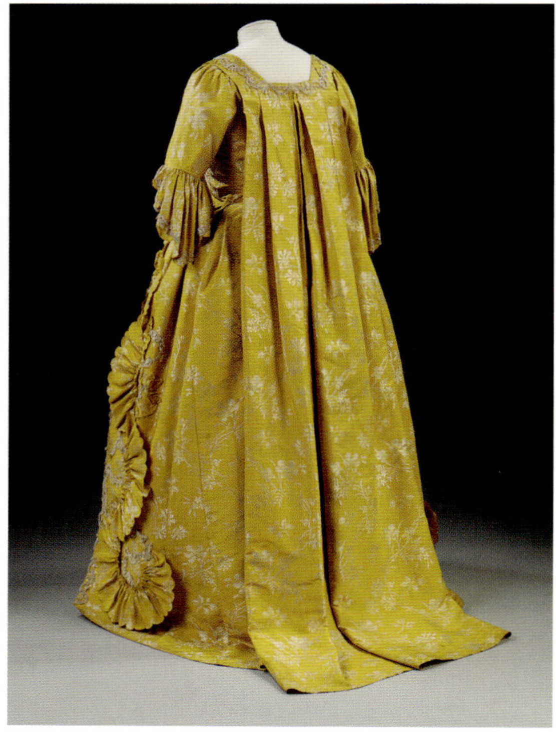

THIS WOMAN'S GOWN IS MADE IN THE STYLE known variously as saque, sack-back or *robe à la française*, its main identifying characteristic being the fullness of the pleats falling from the neckband. The sack-back became a pan-European fashion, worn at all courts. Originating in France at the court of the Regent, Philippe d'Orléans (1674–1723), after Louis XIV's death in 1715, it was initially a loose negligée. It became more tailored and formal as the century progressed. In its earliest form it was considered rather daring, especially outside France, but by the 1770s it had been appropriated into court dress, even in Britain. As the cut changed slowly, it was the textile of which the sack was made that revealed how fashionable it was, as textile designs changed seasonally.

This sack and petticoat (skirt) would have been worn with a matching stomacher piece (now lost) that filled in the triangle from the bosom to below the waist, covering the underwear below. Such gowns gained their shape from their underpinnings – whalebone stays that corseted the upper body, and a hooped petticoat that held out the skirts. Under them, next to the skin, women wore a simple linen chemise. Lace or plain linen ruffles were worn at the end of the sleeves, while a handkerchief or *fichu* filled in the neckline modestly.

While it is not known precisely when this gown was made or for whom, its cut and silk suggest that it dates to the middle years of the eighteenth century, that it was a fashionable day- or afternoon-gown, and that it would have been within the financial means of the nobility or the wealthy merchant or bourgeois classes. The silk has a simple woven pattern, so was more expensive than a plain silk, but much less expensive than one with heavy brocading or embroidery in polychrome and metal threads. The silk was probably made in Spitalfields in London, a major European silk-weaving centre, which offered a stylistic alternative to French patterns, particularly between 1740 and 1765. Very few surviving gowns in such silks have retained their original form, because at the end of the following century they were often adapted for fancy dress.

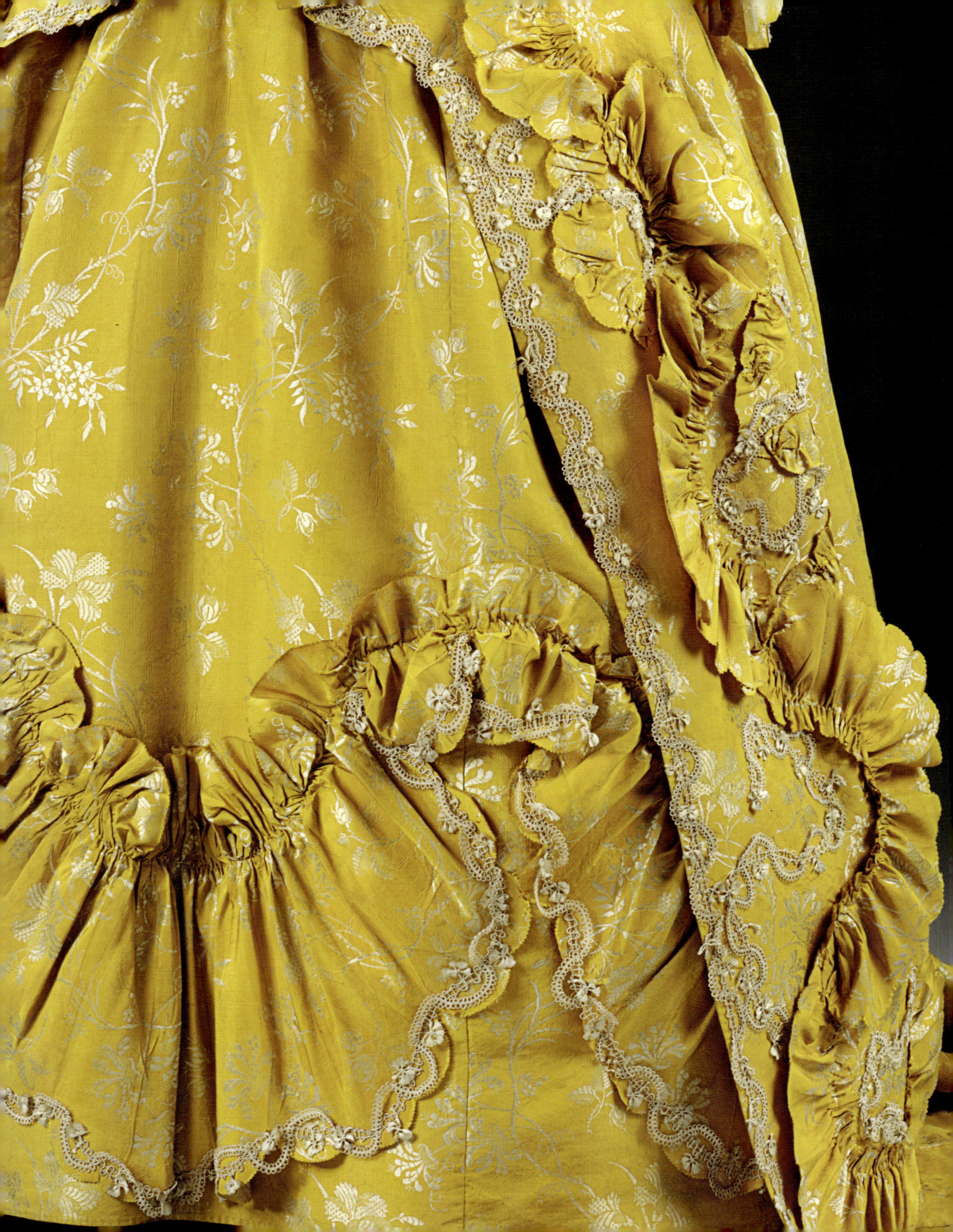

BODICE ORNAMENT

Spain; about 1700
Diamonds set in gold scrolling openwork
V&A: 320–1870; h. 9 cm, w. 13.5 cm, d. 1.9 cm

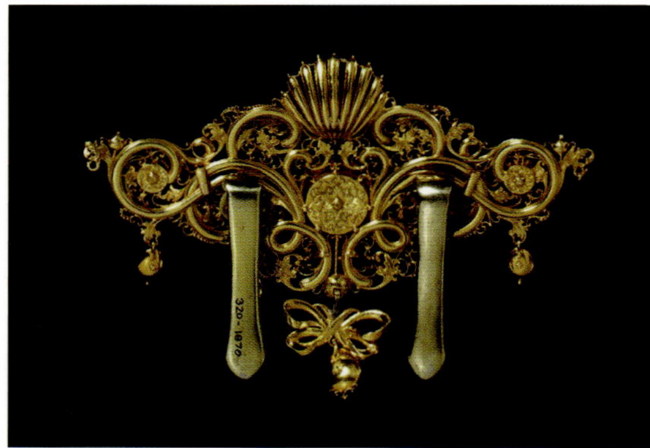

Reverse

THIS WIDE GOLD ORNAMENT OF SPIRALLING acanthus leaves was held in place by two flat hooks at the top of a woman's bodice. Its substantial gold settings secure nearly 300 diamonds. The composition of the design is easier to read on the back (left), where the gold is free from stones. The plain gold stems extend in sinuous curls across the ornament, the leaves are delicately engraved, and the drums that hold the settings for the largest stones are engraved with rosettes of foliage. It finds a parallel in an engraved design for a bodice ornament by Pietro Cerini, made in Rome in about 1675 and now in the V&A Print Room.

The Museum acquired this ornament in 1870 from the treasury of the basilica of the Virgin of the Pillar in Saragossa (Spain) when the church authorities were selling off treasures in order to finance their building programme. The jewel had reputedly been presented to the shrine by Doña Ana María de Flores, Marquesa de la Puebla, probably during the construction of the baroque church between 1681 and 1720. She was evidently one of the Spanish court's great beauties. Her action was in line with the common practice of noblewomen donating gowns and jewellery to religious communities, either as their dowries when they became nuns, or as gifts in life or legacies after death. They were used to dress or decorate statues. Fabrics could also be cut up and made into vestments for the clergy.

During her travels in Spain from 1679 to 1681 the French writer Madame d'Aulnoy (1650–1705) described Spanish ladies' penchant for lavish jewellery, building her commentary outwards from this type of ornament:

> *Ladies wear large jewels set with stones at the top of their bodices, from which fall pearl necklaces or 10 or 12 knots of diamonds which they pin to one side of the body. They … wear bracelets, rings, and [pendant] earrings which are much longer than a hand and so heavy that I don't know how they manage not to pull them from their ears.*

A multitude of hair pins decorated with flies or butterflies set with diamonds completed the richest ensemble.

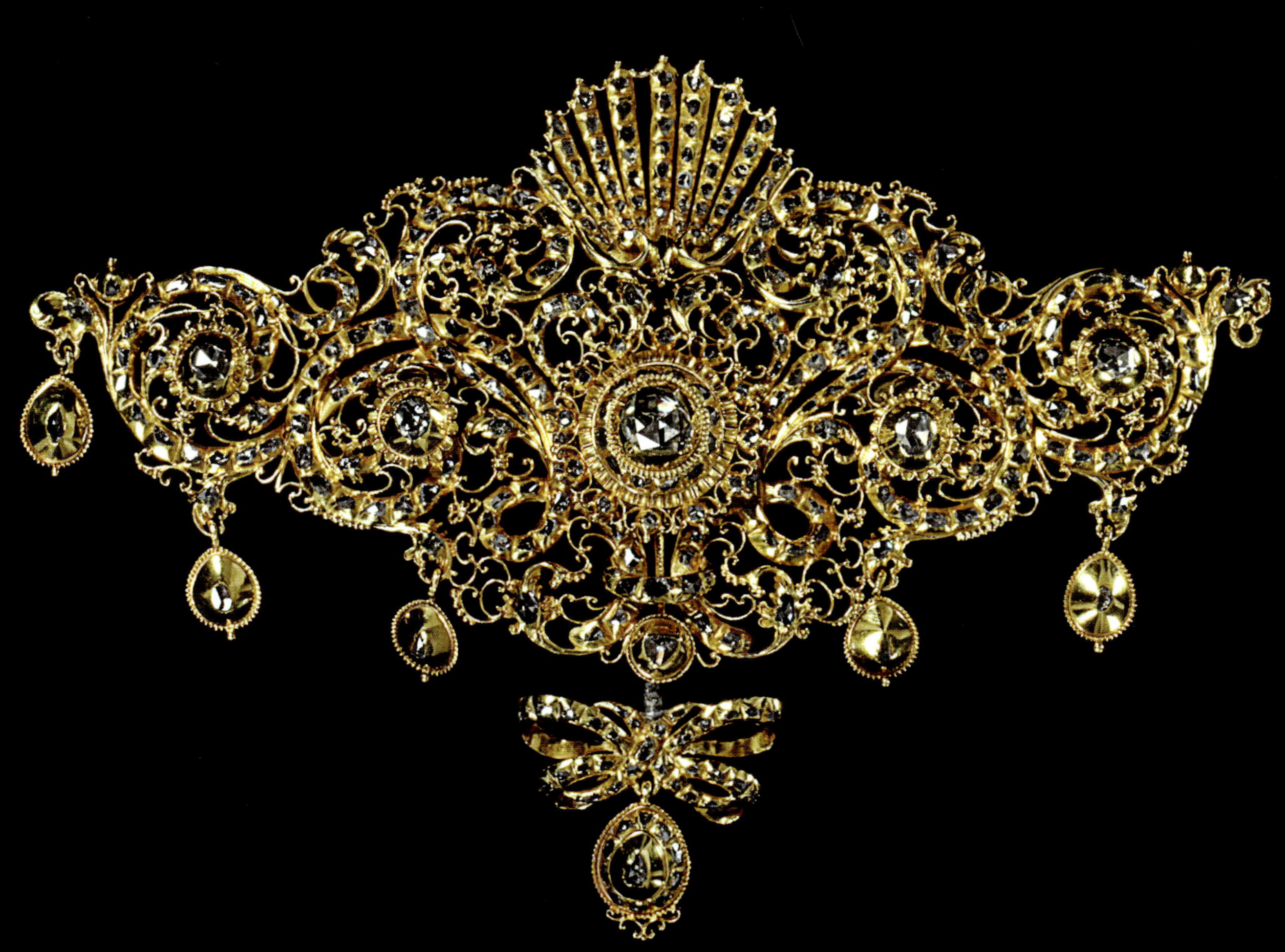

SET OF NECKLET AND PAIR OF EARRINGS

Portugal; 1780–1800
White topaz set in silver
V&A: M.104&A&B–1930; bequeathed by
Mrs A.E. Stuart
Necklet: V&A: M.104–1930: h. 17.4 cm, w. 28.7 cm,
d. 1.6 cm
Earring: V&A: M.104A–1930: h. 9.8 cm, w. 2.7 cm,
d. 0.9 cm
Earring: V&A: M.104B–1930: h. 10 cm, w. 2.7 cm,
d. 0.7 cm

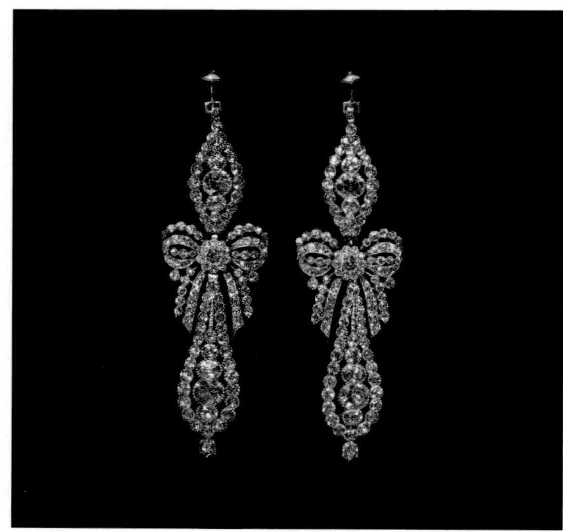

THIS NECKLACE, WITH ITS STRICTLY symmetrical bow from which hang five loops suspending an equally symmetrical bow and pendant, is a typically Portuguese design of the late eighteenth and early nineteenth centuries. With its matching *pendoloque* earrings centred by bows, it forms a *demi-parure* or half-set of jewels. The effect is one of brilliance and light, the stones being white and set in silver in order to enhance their whiteness. They look like diamonds, faceted in the brilliant cut that was introduced in the last decades of the seventeenth century. The facets enhanced the sparkle of the stones, creating a particularly dramatic effect in flickering candlelight. The necklace would have sat on the bare bosom of the wearer, while the earrings would have swung from her ears.

After Portuguese explorers discovered gold in the 1690s and diamonds in the 1720s in the interior of Brazil, the commercial exploitation of precious metal and gemstones brought to Lisbon in large quantities the raw materials of jewellery. While jewels with diamonds, rubies and emeralds continued to be created for the court and aristocracy in the second half of the century, other gemstones were also highly prized in that period. The white topazes in this half-set were among the many gemstones mined in Brazil. They bear a strong resemblance to diamonds, though they would have been considerably cheaper in price – if not as cheap as imitation diamonds made of glass paste, which were also fashionable in this period. Indeed, this set may owe its survival intact to the fact that the stones are not diamonds, and so were not reset into new fashions many times since the eighteenth century. Contemporary portraits suggest that such showy jewellery was only appropriate for court dress, and that for less formal, yet smart dress, pearls were favoured by aristocratic and bourgeois sitters.

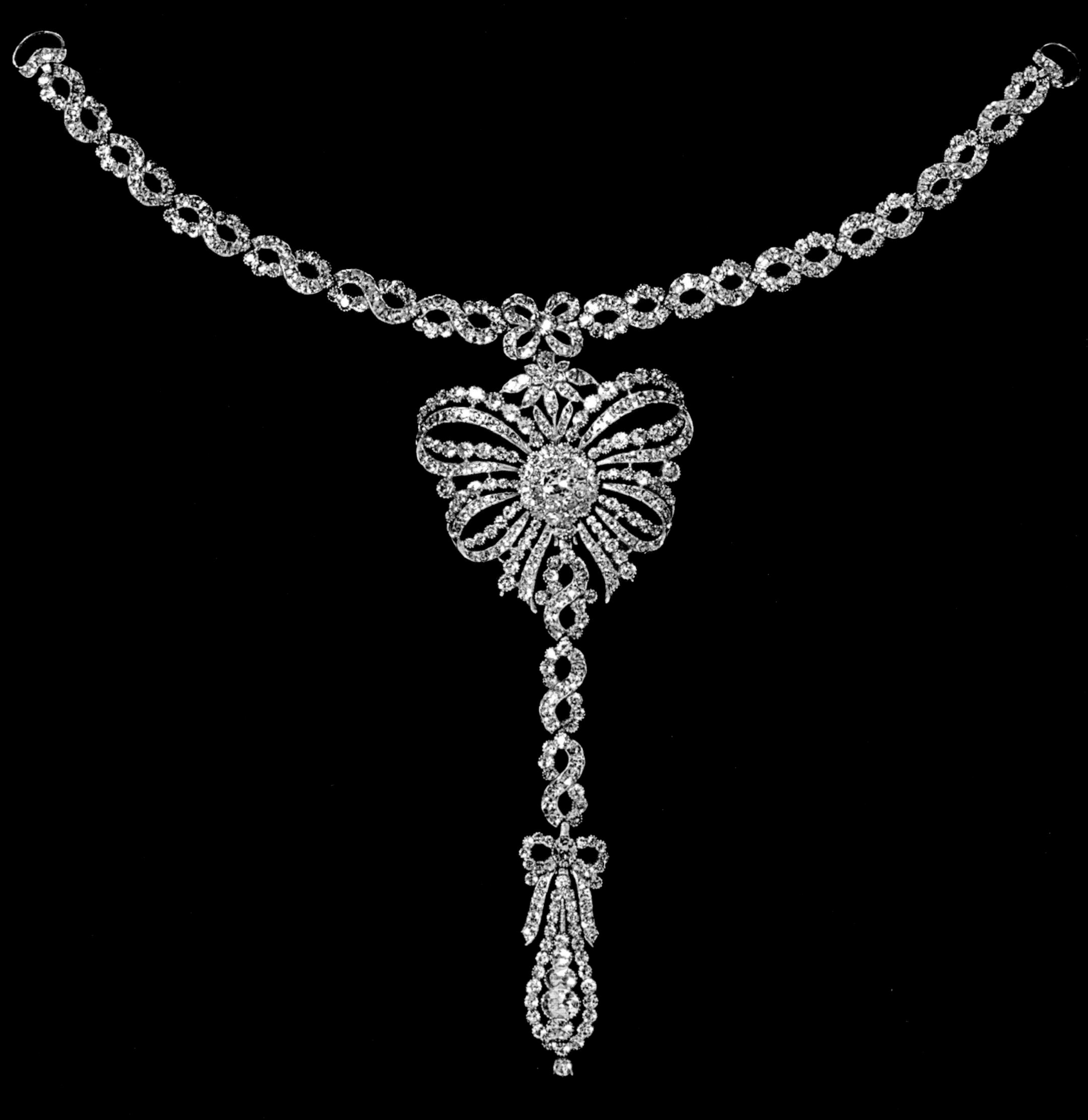

WAISTCOAT

England or France; 1730–39
Silk satin, embroidered with silver thread, silk
thread and spangles
V&A: 252–1906; h. 102 cm, w. 90 cm (max.)

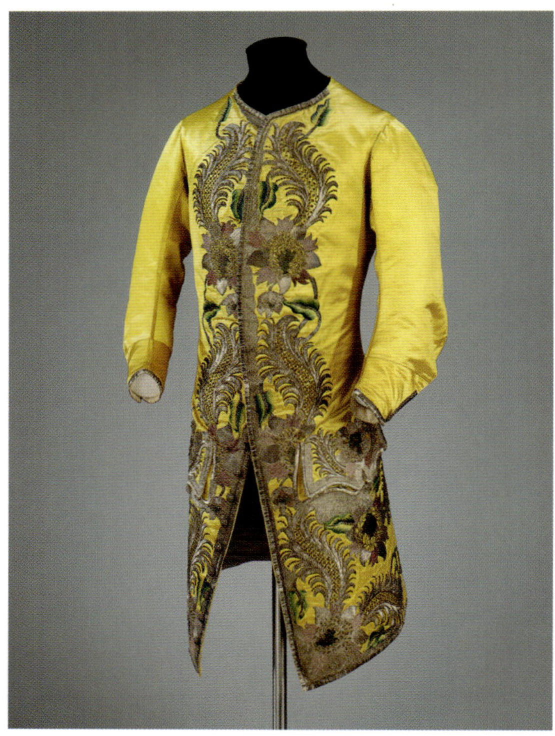

THIS WAISTCOAT EPITOMIZES THE RICH AND colourful attire worn at all European courts in the 1730s for special occasions such as royal birthdays or weddings. It is far too lavish for any other purpose – and unusual in being made entirely of silk, even in areas that would not have been visible below its matching coat. Originally part of a three-piece suit, the waistcoat has survived both coat and breeches. Its decoration would have run parallel to the front opening of the coat from neck to knee, an echo of the coat's embellishment. The lavish baroque design comprises stylized flowers, leaves and feathered scrolls that are bold in scale. Such made-to-measure garments were always accessorized with a fine lace cravat and cuffs, a wig and a sword. In order to manage these accoutrements elegantly, young gentlemen received lessons in both fencing and dancing.

The rich yellow silk of the ground was fashionable in men's and women's dress from the 1730s through to the 1780s. Here, it is a foil for the embroidery of coloured silks, metal threads and spangles (sequins), which would have sparkled in candlelight as the wearer moved through opulent royal apartments. Charles-Germain de Saint-Aubin (1721–86), designer by appointment to Louis XV of France, described the materials and processes of the embroiderer's trade in *L'art du brodeur (The Art of the Embroiderer)*, a treatise published in Paris in 1770 towards the end of his career. He boasted of the prowess of his fellow countrymen in this field:

We French ... have surprisingly benefited from the discoveries of other Nations by changing, improving and adapting them in the best manner to new uses. To be convinced, it suffices to see the masterpieces in the Wardrobe of our King and the number of Foreigners seeking to obtain our Embroidery.

He included as illustrations diagrams of borders from the King's wardrobe. The design of a waistcoat made in 1730, probably by St Aubin's father, is similar in spirit to that of this waistcoat.

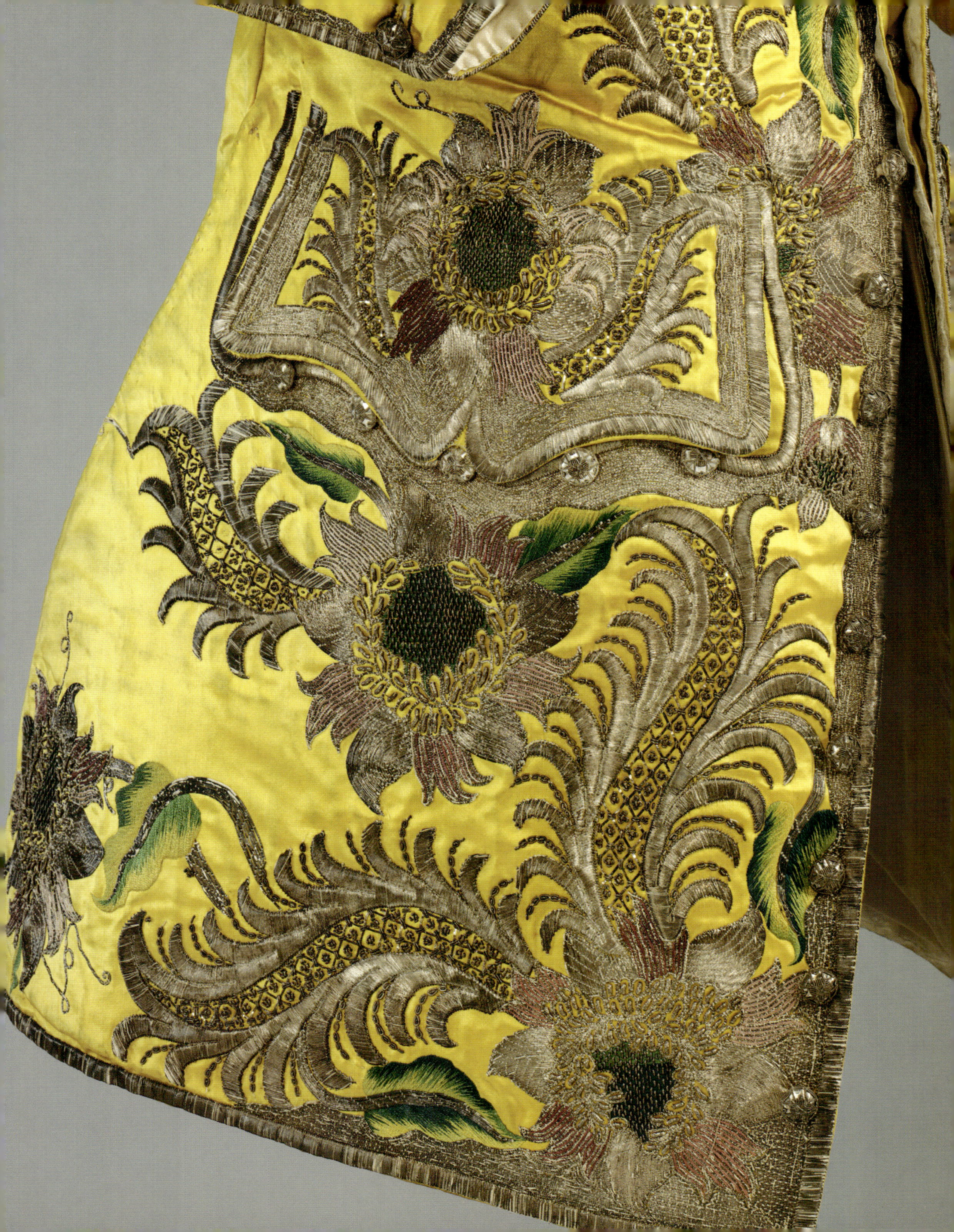

WAISTCOAT

Probably England; 1780–90
Silk, backed and lined with linen; embroidered
with silk and chenille and appliquéd with painted
silk medallions
V&A: 256–1880; circ. 107.5 cm, l. 67 cm (back),
l. 69 cm (front)

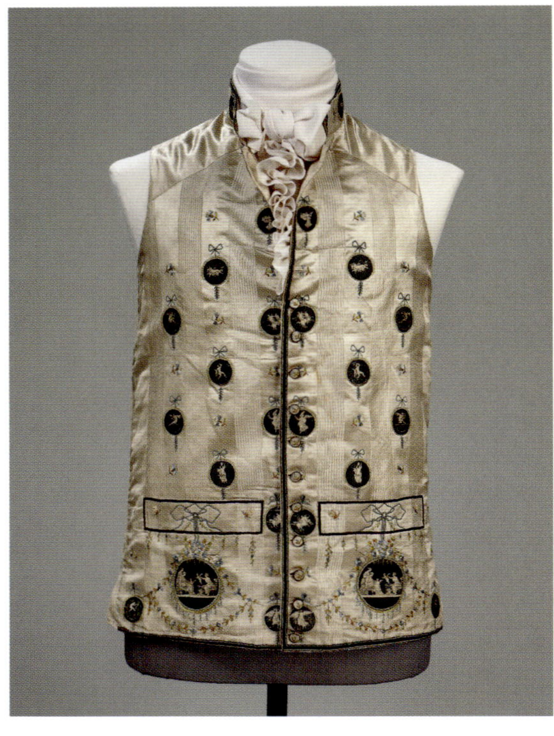

B Y THE END OF THE EIGHTEENTH CENTURY
across Europe fashionable men's coats for
urban day-wear were made of dark woollen
cloth and teamed with dark- or light-
coloured breeches and waistcoats. This
sombre attire was associated in continental
Europe with Anglomania, the late-eighteenth-century craze
for all things English, which contemporaries associated with
constitutional monarchy and freedom of speech. It contrasted
radically with the flamboyance of court dress, which was still
colourful and made predominantly of silk. Waistcoats,
however, brightened men's daily wardrobes, being purchased
independently of other garments and as part of three-piece
suits. Fashion periodicals reveal two styles in the 1780s. The
first, like this one, without sleeves, was cut straight at the
waist (called a *gilet* in French) and probably derived from
sports wear. The second (the *veste*), with or without sleeves,
retained a basque (a short version of the long skirts found on
waistcoats in previous decades) and was more formal.

Most aristocrats purchased large numbers of waistcoats,
some plain cotton, silk or wool, some trimmed with braid or
lace, others embroidered or printed. The son of the Baron de
Montesquiou, for example, bought no fewer than 25 *gilets*
and 26 *vestes* between 1780 and 1787, some three or four of
each every year. Variety in design was crucial for those who
wished to show off the fact that they owned more than one
such garment. In the 1780s nature and exoticism, literature
and literary heroes, theatre and romance, contemporary life
and antiquity were all incorporated into waistcoats, some
imagery being more politically charged than others.

Antiquity was the source for this waistcoat, as it was
for Josiah Wedgwood's ceramics and Robert Adam's interiors.
The neoclassical decoration is elaborate, and its application
required professional embroidery skills, as the motifs are
applied to the ground silk with different qualities of silk
thread and stitching. The circular medallions derive from
recently discovered Roman wall-paintings at Herculaneum,
which were published in the first three volumes of *Le
Antichità di Eroclano (The Antiquities of Herculaneum)*
(1757–92).

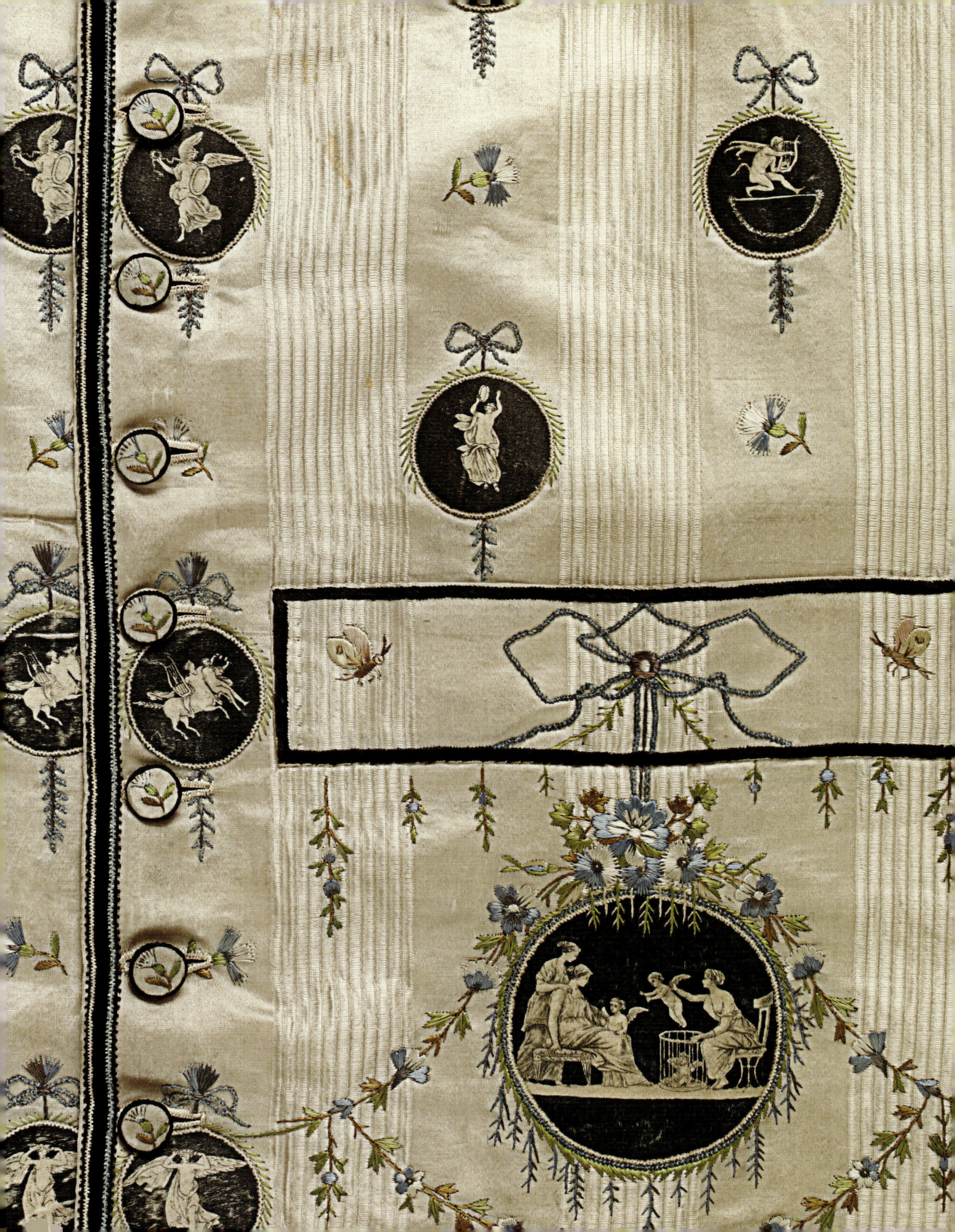

FAN

France; 1760–70
Painted in watercolour on vellum, with carved
mother-of-pearl sticks and guards, decorated with
gilt and silver foil
V&A: T.154–1978; l. 27.5 cm, w. 3 cm (closed),
w. 52 cm (open), d. 2.6 cm

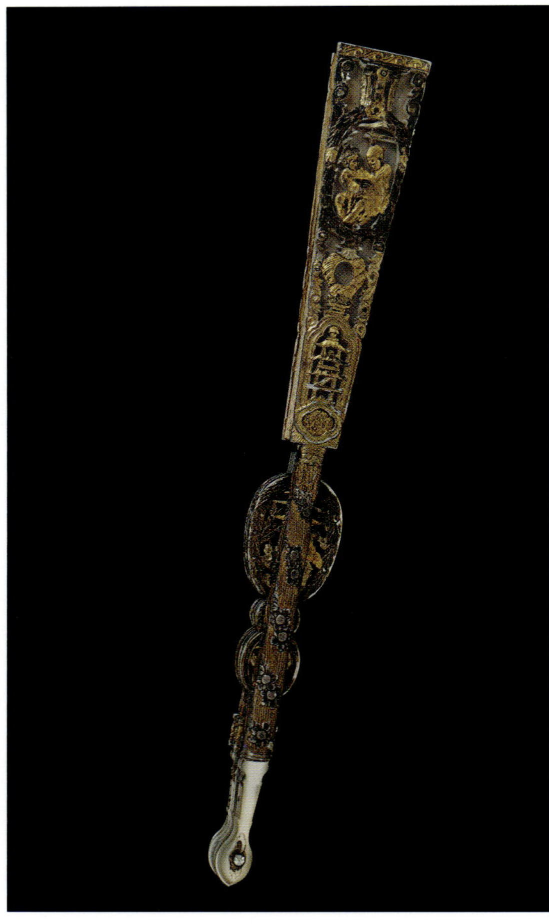

FOLDING FANS BECAME AN INDISPENSABLE
accessory for women at European courts
during the seventeenth century, and by the
eighteenth century were widely used at court
and beyond. They were introduced into
Europe in the sixteenth century, thanks to
Portuguese trading links with Asia. Their form and
decoration changed with fashion and they were sometimes
framed as pictures, rather than being used as what the French
playwright Molière (1622–73) called 'the folding screen of
modesty', a tool of non-verbal communication often
associated with love or flirtation.

This fan is a fine example of the European fascination
with exotic oriental goods, which grew with the formation of
the various East India Companies in the seventeenth century.
Its chinoiserie design combines European motifs with
European interpretations of Asian design. The form is
European, the rounded, paddle-shaped sticks, known by
the French term *battoir*, resembling battledore rackets or
carpet-beaters. The imagery on the fan leaf uses Chinese
subjects and motifs fancifully.

Three vignettes make up the design, showing Chinese
fishermen, Chinese children playing on a seesaw and Chinese
children making music. The fan-maker based these images on
designs by Jean-Baptiste Pillement (1728–1808), a French
artist and designer who had a cosmopolitan career. He
travelled and worked in France, Spain, Portugal, England,
Poland, Russia and Italy, serving between 1780 and 1789 as
court painter of landscapes to Marie Antoinette (1755–93) at
Versailles. His designs spread through print, his first pattern
book of chinoiserie designs, *A New Book of Chinese
Ornaments*, being published in London in 1755, and a second
volume, *The Ladies Amusement*, in 1760. The very title of the
latter publication draws attention to the light-hearted nature
of such ornament, and to its appropriateness for use by
refined women of the leisured classes as a source for their
embroidery or painting. Motifs were also used professionally,
as on this fan.

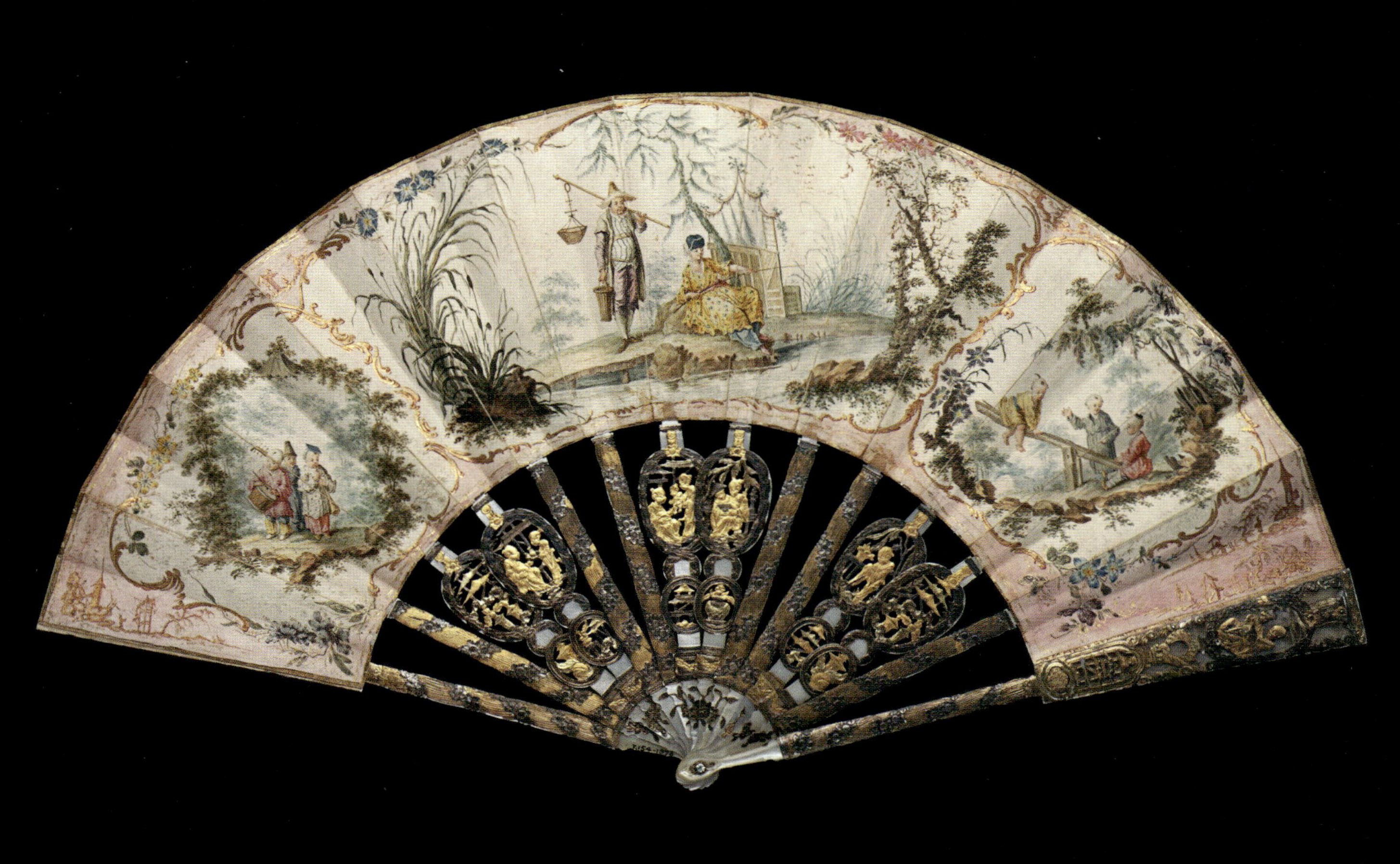

FAN

Made by Antonio Poggi (1769–after 1803);
engraved by Pietro Antonio Martini (1738–97)
Britain; about 1790
Engraved and hand-coloured paper, with carved
and pierced ivory sticks and guards
V&A: T.56–1933; given by Dagmar and Gladys
Farrant in memory of Arthur and Maud Loscombe
Wallis; l. 22.5 cm, w. 1.5 cm (closed), w. 38.4 cm
(open), d. 3 cm

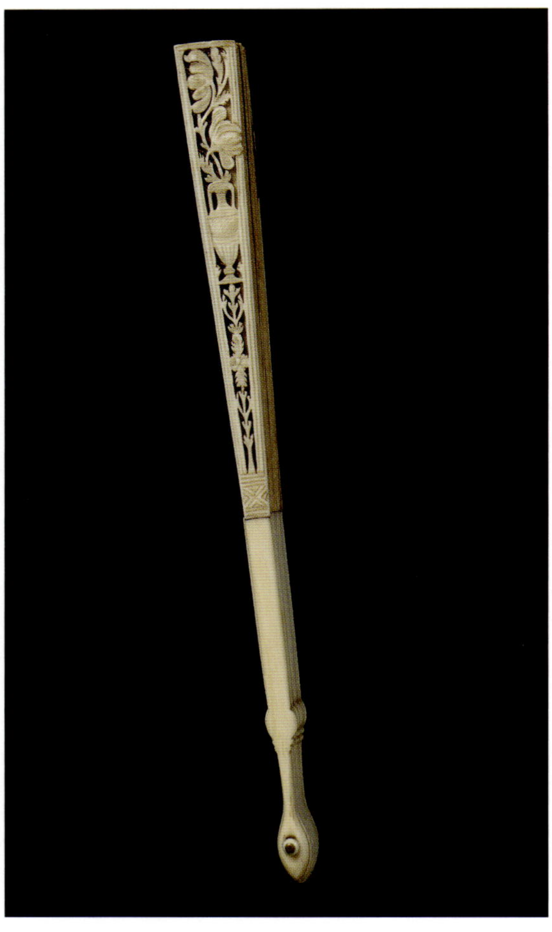

G EORGE III (1738–1820) RECOGNIZED
the importance of creating a positive
image for the royal family, actively
encouraging painters to record his public
appearances. This fan is based on a print
after a painting by the German court
painter, Johann Heinrich Ramberg (1763–1840). It depicts
the King, Queen and their children attending the annual
Royal Academy Exhibition in 1788 in a room at Somerset
House, where the Academy was then based. The original print
by Martini included the Academy's President, the painter Sir
Joshua Reynolds (1723–92), and other leading figures,
whereas a new version of 1790 substituted three of the King's
youngest children for the Academicians, in order to complete
the family portrait.

Fans were an important accessory throughout the
eighteenth century, with all European countries producing
them in considerable numbers. They ranged from simple,
inexpensive styles with bone sticks and paper leaves to highly
ornate versions, which used vellum, gold and silver leaf and
other inlays. This high-quality printed fan, the colours added
by hand, has sticks of expensive imported ivory. The maker
was Antonio Poggi, who had a reputation as both a fan-
maker and painter. He moved from Rome to London in
about 1776. He remained there until after 1803, and himself
exhibited at the Royal Academy in 1776 and 1781. Later in
his career Poggi set up as a dealer in Old Master drawings.
By 1801 he was supplying drawings to the Prince of Wales
(the future George IV, 1762–1830).

The English novelist Fanny Burney visited his shop
with Reynolds in March 1781. She recorded seeing:

*… some beautiful fans, painted by Poggi, from designs of
Sir Joshua [Reynolds], Angelica [Kauffmann], [Benjamin]
West, and [Giovanni Battista] Cipriani, on leather; they
are, indeed, more delightful than can well be imagined: one
was bespoke by the Duchess of Devonshire, for a present
to some woman of rank in France, that was to cost £30.*

In London at that time, this sum of money was
ten times the weekly wage of a skilled artisan, such as a
silk-weaver.

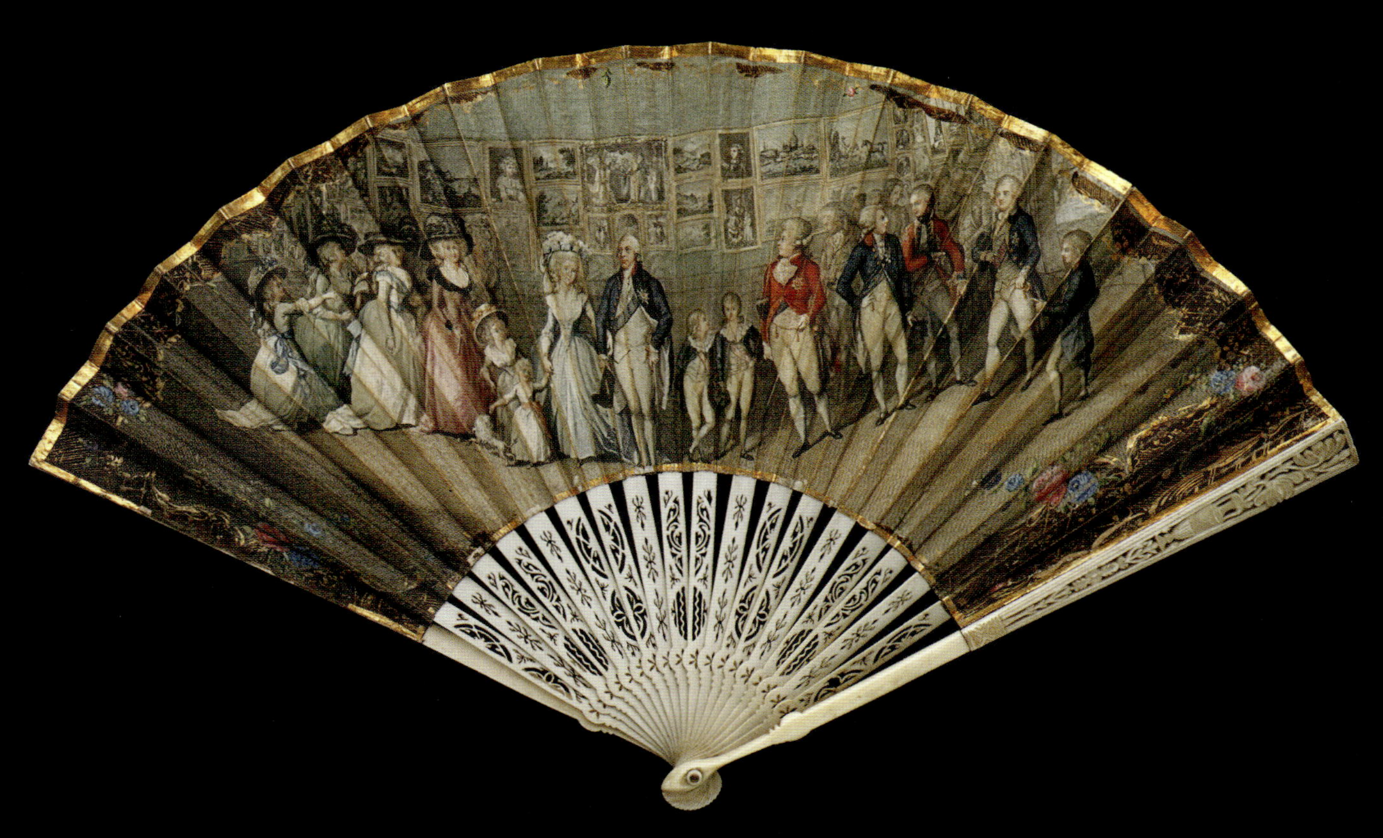

WATCH

Nicolas Bernard (master, 1636–70)

Paris; 1640–50

Gold case decorated in painted enamel; gilt-metal, brass and blued steel movement

V&A: 2359–1855; diam. 5.9 cm, h. 6.7 cm, d. 2.4 cm

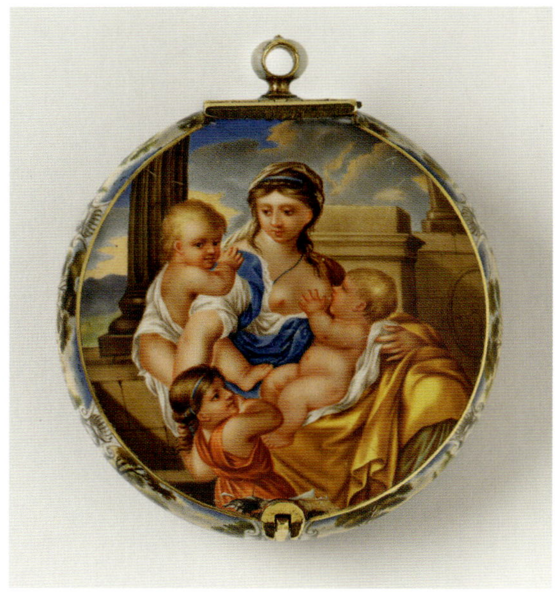

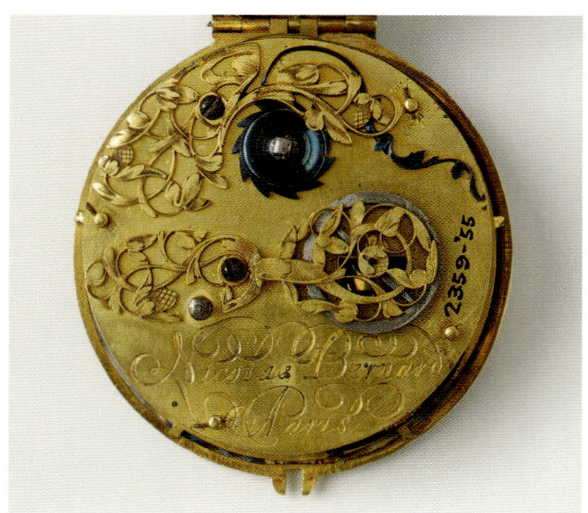

W ATCHES IN THE MIDDLE OF THE seventeenth century were often as much items of jewellery as they were keepers of the time. The finest French watches are celebrated for their superb cases painted in enamel with religious or mythological scenes. By 1630 improved techniques, for which the goldsmith Jean Toutin (1578–1644) was given the credit, made it possible to execute miniature painting in enamel in a wide range of colours. The metal was covered with an enamel ground, usually white, and fired in the kiln. It was then painted with metal oxides mixed with oil. Each colour had to be fired in turn to fuse it onto the enamel ground, beginning with the colours that had the highest melting point. The colours changed when fired, so that the creation of an enamel picture required not only painterly skills, but also knowledge of the colour changes and tight control of the firing process. Such was the potential of the new technique that some watchcases, like this one, became wider and flatter to provide an extensive surface for enamelling. The technique was used to decorate watchcases and other goldsmith's work as well as to paint portraits in miniature.

The key figures in this development were the enamellers and goldsmiths in Paris, Blois and Châteaudun, who had close links with watch-makers. Nicolas Bernard, who put his name to the movement of this watch, was one of these men. He became a master in the Paris Corporation of Clock-Makers in 1636. In 1645 he was one of five watch-makers who put forward 24 articles to provide a new constitution for the corporation, which received the approval of Louis XIV on 20 February 1646.

The case is painted with Charity on the front, Faith and Hope on the back. The sides, dial, reverse of the lid and interior of the case are painted with landscape scenes in the style of the etchings of Gabriel Perelle (1603–77).

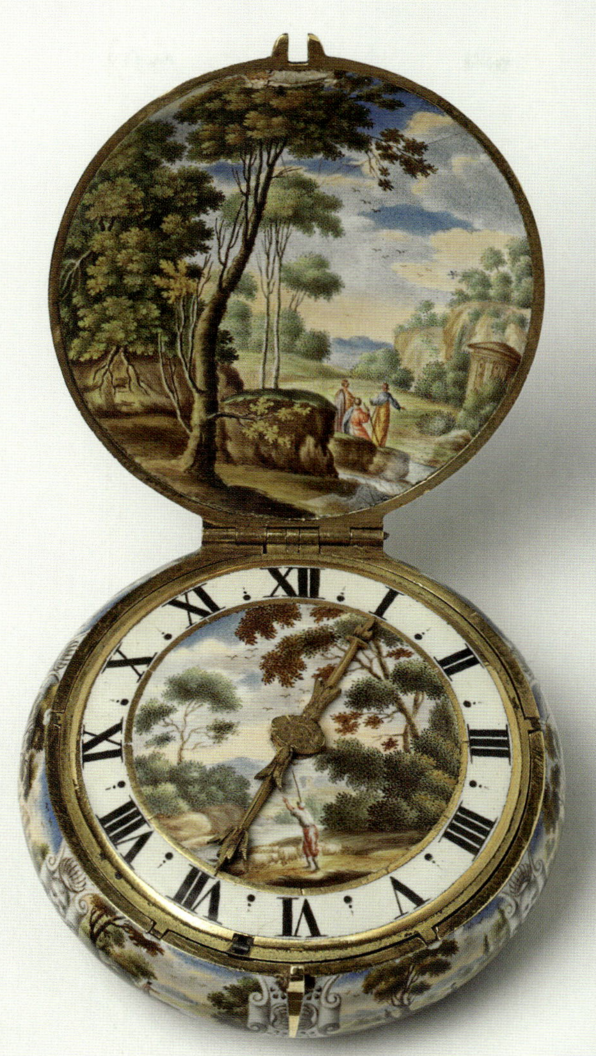

SWORD

Possibly Daniel Sadeler (d. about 1632) or Emanuel Sadeler, after Étienne Delaune (about 1519–83); blade made by Alonso Perez (active late sixteenth century); hilt possibly Prague or Munich, blade made in Toledo; 1590–1625
Chiselled and blued steel, gilt
V&A: M.64–1950; transferred from the Royal United Services Museum; l. 118.8 cm, w. 24.4 cm, d. 12.2 cm

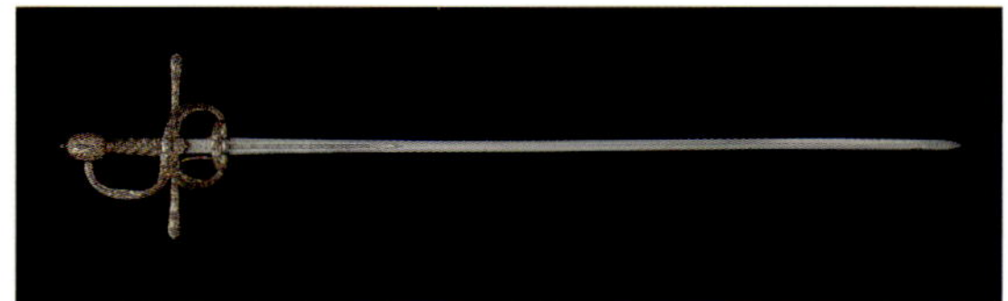

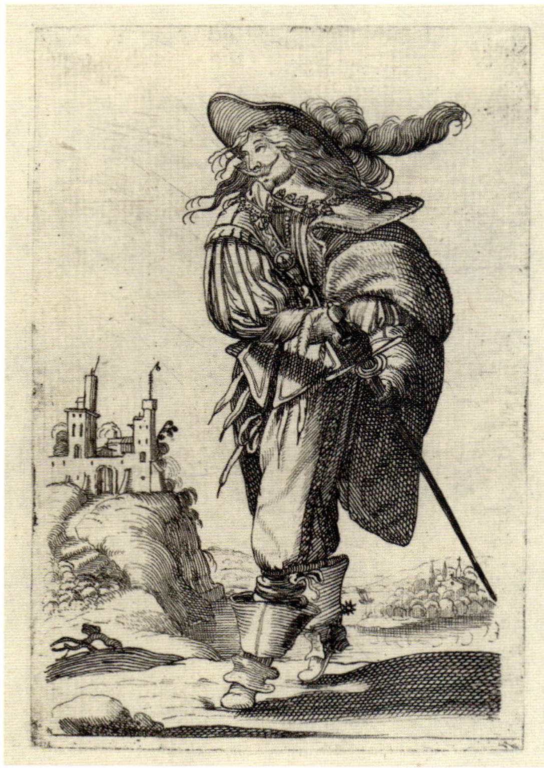

A nobleman, from *Le Jardin de la noblesse français dans lequel ce peut cueillir leur manière de vêtements*, by Abraham Bosse after Jean de Saint-Igny. 1629 (V&A: 26334.4)

THIS SWORD OR RAPIER IS ONE OF THE FINEST in the Museum's collection and may originally have come from the wardrobe of the Electors of Bavaria, as its maker worked at the court there. It would have been worn in its scabbard, suspended from a belt in the form of a sling. The rapier form was most common in civilian dress from the middle of the sixteenth century onwards, the 'swept' hilt between 1570 and 1630. Swords were not merely weapons and a symbol of honour and rank, but also an important decorative element of their wearer's dress. They remained an indispensable feature of outdoor dress for any man with pretensions to status until the late eighteenth century. Indeed, at court the wearing of a sword was mandatory.

The hilt decoration combines mythological figures after engraved designs by Étienne Delaune, with strapwork, foliage, masks, grotesques, fruit and trophies of arms: Mars (god of war) and Diana (goddess of the moon and hunting) are on the pommel, Perseus (the famous warrior king of Macedonia) on the centre of the knuckle guard, Vulcan (god of fire) on the centre of the large side ring, and Ceres (goddess of the earth) in the centre of the small side ring. The town mark of Toledo and a crowned shield bearing the letter S adorn both sides of the ricasso – the bevelled, blunted part between the hilt and the blade.

The fine two-sided Toledo blade was made by the prestigious maker Alonso Perez, whose signature is found in the narrow groove near the hilt – on one side DE ALONSO PE and on the other running down to the point REZ EN TOLEDO. He worked at the shop of the famous Gil de Almau, who produced several swords for the Holy Roman Emperor Charles V (1500–88) and his son Philip II of Spain (1527–98). Sword blades were articles of international trade, made in a few important centres and shipped all over Europe, where they were fitted with hilts in the local fashion. The finest hilts were usually equipped with a Spanish blade, those from Toledo, Valencia and Milan (then a Spanish possession) having the finest reputation in the sixteenth and seventeenth centuries.

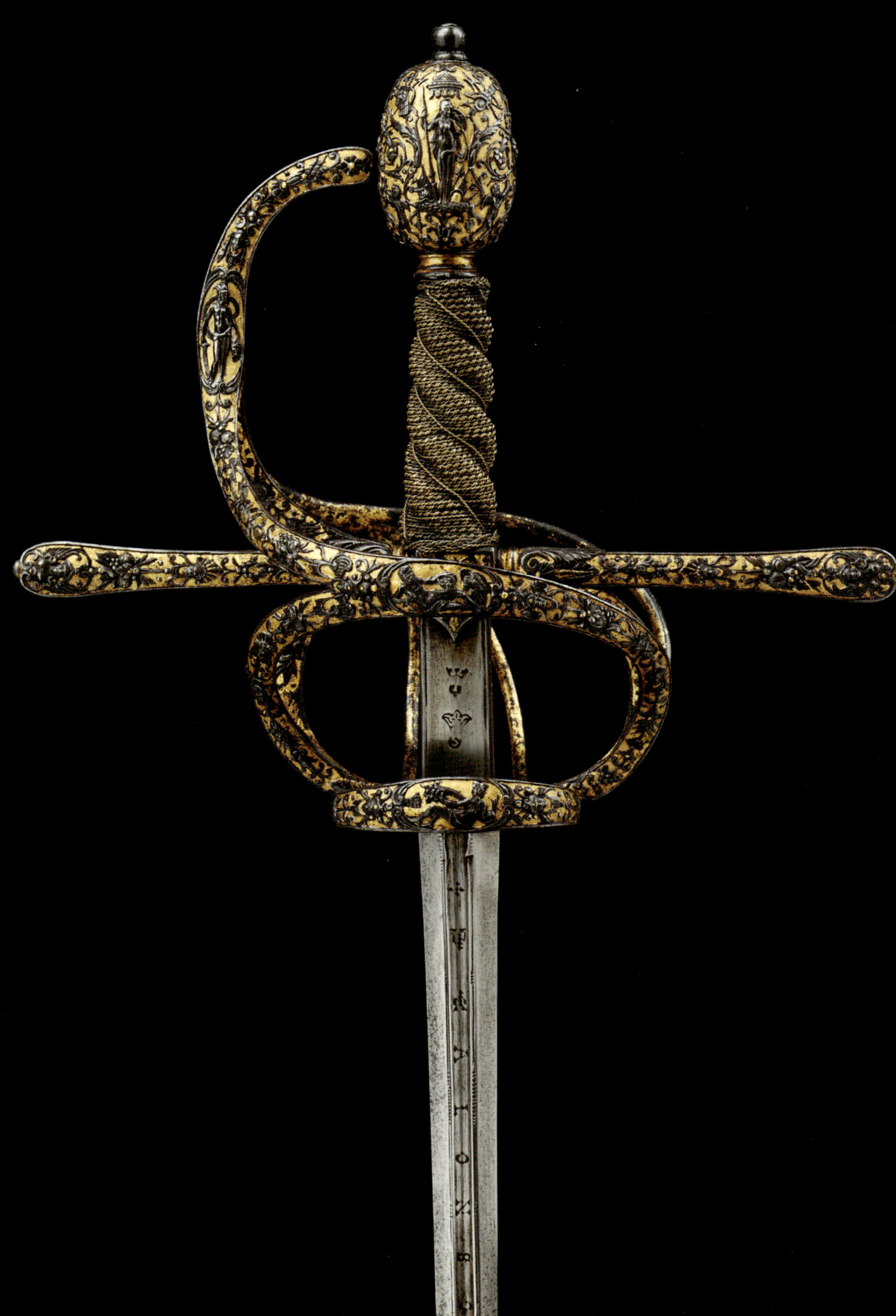

GEORGE III'S CANE

Britain; 1750–1800
Malacca with ivory top, mounted with gold
V&A: 1319–1900; given by Miss Maria Willis;
l. 115.5 cm, w. 2.8 cm

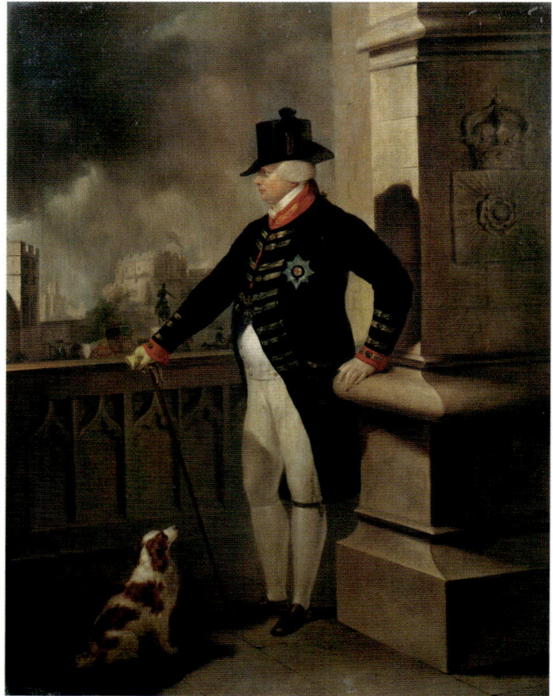

George III, by Peter Edward Stroehling. Oil on copper.
Windsor, 1807 (Royal Collection; RCIN 404865)

PRINCES WERE ALREADY USING CANES IN BRITAIN in the early seventeenth century. Both Charles I (1600–49) and William III (1650–1702) were portrayed carrying cane and sword simultaneously. Canes became, however, a truly fashionable accessory in the eighteenth century, replacing the sword for all but the most formal court wear by the mid-1770s. Associated with the English preference for simplicity, the adoption of the cane merited surprised comment from the Swiss traveller César De Saussure when he was in London in 1726: '[men] wear small round wigs, plain hats, and carry canes in their hands ... You will see rich merchants and gentlemen thus dressed and sometimes even noblemen of high rank.' George III (1738–1820) was renowned for his preference for the simple pleasures of family life over court ceremonial. The painter Peter Edward Stroehling (1768–c.1826) depicted him in 1807, in later life, on a terrace at Windsor Castle in his Windsor Uniform (devised for his private household), leaning on a cane, his faithful spaniel looking up at him expectantly.

This cane is a relic from George III's wardrobe, a fine reminder of how European trading and imperial expansion provided supplies of new materials, which were made up into fashionable commodities in European workshops. Each component of the cane probably came from a different part of the world, from territories colonized by different European powers. The rattan, which is lightweight but strong, took its name from the Malacca Straits, which the Portuguese charted in the sixteenth century; it grows indigenously in Sumatra. The fact that this cane is made of a single piece of rattan reveals it to be a superior product, as it did not need to have joins in order to make it long enough. The ivory probably came from India. The origins of the gold are more difficult to determine, as gold was continually recycled from old items given to jewellers, including coins from different countries.

The cane was given to the Museum in 1900 by a family connection of the descendant of Mr Bryant, to whom George III had given it. He was an acquaintance who lived in Slough (near Windsor) and supplied the King with books and puppies.

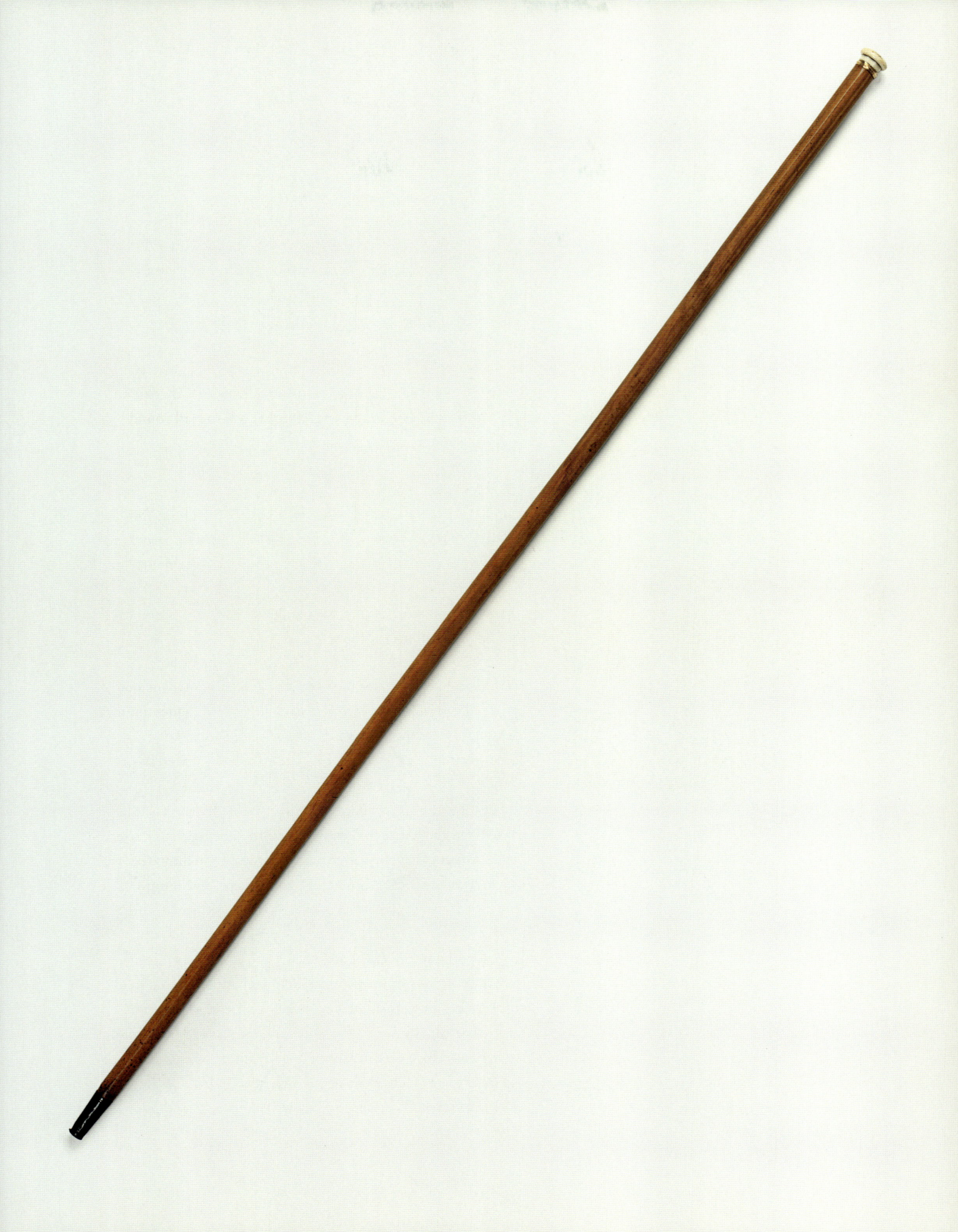

FURTHER READING

Adamson, John (ed.), *The Princely Courts of Europe: Ritual, Politics and Culture Under the Ancien Régime 1500–1750*, London, 1999

Anglo, Sydney, *The Martial Arts of Renaissance Europe*, New Haven and London, 2000

Baker, Malcolm, and Richardson, Brenda (eds), *A Grand Design – The Art of the Victoria and Albert Museum*, Baltimore, 1997

Blanning, Tim, *The Pursuit of Glory: Europe 1648–1815*, London, 2007

Brown, Jonathan, *Kings and Connoisseurs: Collecting Art in Seventeenth-Century Europe*, New Haven, 1995

Buck, Anne, *Dress in England in the Eighteenth Century*, London, 1983

Burton, Anthony, *Vision and Accident: The Story of the Victoria and Albert Museum*, London, 1999

Chadwick, Witney, *Women, Art and Society*, New York, 2002

Childs, John, *Warfare in the Seventeenth Century*, London, 2001

Cuneo, Pia (ed.), *Artful Armies, Beautiful Battles: Art and Warfare in Early Modern Europe*, History of Warfare series, Vol.9, Brill, 2002

Eger, Elizabeth, *Bluestockings: Women of Reason from Enlightenment to Romanticism*, London, 2010

Girouard, Mark, *Life in the French Country House*, London, 2000

Harte, Avril, and North, Susan, *Fashion in Detail: The Seventeenth and Eighteenth Centuries*, London, 1998 (reprinted 2009)

Impey, Oliver, and Macgregor, Arthur (eds), *The Origin of Museums: The Cabinet of Curiosities in Sixteenth- and Seventeenth-Century Europe*, London, 2001

Jones, Colin, *Madame De Pompadour: Images of a Mistress*, London, 2001

Kumin, Beat (ed.), *The European World 1500–1600*, London and New York, 2009

Kunzle, David, *From Criminal to Courtier: The Soldier in Netherlandish Art*, History of Warfare series, Vol.10, Brill, 2002

Mortimer, Geoff, *Eyewitness Accounts of the Thirty Years War*, London, 2002

Rangstrom, Lena et al., *Lions of Fashion: Male Fashion of the 16th, 17th and 18th Centuries*, Stockholm, 2002

Ribeiro, Aileen, *Dress in Eighteenth-Century Europe, 1715–1789*, New Haven and London, 2004 (reprint)

Ribeiro, Aileen, *Fashion and Fiction: Dress in Art and Literature in Stuart England*, New Haven and London, 2005

Sargentson, Carolyn, *Merchants and Luxury Markets: The Marchands Merciers of Eighteenth-Century Paris*, London and Los Angeles, 1996

Scott, Katie, *The Rococo Interior*, New Haven and London, 1995

Snodin, Michael, Llewellyn, Nigel, and Norman, Joanna (eds), *Baroque 1620–1800: Style in the Age of Magnificence*, London, 2009

Somers Cocks, Anna, *The Victoria and Albert Museum: The Making of the Collection*, London, 1980

Thornton, Peter, *Seventeenth-Century Interior Decoration in England, France and Holland*, New Haven, 1981

Thornton, Peter, *Authentic Décor: The Domestic Interior 1620–1920*, London, 1985

ACKNOWLEDGEMENTS

The editors and authors are grateful for the assistance of all colleagues in the Museum who have catalogued, conserved and photographed the objects presented here, in particular: Briony Bartlett-Rawlings, Ana de Benedetti, Clare Browne, Stephen Calloway, Frances Collard, Katie Coombs, Rosemary Crill, Judith Crouch, Oriole Cullen, Richard Davis, Richard Edgcumbe, Edwina Ehrman, Mark Evans, Lara Flecker, Alun Graves, Elizabeth-Anne Haldane, Louise Hofman, Charlotte Hubbard, Kirstin Kennedy, Christopher Maxwell, Leela Meinertas, Luisa Mengoni, Peta Motture, Tessa Murdoch, Susan North, Alicia Robinson, Carolyn Sargentson, Gill Saunders, Jennifer Sliwka, Suzanne Smith, Mor Thunder, Marjorie Trusted, Rowan Watson, Christopher Wilk, Hilary Young, James Yorke, Heike Zech. We also appreciate the research undertaken by Katy Conover, Alice Dolan, Carly Eck, Kasia Maciejowska, Sophie Plender, Jenny Saunt, Rachel Van Greuning and Hannah Wainwright, all students on the V&A/RCA MA Design History and Material Culture. In the Publications and Exhibitions Departments, Tom Windross and Dana Andrew, Caroline Bulloch, Anna Fletcher and Linda Lloyd-Jones have provided support and advice.

We are also grateful to colleagues in other institutions for their scholarly expertise, in particular to Romain Condamine, Susanne Groom, Maria Hayward, Alexandra Kim, Joanna Marschner and Father Rupert McHardy.

PHOTOGRAPHIC CREDITS